# Parliament's Generals

# Parliament's Generals
## of the English Civil War
## 1642–1651

### Neville Lloyd Walford

LEONAUR

*Parliament's Generals*
*of the English Civil War*
*1642-1651*
by Neville Lloyd Walford

First published under the title
*The Parliamentary Generals*
*of the*
*Great Civil War*

Leonaur is an imprint
of Oakpast Ltd

Copyright in this form © 2009 Oakpast Ltd

ISBN: 978-1-84677-934-3 (hardcover)
ISBN: 978-1-84677-933-6 (softcover)

**http://www.leonaur.com**

Publisher's Notes

# Contents

# Introduction

For the purpose of enabling the reader to more fully realise the character of the contests of the Civil War, it is proposed to give a brief description of the arms and tactics of the period, while on a later page will be related the early life of the principal generals of the army of the Parliamentary party.

Two great schools for the art of war existed in Europe at the beginning of the seventeenth century the camp of Gustavus Adolphus, and the Netherlands. The former appears to have principally attracted the Scottish adventurers, while the latter was visited by almost every young nobleman or gentleman in England, as a part of his education.

It would be beyond the scope of this work to enter at any length into the differences and similarities which existed between the systems of war used by the Swedes and the Dutch; but we may say that, while the former studied chiefly the offensive, the others, favoured by the character of their country, were renowned throughout Europe for their skill in defence.

In comparing the art of war as it was in the seventeenth century with the same art in its latest developments, we are at first naturally more struck by the differences which meet the eye than by the points of similarity which may be found. But, in truth, many of these differences, great as they are, are of quite modern growth; for it is scarcely too much to say, that there was less dissimilarity between the tactics of Naseby and Waterloo than there was between those of the latter battle and Gravelotte.

If we look into the history of war, we shall find that strategy and the general principles of tactics have but little changed during the lapse of many years, while the details of the latter have not only constantly varied, but are in fact now undergoing a daily process of change. If we further inquire as to the reason for this fact, we shall discover that the stability of the first is caused by the practically unaltered relations of men and horses to each other, while the last derives its variability from the continual improvement which takes place in the manufacture of arms.

The men of the present day can march no farther than the men of old, they are as liable to hunger and thirst, they are as delicate in organisation, are as easily wounded or killed; and the same may be said of the horses of this era. But if we turn to the arms, how great is the change. The old musket carried about 200 yards, but was not to be trusted above 100; the new rifle will throw with ease a distance of 2,000 yards, and is trustworthy up to 1,000. This last was about the range of field artillery in the old days; the present possible range may almost be described as infinite as far as the gun is concerned, being in practice bounded only by the limits of man's vision.

It is evident that such vast changes as these must make their mark in the manner of conducting the details of the combat; but smaller alterations have played their part also. For example, the invention of the bayonet, that of the iron ramrod, of the cartridge, and of the percussion cap, have all exercised much influence in modelling from time to time the character of fresh orders of attack and defence.

If we examine into any system of tactics we must, for the above reason, commence by considering the nature of the arms with which the soldiers of the clay were provided; by this the manner of their use was decided, as from this it may be deduced.

The strategy of the period, in cases where any knowledge of the art was shown, was not so unlike our own as to call for particular notice, save perhaps that we should mention that it was somewhat modified by the wretched character of the roads, which much delayed the movements of armies, and considerably lengthened the duration of their marches. In our own day, the conditions of strategy have been changed in the opposite direction by the advantage which is gained by the power of moving troops by rail.

In a similar manner, higher tactics, though in principle almost the same as ever, have changed as to their execution, owing to the fact that drill and discipline have made easy of conduct many movements, which would have been far beyond the power of the soldiers of the seventeenth century, and which were therefore not considered in the calculations of the generals of that time.

The altered character of strategy and of the higher tactics may, to a certain extent, be learnt by observation of the history of the campaigns of the Civil War, and it is not, therefore, proposed to again refer to them in this chapter; but the actual details of the combat of great interest, and yet rarely described at any length in the chronicles of the time can only be discovered by the study of the books of instruction which were used to prepare an army for the field. These details, as we have said, have always, in all ages, varied with the changes introduced as to the nature of the arms in use. For this reason it is intended to commence the subject by a description of the armament of the infantry, cavalry, and artillery which took part in the Civil Wars.

The infantry of every army of the period of which we write was armed with two weapons the pike and the musket. The proportions which existed at different times between the numbers of men who carried one or other of these weapons varied considerably; the number of musketeers tending always to increase, and those of the pikemen to diminish, as the arm of the former gained in portability and in accuracy of fire. At the commencement of the Civil Wars, the bearers of the two arms were about equal in number.

The pike was a spear from sixteen to eighteen feet in length, armed with a small steel head, not unlike that of an Indian hog-spear. It was in battle held in one of two ways. Against infantry, it was levelled with the point as high as the enemy's breast, the butt resting by the side of the right hip; against the attack of cavalry, while the shaft was still held with both hands, the butt was placed against the hollow of the right foot, the point being thus raised in the air. The pikeman was armed with breast and back plates, under which he wore a buff coat (to save his body from the pressure of the armour), while his head was protected by a morion or pot-helmet. Light as was his weapon, he was, on account of the weight of his defensive arms, considered as a heavy-armed soldier, and the ranks of the pikemen were filled from the largest and strongest men in the company.

The musketeer, on the other hand, was not as a rule armed with any defence more perfect than a buff coat, but his head was guarded in the same manner as that of the pikeman. He was reckoned as a light-armed soldier, and was expected to be more active than his heavier comrade. The musket was a cumbrous weapon, with a barrel three feet in length, and having a bore which took a ball of twelve to the pound. It was fired from a rest which, on the march, was trailed by a string from the wrist of the soldier. It was loaded from a bandoleer, on which dangled ten or twelve small wooden or tin boxes, which each contained a single charge of powder; the lid of one of these was pulled off with the teeth, and the charge then poured into the barrel.

The bullets were carried in a bag which was worn at the side; but before going into action, the soldier placed two or three balls in his mouth, whence he took them when needed, and dropped them wet into the barrel without wad or patch. The muskets were as a rule matchlocks; that is to say, they were fired by means of a lighted coil of slow-match, which, on the trigger being pulled, was inserted into the pan of the weapon. There were, however, in use some few snaphaunces and wheel-locks, which were fired by means of a flint and steel.

Nor were bows and arrows as yet considered to be obsolete, since in 1643 we find that Essex issued a call for volunteers armed with those weapons; while in a contemporary work they are suggested as fit arms for the pioneers, as being light and portable. But they do not seem to have been much used, the quickness of their fire being more than neutralised by the inability of the arrows to pierce the heavy armour of the day.

In addition to the arms above mentioned, all infantry soldiers carried a straight sword, which was worn on the left side, and hung generally from a baldric or shoulder-belt. Infantry were organised in companies, which varied in size from 100 to 200 men, of whom, as has been mentioned, about one-half were musketeers. These companies were, on the Continent, usually enlisted and equipped by the captain, and were hired as a whole for the service of any state which might happen to be at war. The size of the company in this case depended upon the amount of money which was at the disposal of the captain, or upon his personal character and renown.

The same system doubtless obtained in England at the commencement of the Civil War, with this important difference, that the captains enlisted their companies for the avowed object of serving one or the other side, and were not thus, strictly speaking, "mercenaries;" though, of course, they and the men received pay as soldiers.

Six, eight, or ten companies formed a battalion, which was, as a rule, commanded by some nobleman or distinguished person, and was always known by the name of its colonel. The actual command was, however, generally left in the hands of a lieutenant-colonel.

Each company had one captain, one ensign, four sergeants, and two drummers, while the staff of the battalion consisted of the lieutenant-colonel and a sergeant-major only; the latter seems to have ranked as an officer and to have discharged the duties of adjutant.

Each unit of infantry appears to have fallen in, whether for battle or for parade, in one invariable formation; the pikes were formed into a square, on either flank of which stood a smaller square of musketeers, while the general order of battle for the entire force was in lines of battalions at close interval.

The cavalry were divided into *cuirassiers, arquebusiers, carbineers,* and dragoons, and made up as a rule about one-quarter of the total strength of an army. At the beginning of the seventeenth, century lancers were also used, but they appear to have passed out of date before the commencement of the Civil War.

Cavalry were organised in troops, which were 100 or 120 strong, according to whether they were intended to fight five or six deep; each troop had one captain, one lieutenant, one cornet, three corporals, and two trumpeters.

The *cuirassier* was a heavy-armed soldier, mounted on a large horse, and attended by a boy, who carried his arms and "snap-sack." He was dressed in full armour from head to foot, and used, in addition to a long straight sword, a brace of pistols of 20 or 24 bore, and about 18 inches in length.

The *arquebusier* wore a helmet, a back and breast plate, and a *gorget*, under which was a good buff coat; he was armed, in addition to his sword, with an *arquebus* about 30 inches long and of 17 bore, as well as with a pair of pistols.

The *carbineer* rode a lighter horse than either of the preceding, having, it would appear, no defensive armour; he wore a sword, and carried also a carbine about 27 inches long and of 24 bore.

The dragoon was in truth a mounted infantry soldier, whose horse was used merely a means of conveyance, since the man fought invariably on foot. Dragoons were armed exactly as were the infantry, with pike and musket, and fought in a square in a similar manner. The strength of a troop was usually 132, which allowed one horse-holder to each eleven horses, while 120 was the fighting strength of the troop.

Of these several divisions of the mounted force, the dragoons were pushed forward to seize or to hold any particular post which the general might wish to possess; in this respect, they were the exact type of the mounted infantry of the present day.

The *arquebusiers* and *carbineers* performed those duties which we in our days consider to devolve especially on cavalry; they led the march and protected the columns while on the move, they guarded the flanks of the infantry in battle, and, after driving off the enemy's cavalry, struck at the flanks of the hostile foot.

The *cuirassiers* acted as a reserve to the others, being posted always in rear, in order that they might cover the retreat, if necessary, of the other cavalry, and might thus gain time for the latter to reform. It is obvious that the great weight carried by the horses would prevent the *cuirassiers* from charging over any distance; indeed, their charge, when they did not receive the enemy at the halt, was never made at any faster pace than a trot.

Charges against infantry were rarely pressed home by any one of the various descriptions of cavalry. The general plan of such an attack was a converging rush on the front and flanks of the hostile square, the horses being pulled up when near the front of the infantry to allow their riders to discharge their firearms in the faces of the pikemen; should the latter give way, the cavalry pushed on into the ranks of the battalion, and soon broke it up into a mass of fugitives.

Even against cavalry, the true cavalry weapon, the sword, was never drawn until the pistols or carbine had been discharged, and it is specially recommended by one of the tacticians of the time that the first pistol should be fired at the hostile rider, but the second at his horse; when both had been discharged, the sword was to come into play. He further recommends that a *cuirassier* shall endeavour to advance against the right hand of his adversary, as he could thus use his pistols with greater effect; but *arquebusiers* and *carbineers* are advised to attack the enemy's left, as they could thus rest their weapons on their bridle-arm.

The artillery of the Civil Wars were divided under four heads, as follows:

1. The cannons; including the cannon royal, the whole cannon, and the demi-cannon,

2. The culverins; consisting of the culverin, the demi-culverin, the saker, the minion, the falcon, the falconet, the robinet, and the base.

3. The pierriers, or guns for throwing stone shot.

4. Mortars, closely resembling those of the present day, which threw iron and stone balls.

The following table will give information as to the principal characteristics of the several guns:

All these guns were used for siege purposes, while in the field we occasionally find even so large a gun as the demi-culverin, which was a little heavier than is our present twenty-five pounder, also a gun of position.

Owing to the difficulties of transport, guns were in the seventeenth century a great encumbrance during a campaign; nor could they in battle, owing to the slowness and inaccuracy of their fire, yield sufficient benefit to repay the trouble of their carriage. But a siege train was a necessity in the days when towns were fortified and castles were proof against assault, and since for this reason an army never marched without some guns, it was customary to make use of those guns in action in the open field.

In the case of siege guns there was little difference from the practice of the present day, except that the ranges were of course much less, and the fire much slower, than they are now. The position and the action of the artillery in battle will be considered on a later page.

The heavy guns were drawn by teams of from eight to sixteen horses, each horse being supposed to draw about 500 lbs.; the drivers were sometimes mounted in turn on the off and near horse of each alternate pair.

The operation of loading a gun was as follows: It was, as now, first sponged out; the charge of powder was then taken by means of a brass ladle out of a budge barrel; the ladle, which had a long handle, was pushed to the bottom of the bore and then inverted, in order to pour out the powder; a wad of "hay, grasse, weedes, okham, or such like" was next rammed home; after this the shot, and then another wad of similar materials. Cartridges of linen or paper were sometimes used, in which case they were pricked with a priming-iron.

When the loading had been completed, the vent was primed with loose powder from a horn, and the gun was fired by means of a linstock, which consisted of a stick, around which was a coil

| Names of guns | Diam. of bore in inches | Weight of shot in lbs. | Length of gun in feet | Weight of gun in lbs. | Charge of powder in lbs. | Range with elevation of 7° 30' |
|---|---|---|---|---|---|---|
| Cannon royal | 8 | 63 | 12 | 8,000 | 27 | 1,500 yds |
| Whole cannon | 7 | 39 | 11 | 7,000 | 18 | 1,350 " |
| Demi-cannon | 6.5 | 30 | 10 | 6,000 | 14 | 1,300 " |
| Culverin | 5.25 | 17.5 | 12 | 4,400 | 12 | 1,500 " |
| Demi-culverin | 4.5 | 10.5 | 11 | 2,400 | 7.5 | 1,450 " |
| Saker | 3.75 | 5.25 | 9 | 1,500 | 4.75 | 1,250 " |
| Minion | 3.25 | 3.75 | 7.5 | 1,200 | 3 | 1,000 " |
| Falcon | 2.75 | 2.5 | 7 | 700 | 2 | 1,000 " |
| Falconet | 2.25 | 1.14 | 6 | 500 | 1 | 750 " |
| Robinet | 1.5 | 0.25 | 4 | 300 | 0.5 | 500 " |
| Base | 1.25 | 0.5 | 3.5 | 201 | 0.5 | 380 " |

of slow-match.

An army of the seventeenth century, when drawn up in order of battle, was generally formed in three lines, named respectively the main battle, the battle of succour, and the rear battle; of these, the two last were together about equal in number to the first. The distance between these lines was no more than from twenty to fifty paces; the troops composing them being all formed in column at close interval, the front of the army was short in proportion to its strength.

The infantry of each of these lines was formed, as has been mentioned, in squares of pikemen, on the flanks of which stood smaller squares of musketeers; in the intervals between the battalions of the first line were posted the guns, while the cavalry was divided almost equally between the right and the left wing of the army, and was drawn up five or six deep in two or more lines of troops or squadrons at close interval.

Owing to want of discipline and drill, the operation of forming the order of battle was a very long process, and for this reason was performed while the force was still at a distance from the enemy; after its completion, the army advanced in order against the position of the hostile troops. Since such an advance would hardly be possible over broken ground, it resulted that battles were almost invariably fought on open plains or fields; the small extent of these being of no consequence, since the front of the battle was always narrow in proportion to the numbers engaged. It was considered that the force which stood to the defensive had a great advantage over its enemy, owing to the almost certain effect of the advance of the latter on the arrangement and the order of his troops.

Small but independent bodies of infantry and cavalry were pushed to the front as the enemy approached; these parties, which were styled "forlorn hopes," were intended to delay the advance of the enemy by their fire, and were therefore composed mainly of musketeers, so many pikes only being added as would be needed to protect the others from the hostile cavalry. These bodies "pickeered" between the two armies, while the guns of the defenders fired on the assailants; those of the latter could not fire until the line of battle had been halted.

The cavalry of the attacking force, being on account of their height more liable to injury from the artillery fire than the infantry, were if possible kept under cover until actually needed, but it was not unusual for desperate attacks to be made by small bodies of light-armed infantry or cavalry upon the guns, in the hope of silencing or spiking them.

When the two armies were at a distance of from 300 to 400 yards apart, they both as a rule halted and stood watching each other, while the guns continued their fire. After a pause of shorter or longer duration, varied only by the skirmishing of the advanced troops, one or the other force would decide to attack. An advance was made, the forlorn hopes were driven in, and the true battle began. As soon as it was obvious that the enemy meant to close, the guns of the defenders were withdrawn through the intervals, and formed up in line with the battle of succour.

While the infantry were slowly picking their way across the intervening space, the horse of each army would charge that of the other; advancing towards their enemy at a hand-gallop, they would fire their pistols in each other's faces, and then join in a hand-to-hand fight with swords. This irregular engagement, which the cavalry fought out for themselves regardless of the necessities of the infantry, was typical of the tactics of the Civil Wars, in which, owing to the lack of discipline in either army, a battle became a series of single combats, without purpose and often without result. The cavalry of either side being thus well occupied, the infantry, closing in on each other, drew forward to close combat.

On the advance of the hostile army, the musketeers of each battalion were sent to the front, marshalled in files ten deep, and posted so as to cover the flanks and front of the pikemen. As the musketeers of the enemy, who were formed in a similar manner, came within shot, the leading man of each file fired his musket; this done, he wheeled to the right-about, and fell back to the rear of the file in order to load. Files which were advancing moved up to the front to fire, and stood their ground to load.

As the two lines drew yet nearer and nearer, the musketeers of either army drew away from the front of the pikes, and formed up on their flanks; when the latter came actually almost in contact, the musketeers either ranked up in rear of the square or placed themselves inside it, and fired on the enemy through the intervals between the pikes.

At last both squares of pikemen closed, and the fight was fought out hand-to-hand and knee-to-knee, with little hope of escape for the wounded, who were trampled to death as the mass of the combatants swayed above them; at length one or the other side would break and fly, with the view of rallying on the battle of succour.

At once from out of and from in rear of the square, the musketeers poured forth and pursued the retreating battalions with their fire; but soon, not being able, owing to the clumsiness of their firearms, to follow them far, they returned to their pikemen and prepared for a renewed defence.

So the wave of battle swayed backwards and forwards; for, since there was seldom any connected plan of attack or defence, each battalion fought out the fight for itself, and an army victorious on its right might nevertheless be routed on the left; in which case the final victory generally rested with that force which had its reserves close at hand.

In the battles of the Civil War, the infantry combat had never come to a decided end before the return of the cavalry of one or the other party; and thus it happened that in almost every action the result of the battle followed that of the cavalry contest.

On the return of the victorious horse to the field of battle, their efforts were at once addressed to breaking the infantry squares, either by charging these in flank while the infantry attacked them in front, or by their own independent action. In the latter case they rode up to the pikemen and fired into their ranks, then wheeling away retired to reload their pistols; so the fight went on, until either the cavalry had been repulsed by the fire of the musketeers, who lay under the front pikes or fired from the interior of the square, or some unsteadiness having shown itself among the pikes, the horsemen could push into the battalion square and could disperse the men in all directions.

When the horse had been driven from the field and the squares of the infantry had been broken up, in spite of their efforts to rally on the lines in rear, then indeed the battle was lost and the pursuit began, of all parts of the action the most costly to the defeated party. For, cumbered by their arms, and having too little discipline to rally, the retreating troops fled without order to any point which promised momentary safety, and thus fell an easy prey to the swords of the pursuing cavalry, who drove them from shelter to shelter, with but small loss to themselves, until the army was not only defeated but dispersed never to rally again.

Unlike as is a modern European battle to such a contest as has been described, with regard to the numbers engaged, the space occupied on the field, the mode of attack, and in the manner of the use of cavalry, in nothing is it more unlike than in the conduct of the pursuit. Whereas in the seventeenth century the larger portion of the losses of the defeated army were incurred during its flight, it is now the case that, owing to the extreme ranges at which a battle is fought, there is in practice hardly any such thing as a pursuit; from this it results, that in almost every action the army which attacks, though it may be victorious, loses more men than that which assumes the defensive.

We may here remark that, in spite of their experience in the Netherlands, the leaders on either side, at the commencement of the Civil Wars, showed but little skill either in tactics or strategy; and that the few lessons which may be drawn from the history of these campaigns teach us for the most part only what to avoid in war.

Before beginning the narrative of the Civil War, it may be interesting to briefly recall the extraction and analyse the characters of some of the principal leaders of the forces of the Parliament.

Of these, the foremost in point of time, though by no means the most remarkable as a general, is Robert Devereux, the third Earl of Essex,

He was the son of the unfortunate favourite of Elizabeth, and was born in London in 1592, so that at the outbreak of the war he was about fifty years of age.

His first wife, Lady Frances Howard, deserted him for Carr, Lord Rochester, the unprincipled favourite of James I. Essex, weary of England, passed over to the Netherlands, where he served for some time, attained high distinction, and was much beloved by his men.

On his return to his native land, his sympathies were altogether in favour of the popular party, though the King, with the object of detaching him from it, bestowed upon him the office of Lord Chamberlain.

This place was shortly after, on his refusal to follow the King from London, foolishly taken from him, and the earl was thus left free to accept without scruple the command in chief of the forces of the Parliament.

If we judge of his military abilities by the results of his campaigns, we are forced to admit that they were but moderate; no skill is shown in the general conduct of the war, while his movements, when not forced by circumstances into some certain direction, appear to have been for the most part objectless, for during his three years of command he effected little or nothing towards the favourable conclusion of the contest; this failure to obtain marked success against the King may, however, have been the consequence rather of his political policy than of his incompetency for command, since he was undoubtedly as averse to the complete triumph of the Republican party as he was disinclined to allow the return of the King to such despotic exercise of his power as would be possible should he entirely crush the rebellion of his subjects.

But he was not sufficiently strong for the times. The men whom he proposed to use as tools to forward his personal aggrandisement, so soon as they realised that he was inclined to play his own game and not theirs, caballed against him, and, aided by the common-sense of the people, who saw that thus conducted the war would never end, they succeeded in ousting him from his high post, and laid him by in honourable obscurity.

Sir Thomas Fairfax, the successor of Essex, was the son of Ferdinand, Lord Fairfax, on whose death, March 13th, 1648, he assumed the title. He was a member of an old Yorkshire family, and on the outbreak of the Civil War threw the whole weight of his personal influence in favour of the Parliamentary cause. His father at first led the Roundhead party in the North, but the youth and energy of the son soon raised him to the real, though not the nominal, command, and the name of Ferdinand, Lord Fairfax, is chiefly known in history as that of the father of Sir Thomas.

The latter in his early youth had served in Holland, and had brought back thence the repute of a skilful soldier. His continued, though at one time almost hopeless, struggles against Newcastle in the North made his name famous; and there does not appear to have been one dissentient voice raised against his appointment as commander-in-chief in succession to Essex.

He was gentle and kind in private life; his countenance and mind were strongly marked with melancholy, the result possibly of continual ill-health, for he suffered during his whole life from the effects of his hardships in the Netherlands; but in action he was fierce and uncontrollable, so that in battle men dared scarcely speak to him. It may be doubted whether, as a soldier (not as a leader), he was not, at least the equal of Cromwell; he certainly knew more of war, and his blows, if less heavy, were perhaps more skilful than those of his great successor.

In comparing the two generals, we must remember that Cromwell never commanded in chief against better troops than the indifferently armed and undisciplined Scots and Irish, whereas Fairfax in one campaign defeated the Royalist army and ruined their cause, at the very moment when its partisans were most full of hope.

To those who read the history of his times with care, the name of Fairfax shines forth as that of the most unselfish and most noble gentleman of his party, though, being more a soldier than a politician, he never acquired the renown of Cromwell, for the reason that he served in war with no ulterior or personal motives.

Of Cromwell, the foremost figure of the latter years of the war, as he was the guiding spirit of much that was done during the earlier period, it is unnecessary to speak at length, since his life is in great part the history of England.

He was born in the year 1599, and was the son of a gentleman of Huntingdon, of good family in that county.

At the commencement of the disagreement between the King and the Parliament, he strongly supported the cause of the latter, and, when hostilities between the two became inevitable, he used his great local influence for the purpose of raising troops in the eastern counties. At first merely the captain of a troop, he soon worked his way to the rank of colonel; but his greatest task at this time was the formation of the Association of the Eastern Counties, a league which was never broken, and which added immensely to the strength of the Parliamentary party.

With respect to his character as a general, we may note that, gifted with a natural genius for organisation, and with that peculiar power over the minds of men which stamps the true leader, he raised the first body of "soldiers," and with them leavened that army, which before his coming was a mere rabble of "tapsters and serving-men."

Devoted to religion but broad in his views, he at the same time made use of the fervour of the zealot, and accepted the good service of those who differed from him in their dogma; "the cause" was to him the touchstone of a man's worth, and none were rejected who were "honest men."

At a later period, when higher command fell to his lot, he showed the same talents as a general which had already distinguished him as a captain; he was a good judge of men, and, being thus secure in his confidence in his subordinates, ventured to undertake movements and marches which, to the majority of the armies of those days, would have been impossible to execute and dangerous to attempt.

His success, reacting on the influence over men which had made that success possible, raised him to a pinnacle of power, whence other men appeared but pigmies, as small and as mean as their ends; while, accustomed to the obedience of the soldier, he sought, as have all those who have risen by the sword, to treat a nation as an army.

While he lived, England endured this attitude, but at his death she gladly flung his sons back into obscurity, and destroyed with ease that political condition which he had brought about at the cost of the best years of his life.

Sir William Waller was a gentleman of Kent, and was born in the year 1597; he was, therefore, at the beginning of the war about forty-five years of age.

He had in his youth much distinguished himself in war on the Continent, and was on his return knighted by Charles I. as a reward for these services. But a quarrel with a relative, which found its crisis in a blow delivered within the precincts of the Palace of Westminster, brought Waller before the Star Chamber, from whose clutches he with difficulty escaped at the cost of a heavy fine. After this incident he threw himself headlong into opposition to the Royal party, and was rewarded by a command at the first outbreak of the war.

He had no talent as a soldier, and the history of his campaigns is an almost unbroken list of defeats; yet he was popular, partially on account of his rivalry with Essex, and might, but for his ill-success in war, have succeeded that general in his command.

Waller is a remarkable example of a case in which the man's reputation was so much greater than the man, that its possessor was eventually broken down by its weight; for he does not appear to have been in any respect above mediocrity; he had so little influence with his soldiers that he was even unable to preserve discipline, while, to speak charitably, his fortune was so bad that he was defeated in a large majority of the battles in which he commanded.

Of the leaders who came into notice at the latter end of the Civil Wars, the first to claim our attention is Henry Ireton, the friend and son-in-law of Cromwell.

He was born in Nottinghamshire, in the year 1610, and served the Parliament from the commencement of the war up to his death in 1651.

This event was of national importance, not so much on account of the share which Ireton had taken in the military and political conduct of the Civil War, as by reason of the effect which his counsels and opinion might have had on Cromwell, had he lived to see the latter supreme. Having been educated as a lawyer, Ireton had the principal hand in drawing up the various declarations and remonstrances which were presented to the Parliament by the Army. But he was a strong man in action as well as with his pen, being very energetic, industrious, and firm, and, as a soldier, able and stout in the field. No man had such influence with Cromwell as he, none was so trusted and none so respected. He was in heart and soul a Republican, and it may be doubted whether, had he lived, Oliver would have ventured to assume the Protectorate.

Charles Fleetwood, who married Ireton's widow, was the son of Sir William Fleetwood, who was cupbearer to James I. and Charles I.

He had sufficient military skill to enable him to carry out the plans of better men than he, but was wanting in energy, in daring, and in self-confidence. Timid, wavering, and cunning, he was, perhaps, of all the leaders of the forces of the Parliament, the one least worthy of his place in the history of the times, which was probably, in great part, due to his relationship to the Protector.

Of far other metal was the bold, ambitious, and unscrupulous Lambert, who was early marked by Cromwell as a useful but dangerous man.

He was born, of good family, about 1620, and was educated for the Bar, but abandoned his profession on the outbreak of hostilities.

As a leader of cavalry he had no equal in those days, and he appears to have been fully acquainted with his whole duty in war. This was especially shown in the campaigns against the Scots in 1648 and 1651, where, though he had every temptation to strike an independent blow at the enemy, he entered so fully into the plan of the campaign, that he held his hand until the number of troops at the command of the Parliamentary leaders rendered the defeat of the Northern army not only certain but disastrous.

In political matters his action was bold to rashness, open and determined; and he was in consequence, on the elevation of Cromwell to the Protectorate, dismissed from his offices in disgrace. Compared with Cromwell, he was deficient in the art of ruling men, and had not the power which Oliver possessed of concealing his intentions until they were ripe for execution; but as a soldier he was not far behind his great leader.

The name of Blake should not perhaps be included among those of the generals of the Parliamentary party, but it is one of such mark in English history that it cannot be altogether passed by.

Robert Blake was born at Bridgewater, in Somersetshire, in the year 1594. On the commencement of hostilities between the King and the Parliament, he joined the army of the latter, and distinguished himself in the defence of Bristol against Prince Rupert. His most gallant service was performed in 1645, at Taunton, which town he defended during two sieges.

In 1649, when in his fifty-fifth year, he received the command of the Parliamentary fleet, and in that position gained many most important successes over the Dutch. He was a severe disciplinarian, a rigid Puritan, and in politics a Republican.

In view of the importance of the after action of Monk, we may perhaps also give a short record of his birth and early life.

George Monk was the second son of Sir Thomas Monk, of Petheridge, Devon, and was born in 1608. He served in the expedition to Cadiz, and also in that to Rhé. In 1629, he passed into the Low Countries, where he served with distinction; in 1639 he returned to England, and was engaged in the two campaigns which Charles I. made against Scotland.

In 1642, he was sent as a colonel to Ireland, but was recalled when the King, having concluded a truce with the rebels, drew the army of Ireland to his aid in England. Though suspected of a leaning to the Parliamentary cause, Monk succeeded in justifying himself to the King, and was appointed to serve with the Irish force which landed in North Wales at the end of 1643.

He was there taken prisoner by Sir Thomas Fairfax, and was committed to the Tower. His subsequent fate, and his actions in the service of the Parliament in Scotland, will be related in the following chapters.

Having thus briefly introduced to our readers the principal leaders of the Parliamentary party, we may pass on to the narration of the events with which they were connected.

# CHAPTER 1

# 1642

Among the most prominent failings of the Stuart kings may be placed their blindness, complete as it was unconscious, to the signs of the times in which they lived; this again was a consequence of their entire inability to understand the character of the English people.

James I., the *pedant-debauchee*, held a very different position in the eyes of England to that occupied by his imperious predecessor, but it may be doubted whether he ever realised how entirely the heartiness of the welcome accorded to him sprang from fear of the two powers, which to the minds of most Englishmen represented the Antichrist, namely the Pope and Spain. As far as James could be said to hold to any form of faith, he was a Protestant, a fact which to men of those days meant more than we can now imagine, we who view the Papacy as an interesting relic of earlier ages, venerable from its antiquity and harmless for the same reason.

Passing on to the successors of James, we find that the poison most constantly used to envenom the attacks on Charles I. was the repetition of the statement that his army was mainly composed of "Papists," while in all probability, of all the errors which he committed, none heaped upon him so huge a load of contumely and hatred as his hesitation to issue proclamations against the Catholic rebels in Ireland.

James II. lost his crown by his intolerant devotion to the Church of Rome, while Charles II. earned forgiveness for his well-known though disguised leaning in the same direction, only by persecuting most strenuously in public that Faith in which in private he was, as far as any belief in him lay, a believer.

If we turn from the religious to the political doctrine of the Stuart kings, we shall here again find them at variance with the spirit of the times. From the first to the last of the race they assumed that the Kingship was theirs by indefeasible right, and that England was, so to speak, their farm, in which the nobles were bailiffs and the people labourers, and of which the entire profit was for their sole use, and subject to their disposition alone. Such was not at all the view taken by the people of England during the earlier part of the seventeenth century.

The last of the purely English line of kings was dead, and the ruler of an alien race, of one moreover allied from old time with hostile France, was accepted as the wearer of the crown, and this not so much because this ruler was desired or desirable, as from fear lest worse things should otherwise befall them. The position of the Stuart kings with respect to England was thus very different to that of their predecessors, while their demands on the unhesitating loyalty of their subjects were such as might well have strained the bonds between Elizabeth and her people. The spread of education, bringing with it the habit of independent thought, and the same striving after liberty in speech and action which had led to the rupture of the chains of Rome, made men criticise such things as seemed to them doubtful, and condemn much which earlier ages had revered.

The attitude of the England of those days closely resembled that of a youth who has reached that stage of his development when the fairy tales and fables of his childhood have no longer an interest for him, since he has begun to learn that there is in him a something which demands stronger food; he is no longer to be held back by "wise saws and modern instances," but insists upon a voice in matters affecting his interests. The king, on the other hand, resembled the father of such a stripling who is unable and unwilling to understand that there is a well-marked stage between the child and the man, and who strives to repress, by means which perhaps only last year were sufficient, that personality of his son which is now independent of all but his love. If to further extend this simile we suppose the son, as is not rarely the case, to awake one day to the fact that his father is not infallible or immaculate, while the sire in his turn ventures to resort to violent means for the subjugation or the punishment of his heir, we shall find, as the result of the opposition of the two kindred wills, a struggle which may serve as a fair type of the great Civil War.

On the 27th of March, 1625, died James the First of England, and Sixth of Scotland, leaving, as a heritage to his son, a war with Spain, a half-healed quarrel with the Parliament on the subject of that son's marriage, an exchequer burdened with gifts to the favourites and satellites of a debauched court, and a people oppressed with the load, hourly felt and cursed, of monopolies on many of the articles of common USQ, laid upon them by the Crown for no public purposes, but for the maintenance of the lowest creatures of both sexes.

Charles, the inheritor of this fortune so full of promise of evil, was a man who in many respects deserved a better fate. He was, as men then went, virtuous; he was in any case decent; and his accession was the signal for a notable cleansing of the court; he was brave, generous, and chivalrous, a good husband and a most loving father; but he was weak, and of his weakness deceitful. His manner was wanting in cordiality, while his knowledge of men was small, and he thus at no time had any real power (apart from his position as king) over those by whom he was surrounded, while, strange as it may seem when we think of the love lavished on him when dead, he does not appear to have been loved by any one friend at any time during the whole of his life.

But another characteristic far outdid all these in its result on his reign. He had, in an inordinate degree, the Stuart belief in the "divinity that doth hedge a king." As his misfortunes and death have raised to him myriads of posthumous adorers, so the errors and failings of his life have drawn from others words of scorn, such as are scarcely deserved by one who, false as his lights were, lived up to them as far as he was able.

Charles appears to have fully and truly believed that the kingship was a thing of a nature so divine that it was holy, not only to all subjects, but even to the king himself. He wore his crown as a direct gift from God, holding it to be a symbol as sacred as the sacramental cup, a thing not to be touched by profane hands, not to be approached but with bared head and downcast eyes. The man, he felt, might err, but the king never; and such deeds as were done by him as king, though they might appear inscrutable or even unreasonable to others, should be by them received as the acts of an inspired being too high for cavil, too holy for criticism.

He held, in a very different sense to that in which we now use the words, that the king could "do no wrong."

Even more, he believed that for a king there were no such qualities as right and wrong. Opposition to him was heresy abuse of him, blasphemy; as to honour him was worship, and to love him the whole duty of man.

Up to this point we shall, according to our hearts, pity or deride King Charles. The moral results of this phase of his character we must all condemn; but for the steadfastness with which he held to that which he thought to be true, we must all feel that admiration which is due to any belief for which a man may dare to die.

Of his kingship, Charles felt himself to be but the depositary; and thus, even during his times of utmost suffering, we find that the paramount idea in his words and actions is the absolute duty that lay upon him, that by him no stain should fall upon the brightness of this inestimable jewel. The crown was to him as was the breastplate to the Jewish High Priest; in it were the Urim and Thummim, and it were better for him to die better even that he had never been born than that the glory of this ensign should be abated through any deed, or even through any scruple, of his own.

From this inordinate reverence for the kingly office grew a great evil, for with a perverseness of reasoning which we name

Jesuitical, Charles held that for the advancement of so holy a cause as that of the king must ever be, no means, however vile or mean to the common eye, could be in verity aught but virtuous and true. To this Moloch he sacrificed his children, as he had previously surrendered his home, his wife, and his happiness; to this idol he offered up the love of his subjects, the hope of his house, and the good of his country; for this he became an outcast, a vagrant, and a prisoner; and when love, friends, and liberty had been swallowed by the burning fiery furnace, he flung in with them his honour and his fair fame for ever; it was then no hard matter to die for the god. Let those only judge him for whom there exists a Truth so living.

Such was the King who, on the 4th of January, 1642, came to the House of Commons attended by about two hundred of his courtiers and soldiers of fortune, and, passing alone into the House, demanded, from his station by the Speaker's chair, that the five members should be surrendered to him. This act, of so threatening a character, rendered reconciliation all but impossible, and Charles, finding that the feeling of the City of London (where the five members had taken refuge) was altogether on the side of the Parliament, withdrew from his capital, which he was never to re-enter save as a prisoner.

The House of Commons, on the other hand, knowing their insecurity in the case of an appeal to arms, unless they could succeed in getting the government of the militia into their own hands, endeavoured to induce the King to agree to the appointment of such persons as they should select to "settle" that force.

This point now and ever, Charles refused to grant. Finding that the almost certain end of such proposals would be civil war, he despatched the Queen whose unpopularity far exceeded his own to Holland, with a considerable portion of the Crown jewels. On these she was to raise money for the purchase of arms and munitions of war. He himself moved towards the north, and at the end of March, 1642, was at York.

At the time of the abandonment of the ill-omened campaign against the Scots, in 1640, a large store of arms and powder, prepared for that expedition, had been left in Hull. This the King was as anxious to seize as the Parliament was desirous to deny it to him. The latter wished to bring the whole to London; but, finding that the King would not permit them to do so, sent Sir John Hotham, in whom they had entire dependence, as governor to Hull, with direct orders to deny admission to the King, should he demand it.

On the 23rd of April, Charles, with a train of no great size, presented himself at the gates of the town, which on his approach had been closed. On his demand for admission, Hotham, speaking from the walls, declared on his knees that he could not admit him without breach of his trust to the Parliament. Charles, after a useless effort to gain by negotiation that which he could not win by arms, returned to York, contenting himself, perforce, with the empty proclamation of Hotham as a traitor.

Each party, seeing now that war was inevitable, made every effort to raise forces for the coming struggle. The Parliament passed an "Ordinance for the Militia," which placed the command of that body in the hands of lieutenants of their own selection; while the King, after raising a bodyguard of about six hundred men in the county of York, sent out his Commission of Array. Each, as might have been expected, declared the action of the other to be illegal, and in this each was probably warranted by facts. But the time was past for all constitutional proceedings, and the result was that every man served in that army which either appeared to him to have the better cause, or which promised to himself personally the greater present or ultimate gain. But of even greater urgency than the question of the supply of men, was that of the provision of money.

For this the Parliament principally relied on the City of London, which responded with the very utmost alacrity, cash and plate being freely offered by the citizens, even the women bringing their jewellery and ornaments to add to the public store; while on the passing of a vote "that an army should be raised for the defence of King and Parliament," recruits willingly flocked in. It is certain that the support of the City of London alone enabled the Parliament to commence the struggle; since the capital, which contained by far the greater part of the wealth of the country, furnished to its defenders not only pay and provisions, but also, as will be seen at a later period, a force of infantry which had no superior in the field.

The King had no such ally, but was indebted for his supplies of money and arms to the contributions of those nobles and gentlemen who favoured his cause, and especially to the generosity of the University of Oxford, of which the Colleges did not even deny that plate which was a great subject of their pride. It may be of interest to note here, though the occurrence took place in 1643, that a similar contribution on the part of the University of Cambridge was rendered impossible by the swift action of Oliver Cromwell, who occupied the town, and overawed the Heads of Colleges; he was at that time the Captain of No. 67 Troop of the Parliamentary army, and was employed, under Lord Willoughby of Parham, in organising the popular forces in the eastern counties.

Charles, after having levied a small force in Yorkshire, where, however, his action was much hampered by the counter-influence of Ferdinand, Lord Fairfax, and of his son Thomas, moved slowly towards the south, in the hope of raising recruits in the midland counties. He was defeated, by the thoughtfulness of the Earl of Stamford, in an attempt to seize the armoury at Leicester, and, Coventry having refused to receive him, he retired to Nottingham, where, on the 22nd of August, 1642, he raised his standard.

Of this proceeding, the actual ceremony was devoid of grace. The standard, which was of scarlet silk, "in form of a scutcheon," "bore on it the King's arms, with the motto, *Give Caesar his due*; it was at first pushed from one of the upper windows of the castle, but, as the King considered that it was not thus fully displayed, it was on the following day carried into the park, and there, with much difficulty, owing to the hardness of the ground, finally raised, which operation was, however, conducted in so unskilful a manner, that on the same night the standard, with its pole, was blown to the ground, which, being taken as an omen, seemed an "ill presage to melancholy men."

The practical found a worse augury in the fact that during a stay of about three weeks at Nottingham, scarcely any recruits joined the King's forces; he had thus no infantry and few arms, and was dependent even for the safety of his person on the trained-bands which the Sheriff of the County had called out. So early did it become evident that Charles could not expect support from the Eastern half of England.

The Parliament had in the meantime fixed the head-quarters of their army at St. Albans, whence, when the organisation had been in some degree completed, they were, in the middle of September, moved to Northampton, an advance which compelled the retirement of the King. The total strength of the forces of the popular party was about 15,000 men, divided into horse, foot, and dragoons, the latter being in practice mounted infantry.

The command of this considerable body of men had been given by the Houses to Robert Devereux, Earl of Essex, who had held charge of all south of the Trent during the Scottish war, a post which had afforded him little opportunity of distinguishing himself. He was appointed at a later period,, as has been mentioned, to an office near the person of the King, which Charles, with the characteristic folly of the Stuarts, took from him at the very moment when it was of the last importance to bind him to his side. What wonder, then, that Essex threw in his lot with the party to which he was at heart attached!

To the Parliament his presence was of the greatest value; brave, generous, and the darling of all such as had served under him in the Netherlands, his very name was a tower of strength to the cause which he favoured, and "honest Robin" as the men named him was, both in popularity and in warlike renown, the first of the then generals in England.

Born in 1592, he was at this time in the full vigour of manhood, and having lived, owing to his domestic misfortunes, much abroad in camps and bivouacs, stood forth as the natural leader of the Parliamentary forces; though subsequent events led many to doubt both his military skill and the purity of his political principles.

On the 9th of September, 1642, Essex, accompanied by many members of both Houses of Parliament, joined his army at St. Albans, and there took up his command. From this date we may assume the undoubted existence of a state of war, though both before and after that event efforts at negotiation were constantly made by those who thought no scheme should be left untried which might avert from the country so terrible an evil as civil war.

But such efforts could have no result, for both King and Parliament were now determined to fight, since matters between them had come to such a pass, that no reconciliation was possible, save on the condition of the absolute submission of the one to the other, which again on either side could follow only as the result of a decisive defeat. Yet all men thought that the struggle, bloody though it might be, would prove but short; while each party felt secure in such certainty of success as was born of their entire ignorance of the many possible sources of failure. The general feeling of the country was that one battle would decide the contest; and, with that want of knowledge of military matters which always results from a long peace, men imagined that war needed no skill but only courage, and that a victory if bloody must necessarily be decisive.

With regard to the adherents of either party, we may say that, broadly speaking, the nobility and county magnates were, as might be expected, on the side of the King, and were followed in their actions, if only partially in their principles, by their tenants and dependants; while the supporters of the Parliament were the traders, the manufacturing and seafaring population, and, in some parts of England, the yeoman freeholders. From this division it followed that, as a rule, the principal sea-ports and the large towns, including the capital, were in arms against the rural districts, including the garrisons of the various castles and manor-houses in the kingdom.

From this fact there at once grew a great advantage to the Parliamentary party, since a town, if in any way capable of defence, can spare from its garrison some considerable quota to the strength of the field army; whereas the fair castles and noble houses of the supporters of the King were too small as a rule for a prolonged defence, while the natural tendency of each man to protect his house and family led to the retention in such tiny garrisons of bodies of men who might, in the aggregate, have added considerably to the marching force of the Royalists.

If we consider the political principles of the time from a geographical point of view, we shall find that the east and south-east of England, with, part of Yorkshire Lancashire, as also a portion of the south coast, favoured the Parliament, while the cause of the King, which found its largest number of recruits in Wales and the west, was popular also in many of the midland counties and in the north.

Space will not admit of the particularisation of the districts and towns which adhered to each party, but the above may be taken as generally true; while in many parts the local magnates were so evenly divided as to numbers and influence between the combatants, that, especially during the earlier part of the war, such districts became the scene of many skirmishes and combats which, without result to their action or cause for their undertaking, were as useless as they were destructive, and, as we read of them, remind us, in their futility and rancour, of the private wars which raged under the feudal system.

One peculiar phase of this method of making war is worthy of mention. In Yorkshire at this time and a little later in Cheshire, as also in Devonshire, a private truce to their private war was arranged between the leaders of the Cavaliers and Roundheads in the several counties, such truces having for their object the preservation of the inhabitants of the particular district from the invariable sufferings caused by the passage and contests of armed forces, and for their reason the certainty which all men felt that the war would be decided by the first great battle between the main armies.

The opening event of the war was very unfavourable to the Royal party. Portsmouth, Hull, and London were at this time the principal arsenals of the kingdom, and of these the two latter were in the hands of the Parliament; but the first, under Colonel Goring, held for the King, who had thus a sea-port on the south coast, by which he could communicate with France. The Houses, realising the importance of this possession, sent Sir William Waller to besiege Portsmouth, to whom after a feeble defence Goring surrendered "the strongest and best fortified town in the Kingdom." Thus in the beginning of September, Newcastle was the only port in the hands of the Cavaliers.

The war at this period divides itself into four main theatres, *viz.*

1. The Eastern Counties.
2. The North and Yorkshire.
3. Cornwall and the West.
4. The Midlands.

**1.** The progress of events in the eastern counties, of which want of space will not permit the examination of every detail, is mainly remarkable as giving the first proof of the vigour of the mind and the hand of Cromwell, who, with Lord Grey of Wark, was during this year and the next working hard to form the Eastern Association. This, which consisted at first of Norfolk, Suffolk, Essex, Cambridge, and Herts, in time included also Lincoln and Huntingdon.

From these counties Oliver drew that cavalry whose name will endure as long as his own, and, flying with them hither and thither as need might call, he allowed no Royalist rising, he permitted even no Cavalier's presence, to disturb the peace of the district which thus, during the whole course of the contest, stood alone in its almost absolute immunity from the horrors of war.

**2.** The northern counties and Yorkshire were at this time for the most part Royalist, though Hotham held out in Hull, while

Ferdinand Lord Fairfax endeavoured to raise a party for the Parliament in the West Riding. His son, Sir Thomas, succeeded during the autumn in securing Leeds, Wakefield, and Doncaster, upon which the Earl of Newcastle was sent from the north, as the King's general, to defend the county.

In December, Lord Fairfax, who had been appointed general in Yorkshire for the Parliament, was attacked at Tadcaster by Newcastle with very superior forces, but the former, after a fight which lasted five hours, drove the Earl back to York. Each party, however, was at this early period of the war in such small strength that no decisive action could be expected from them.

**3.** When the King leaving York advanced towards London, he detached from his person the then commander-in-chief, the Marquis of Hertford, with orders to make his way into the west and to there organise the Royalist forces. Hertford having fixed his headquarters at Wells, called in the trained bands to his standard, but finding that recruits came in but slowly, while on the other hand the Earl of Bedford was in the field with a large body of the troops of the Parliament, he fell back into Sherborne Castle. Hearing at this place of the surrender of Portsmouth, which it had been his purpose to relieve, he crossed the Bristol Channel into Glamorganshire, and, after a time, rejoined the army of the King. The Earl of Bedford, for his part, made his way to the Earl of Essex, as did also Sir William Waller, as soon as Portsmouth had surrendered to him.

**4.** But though these smaller events were important to the actors in them, the eyes of the country were fixed, to the exclusion of other interests, on the movements of the two principal armies under Essex and the King.

The latter in September, on the advance of the Parliamentary forces from St. Albans to Northampton, finding that he could in Nottingham obtain no accession to his strength, moved by way of Derby and Stafford into the west, and was on the 20th of September at Shrewsbury. Here his forces were so largely increased by the number of recruits who joined from Wales, that it now became a matter of very great difficulty to supply them with either arms or money.

Essex, who had undoubtedly lost a favourable opportunity, since he might easily have crushed the small following of the King while they lay at Nottingham, now, when it was too late, marched after him with the object of hindering the junction of his reinforcements, and this movement brought about the first action of any importance.

A body of the Parliamentary cavalry, which, under Nathaniel Fiennes, formed the advanced guard of the main column, on arriving at Worcester found at that place a considerable force of the Royalist horse, which, led by Prince Rupert and Goring, had been sent thither from Shrewsbury to serve as escort to a convoy of money, and between these parties, on the 22nd of September, took place a skirmish, much thought of at the time, but of which the memory was afterwards almost lost in that of the severer actions of the war. The manner of it was as follows:

An advanced guard of the Roundhead cavalry, consisting of about 1,000 horse and dragoons, having crossed the Severn, moved on Worcester by way of Powick, where was a bridge over the Teme. On false information that Sir William Balfour, the lieutenant-general of the main body of cavalry, had ordered his force to advance in support, the officer in command pushed on across the Teme, and up a narrow lane where five or six men only could march abreast. While so moving they suddenly found themselves in the presence of about 1,600 of the Royalist cavalry, who, wearied with their long ride, were lying idly on the ground.

Prince Rupert, at once seeing his advantage, had in a moment mounted his men, and burst upon the enemy before more than five troops had found time to deploy for the charge. The Parliamentary horse, surprised and outnumbered, yet made head for a while against the attack of the Cavaliers, but were finally routed and driven back in disorder across the river, with the loss of their colonel (Sandys, who was mortally wounded), and of about thirty other officers and men.

The moral effect of this small engagement was out of all proportion to its real importance, since it "rendered the name of Prince Rupert very terrible." To us, who can view the history of the war as a whole, it further brings the thought whether this success, so easily obtained, may not have been in some degree the originating cause of much further disaster, in that it encouraged to rashness the inconsiderate valour of the Prince.

It is interesting to note, as showing the worthlessness from a military point of view of the Parliamentary troops at this time (the tapsters and serving-men of Cromwell's celebrated saying), that we learn from Ludlow, then a private in the general's body-guard, that even that force of picked men so little understood the meaning of a word of command that, at the order to "wheel about," they "shifted for themselves," and rallied only on the following morning at head-quarters, where they naturally met with but a cold reception from the general.

The King, having by the beginning of October raised about 8,000 men,[1] of whom 6,000 were infantry, prepared to take the field, although his troops were most insufficiently supplied with the necessaries of war. For, in order to provide arms for even so small a force as the above, he had been compelled to seize the arsenals of the county trained-bands, and could then find no better weapons than cudgels for some 300 or 400 of his soldiers, while none of the pikemen (the true strength of the infantry of the day) were provided with corslets; moreover the cavalry, who were for the most part gentlemen, had no other arms than their swords, and were as a rule without the defensive armour which was then deemed essential to the safety of a horseman.

The Parliamentary troops, on the other hand, were generally well armed, for the great arsenal of the Tower of London was in the power of the Roundheads; thus, after the skirmish at Worcester, bitter complaints were made by Rupert's men that their swords could not touch their enemies, who rode in armour of proof, while of pistols the Cavaliers had few or none.

In spite, however, of such disadvantages, it was determined

---

1. According to other accounts lie had 6,000 foot, 3,000 horse, and 1,500 dragoons.

that with what force he had the King should march on London, for it was felt that this movement would certainly be followed by Essex, and that from it a battle would result, of which the issue would without doubt be favourable to the Royalists, and which would at one blow decide the quarrel. Accordingly the Royal army, leaving Shrewsbury about the middle of October, marched by Bridgenorth, Wolverhampton, and Birmingham to Edgecot, at which place, about four miles from Banbury, it arrived on Saturday, the 22nd of October.

This movement put the Parliament and the City into "no small apprehension," and they used all means to obstruct Charles's march and to hasten Essex after him. The latter, on learning of the King's advance, at once broke up his camp at Worcester, and, following the Royal army, was at the above date at Kineton, a village on the borders of Warwick-shire and Oxfordshire, about six miles from Edgecot. On the following day, Sunday, October 23rd, took place the battle of Edgehill, the first of that war of which the last engagement, contrary to the hopes and beliefs of most men, was not to be fought until nearly nine years later.

The main body of the Parliamentary army, about 10,000 strong, had been ordered to rest for the Sabbath in the village of Kineton, whither, however, in the morning, as the leaders were on their way to church, news was brought from the advanced scouts that the enemy were moving forward, and about 9 a.m. the leading Royalist troops were observed in position on Edgehill, an eminence about three miles to the south-east of the camp of Essex.

This movement of the Cavaliers had been caused by a report which Rupert, about midnight on the 22nd, had sent in to the King, of the presence of the hostile army at Kineton, on receipt of which orders were at once issued for the occupation of Edgehill; this position was not, however, fully held by the King's troops until noon on the 23rd, on account of the distance, seven or eight miles, which some of the regiments had to march. Thus, had Essex been properly served by his scouts, he might easily have seized such advantage as could be derived from the nature

41

of the ground.

Between Edgehill and Kineton lies the Vale of the Red Horse, which is described as being on the day of the battle a "great broad field," but somewhat intersected with hedges,, especially in that part of it which lay near the village. On this plain, posted on some slightly rising ground, the army of Essex, marshalled in line of battle, awaited until 1 p.m. the advance of the enemy.

Their order of battle, as nearly as can be discovered in the confusion of contemporary accounts, was as follows: The centre of the line consisted of three brigades of infantry, echeloned on the right brigade, which was commanded by Sir John Meldrum, the other brigadiers being Colonel Essex and Colonel Hollis. In support of this force there was a reserve, consisting of one brigade under Colonel Ballard.

On the right stood three regiments of cavalry, two in first line and one in reserve, commanded by Sir Philip Stapleton, Sir William Balfour, and Lord Fielding. The left wing was composed of twenty-four troops of horse, led by Sir James Ramsay, while Hampden, with another brigade, which was serving as escort to the artillery (of which the advance had been very slow, owing to the want of draught-horses), was at this time drawing near to Kineton by the Stratford-on-Avon road.

The Royal army, which was commanded by the Earl of Lindsey, moved down the hill about 2 p.m., in a similar order; the foot, in nine *tertia* or battalions in line, formed the centre, while the left was composed of ten troops of cavalry under Lord Wilmot, the remainder of the mounted arm being placed on the right, and being led by Prince Rupert in person.

The advance of the Royalist army appears to have been but. indifferently executed, since a wide interval (about half-a-mile) divided each wing from the centre, while some of the infantry regiments lagged in their march so far behind the front line, that the main army might have been defeated before they could have come up. This carelessness was no doubt in part due to the assurance of victory which the Cavaliers felt, of which a yet stronger proof was given by their voluntary abandonment of a good de-

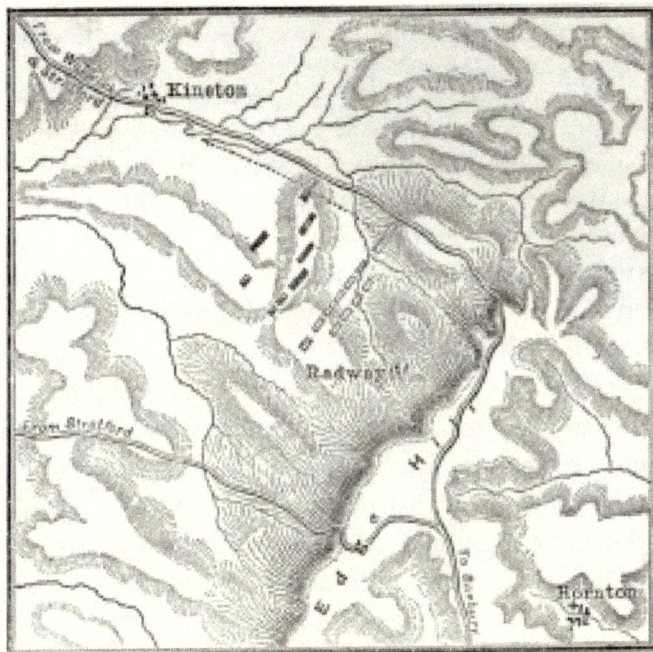

The Vale of the Red Horse
between Kineton and Edgehill,
where the Battle of Edgehill was fought,
October 23rd, 1642

fensive position which, lying between the enemy and London, compelled an attack under every disadvantage.

Thus, despising their adversary, the Cavaliers gave up every point in their favour and pressed forward to the attack, though many of their men had marched eight miles to the battle and others had not tasted food for forty-eight hours. The advice of some of the more prudent of the King's officers, that the battle should be deferred until the morrow, was overruled, on the ground that delay would not bring with it any accession of strength to themselves, while the forces of the Parliamentary army were being daily augmented, thanks to the efforts of the House of Commons and the City.

The army of Essex stood quietly awaiting the approach of their enemy until about 3 p.m., when, after the exchange of a few shots from the artillery of either side, the battle was begun by an attack of the Royalist foot on the leading brigade of the Parliamentary army, followed a moment later by a furious charge of Rupert against the cavalry of Essex's left wing, of which the effect was much increased by the desertion, from Sir William Waller's regiment, of Sir Faithful Fortescue and his troop, who, firing their pistols into the ground, rode into the ranks of the Cavaliers.

By this charge the Parliamentary horse of the left wing was entirely routed, and they, flying before their foes, burst their way through the ranks of Hollis's regiment of foot, which, being further pressed by the victors, broke up and fled for their lives to Kineton. Thither they and the remnant of the horse were pursued by Rupert, who, rushing in upon the Roundhead camp, proceeded to wreck and destroy all that he found there, careless of the fact that, as might have been expected, all discipline was quickly lost in the universal search for plunder.

The centre of the army of Essex, giving way to the contagion of fear, was also partially broken up, and for a time matters looked ill for the Parliamentary party, but all advantage which might have been reaped from this good fortune was lost to the Royalists, owing to the failure of Rupert to appreciate the situation, and to improve it by attacking with his victorious troops that portion of the enemy's line which yet held its ground.

The cavalry on the King's left, having with dragoons driven in some musketeers who lined the hedges in their front, charged the two regiments of horse who formed the first line of the Parliamentary right, and were to some extent successful, but the Roundhead regiment, which was in reserve, having charged in its turn, they appear to have been beaten from the field, since we hear no more of them.

The right or foremost brigade of the *echelon* of the Parliamentary foot, having been reinforced by some of the better-hearted of the men of the brigades in rear, stood its ground firmly, and, assisted by the cavalry on its right, which forced the enemy's musketeers to seek refuge within the squares of the pikemen, bravely repulsed all attacks.

Each of the two armies had by this time practically changed front to the left, as they now stood facing, the Royalists the south, and the Parliamentarians the north. After a pause in the action, for each party was unwilling to retire though neither dared to attack, a fresh charge was made against the King's left flank by the three regiments of cavalry of Essex's right wing; to this attack Charles had no horse to oppose, since his bodyguard, who, according to the custom of the time, should have formed his reserve of cavalry, furious at being jeered at by the other troops as merely "men of show," had begged permission to charge at the head of Rupert's columns, and were thus, at the hour of need, engaged with the others in the plunder of Kineton.

The cavalry regiments of Colonel Ballard and Lord Brooke broke up two of the King's squares, entirely disorganising and destroying the battalions which composed them, while Sir William Balfour, with the aid of a frontal attack by the infantry, dispersed the whole of two other of the Royal regiments of foot. In this charge the King's standard-bearer, Sir Edward Verney, was killed and the standard captured; it was presented to Essex, who handed it to his secretary. From the latter it was recovered at a later period of the action by an officer of the Royal army, who, disguised by wearing an orange-tawny scarf (the colour of Essex), pressing through the enemy snatched it from his hand, saying, "no clerk should carry it," and thus unobserved escaped with it to the King.

The lull which after this sharp engagement fell over the field was interrupted by the return of Rupert, who had been driven from Kineton by the advance of Hampden's brigade, with so much of Hollis's force as the latter had succeeded in rallying. Pressed from their plunder the Cavaliers swept back towards the King, but as they passed over the ground where, at the commencement of the action, the Parliamentary left had rested, they were charged by some of Essex's Life Guards; flying from these and in great disorder, they at length arrived to the support of the Royal infantry, but were too exhausted or too disheartened to attempt a new attack.

The condition of the Parliamentary troops was no better than that of their adversaries, and thus, since neither army had any further reserves or fresh battalions, the opposing lines stood facing each other, like two dogs, weary with fighting, each on its guard against the other, but neither capable of attack. On this attitude the short October day drew to a close.

During the night the King withdrew his forces on to Edgehill, while Essex made his bivouac on the field of battle, and thus, in the eyes of the Parliamentary party, proved himself to be the winner of the action, which however, save in respect to the losses incurred in it, left each of the opponents in the same condition in which he was before it took place.

On the following day Essex paraded his force at about 9 or 10 a.m., but, though he had by that time been reinforced by Hampden's brigade (2,000 foot and 500 horse), he attempted no attack, but stood merely on the defensive and watched the King's army file off the hill; when the last man had disappeared he in his turn, having completed the burial of the dead, retired by way of Warwick on Coventry. Charles having received the surrender of Banbury Castle, the garrison of which was overawed by the supposed victory of the Royalists, pushed forward to Oxford on his way to London. Rupert however, hearing of the retreat of Essex, returned to the field of battle, whence he followed the Earl towards Warwick, having, so said his enemies, in passing committed great cruelties on the wounded of Essex's army who had been left at Kineton.

On the strength of this movement the Royalists, for their part, claimed to have been last in possession of the field. The loss of the two armies in this battle amounted altogether to between 5,000 and 6,000 men, of which the King's admitted only 2,000 as their share. This assertion may probably have been correct, since it was noted that those of the Parliamentary army who fled suffered more than those who stood, while the contrary was the case in the King's force; while it is an undoubted fact that in the battles of that time the greatest slaughter invariably took place during the pursuit.

It is perhaps scarcely reasonable to judge the tactics of that period by the scale of modern knowledge and experience, but it is impossible to escape the conviction that Charles committed a grave error when he abandoned his position on Edgehill; so long as he stood there he was placed in such a manner that, while Essex by the necessity of the situation was compelled to attack (for otherwise he could not relieve the pressure upon London), the assault of the Parliamentary troops must have been made under such conditions that, considering the rawness of their soldiers and their doubtful mobility, the probabilities of success would have inclined strongly to the side of the Royal army.

The King, in fact, abandoned all such advantage as he might have gained from the character of the ground, and assumed the offensive at a time when the defensive would have been the safer, if less brilliant, form of tactical attitude. He was probably pushed to this line of action by the same force which rendered attack dangerous, and as it proved disastrous, namely, the headlong valour and the ignorant zeal of the Cavaliers, who appear to have been peculiarly liable to that English failing, contempt for their adversaries.

There can be no doubt but that, man for man, the army of

the Parliament was at this time inferior to that of the King; but their very inexperience, and consequent dependence on the few men who knew anything of war, combined with the fact that in this, their first battle, the infantry stood principally on the defensive, tended to prevent that extravagant precipitation, that "eagerness" to use Lord Clyde's words which lost in after time so many battles to the King.

Whether Essex so failed in ignorance of war, or whether he was unwilling to push his advantage to the end, it is certain that he committed a great fault in not pressing on after Charles, whose troops were weary and in retreat, with the fresh forces which Hampden and Lord Willoughby of Parham had brought up. Had he done so, it is probable that he would have demoralised or even dispersed the army of the King, while he would certainly have saved Banbury from capture, and have secured for himself the honour of undoubted victory. As it was, each army claimed to have won the field; but we, can at this distance of time be impartial, prefer to say that victory was at various times in the grasp of either, but that each failed to seize the opportunities which fortune rather than skill offered to it.

The results of the battle were, for the above reasons, insignificant; but, even had the King gained a decisive victory, its fruits would have been lost, owing to the long stay which he made in Oxford, where he remained idle until the first week of November, in place of marching at once on London.

In November he at last moved, and having learnt from his scouts that Reading had been abandoned by its garrison while Essex was still at Warwick, he occupied that town, where he received proposals of peace from the Parliament. While negotiations were proceeding, Essex, taking advantage of the pause in military operations, transferred his army to the capital, which by this time had become a huge camp, since the trained-bands and apprentices had been called to arms; while, by order of the Houses, all shops had been closed and all business suspended. The Surrey forces were concentrated at Guildford and the City troops were in camp on Turnham Green, while Brentford was held by the two regiments of Hollis and Hampden.

The Royal army, preceded by Rupert and his cavalry, pushed on, while the discussion of the treaty was yet unfinished, through Colnbrook towards London, the Prince making on the way an unsuccessful effort to secure the surrender of Windsor Castle. On the 12th of November, the King's advanced guard came in contact with the outposts of the Parliament in front of Brentford, and, being reinforced by the main body, attacked the entrenchments with, which the town was defended; after a sharp struggle the assailants were completely successful, the garrison were driven out, and the town occupied by the Royalist forces.

This action occasioned loud outcries from the Roundheads, who angrily protested against such an interruption of the negotiations for peace. During the whole of the night which followed this attack, the citizens of London trooped out to the westward, and the morning of Sunday, the 13th of November, found 24,000 of them in arms facing the Royal forces on Turnham Green.

The Surrey trained-bands had been by this time brought up to Kingston, and the suggestion was now made that these should, under the above circumstances, move on to Hounslow, with the object of threatening, if not of cutting off, the retreat of the Cavaliers; but the order which was at first given to this effect was soon counter-ordered, as was also one for a similar movement of two regiments of horse and one of foot by way of Acton.

Whether these counter-orders were dictated by a desire not to bring matters to a final issue, or by a cautious wish to provide a golden bridge for the King's army, will never be known; but the Cavaliers, after facing the City troops for some hours, were permitted to draw off without opposition and retreated leisurely on Reading, alleging afterwards as their reason for retiring, that the greater part of their ammunition had been expended.

Thus, like all other military movements of King Charles, which, even when they had in their conception some appearance of that boldness which forces victory, failed invariably from the weakness of their execution, this march on London—of which even the failure created a panic, while the success of it would have conquered a kingdom—dwindled into a mere military promenade, futile as regarded its immediate object, while the attendant details of plunder and rapine raised up numberless enemies to the Royal cause.

During the remainder of the year 1642, no movement of importance was undertaken by either of the main armies, who both, as was the custom in those days, passed the bad weather of the winter in quarters, a measure no doubt rendered advisable by the fact that marching was impossible except in the drier and warmer months, on account of the bad condition of the roads.

It remains only to notice some of the smaller events which happened during the year. In Cornwall, Sir Ralph Hopton and Sir Bevil Greenville (or Grenville), having called out the militia of the county, seized Launceston for the King, and thus commenced that war in the west, which at one time promised to replace Charles in power.

In Yorkshire, at the end of the year, Newcastle was joined by Goring, who had returned to England; but the former, devoting his attention principally to the organisation of his army, permitted Fairfax to retain for the present an uninterrupted occupation of the southern half of the county. In Lancashire, the Earl of Derby, trusting in his personal influence, endeavoured to raise a force for the King, but the general spirit of the county was so entirely for the Parliament, that in this he signally failed, and was finally defeated and forced to shelter himself in Latham House.

In the southern counties Sir William Waller succeeded in capturing Farnham Castle and the town of Winchester, while towards the end of the year he reduced Chichester, which had been garrisoned by some of the gentlemen of Sussex, who having raised a force with the intention of joining the King at Brentford, found themselves isolated on his unexpected retreat.

As a summary of the operations during the year 1642, we may say that by them the relative positions of the contending parties was not materially altered, but that now, all hope of accommodation being at an end, men were for the most part decided as to the attitude which they intended to maintain; yet many on each side, though they were committed to a distinct policy, were but half-hearted in their wishes for the complete triumph of either party.

The King remained master of the north and Wales, whilst his headquarters at Oxford were, by the natural advantages of the position of that city, absolutely secure from attack. But already symptoms were to be seen of that disagreement between the leaders of his army which was to work such evil to him, for the great nobles of England found it hard to endure the abrupt manner and hasty speech of Prince Rupert,, who, too young to understand the art of ruling men by their weaknesses, did not hesitate to chide their failings, and, confident in his position as one of royal blood, forgot that to Englishmen he seemed rather a foreigner than one of themselves.

The Parliament, on the other hand, held possession of every sea-port except Newcastle, and were steadily gaining ground towards the west in the southern counties, while their forces in Yorkshire were now organised for resistance, and the Eastern Association, growing daily in strength, formed with the City of London a bulwark, against which the undisciplined forces of the King might dash themselves in vain.

None of those suspicions, which were afterwards so rife, seem yet to have arisen with regard to the goodwill of Essex, nor were there any signs at present of the ill-blood which at a later period prevented the co-operation of himself and Waller; while the latter, whose name in a few years became synonymous with defeat, was still saluted by the citizens, who adored him, as "William the Conqueror."

CHAPTER 2

# 1643

It is almost impossible to give any connected history of this period of the contest, when every town was warring with the country around it, and each county became the scene of a petty campaign. Thus Cheshire was divided between Sir William Brereton, who had fortified Nantwich for the Parliament, and Sir Nicholas Byron, who held Chester for the King; while Lancashire, in spite of the persistent efforts of the Earl of Derby, assisted the former, as the Royalists were aided by Shropshire and Wales.

Northamptonshire, Warwickshire, Derbyshire, and Staffordshire formed an association under Lord Brooke against the King, while Berkshire and Oxfordshire were in his favour, the remaining midland counties being possessed by the one or the other party as the fortune of war might decide.

The first actions of the year took place in Yorkshire, where Lord Fairfax, repulsing the efforts of Newcastle to drive him from Leeds, Bradford, and Halifax, succeeded for a time in holding the south-west corner of the county; but about the middle of February the Queen, having landed at Bridlington Bay, gave such assistance in arms and money to the Earl, as enabled him to raise an army superior to any that Fairfax could collect, and the latter thus was able only with great difficulty to hold his own.

The country between York and Oxford was, however, still for the most part in the power of the Parliamentary party, and the Earl therefore placed a garrison in Newark with the object of keeping up communication with the headquarters of the King. Thence a little later he was able to extend his operations into Lincolnshire, where Cavendish, a brother of the Earl of Devonshire, succeeded in occupying Grantham. In addition to, or in consequence of this good fortune, the Governor of Scarborough Castle gave in his adhesion to the Royal cause, while Hotham, the Governor of Hull, whose faith in the Parliament had long been wavering, was with his son made a prisoner and sent to London, on a suspicion of a similar intention.

Returning now to Cornwall, we find that the Parliamentary leaders in that county, Buller and Carew, had, on the advance of 3,000 men under Hopton to Launceston, fallen back into Devonshire, whither the Royalists followed them, after a short delay caused by the necessity of raising volunteer regiments, since the militia, which composed their present force, could not be called upon to serve out of their county. Ruthven, the Parliamentary Governor of Plymouth, was defeated by Hopton at Braddock Down, and the Royalists gallantly carried Saltash by storm. This petty war was ended by a private peace, concluded in all due form between the counties of Devon and Cornwall, a peace promptly annulled by the Houses, who further at once ordered Waller to the west.

In Staffordshire the siege of Lichfield cost the Parliament the life of Lord Brooke, who was shot from the close, as he sat at a window watching the operations of the besiegers; but the city was soon after stormed by Sir John Gell, the Roundhead leader in that county, against whom in turn the Earl of Northampton advanced from Banbury.

Gell, pressed by the superior forces of the Earl, abandoned Lichfield and fell back towards Nantwich; he found there Sir William Brereton at the head of nearly 3,000 men, who returned with him against the Earl. The two forces met, about the middle of March, on Hopton Heath, near Stafford, where a battle ensued, in which Northampton was killed at the head of his troops. Each party claimed the victory, but a good proof that fortune on this occasion favoured the Cavaliers is given by the fact, that Lichfield was in April surrendered to them.

Gloucester, of which the governor, Massey, had acted with great vigour in reducing the castles in its vicinity, was in the early part of the year threatened by the Earl of Worcester, who, at the head of a mob of raw Welsh troops, moved against it from the west; but when the so-called siege had lasted only five weeks, this undisciplined rabble was easily defeated by Waller, who had been detached to the relief of the city, and was by him driven back in disorder into the hills. After the completion of this light service, Waller possessed himself of Hereford and Tewkesbury, and having provided them with garrisons, himself returned to the main army under Essex, who was at that time before Reading.

Let us now return with him to the Lord-General. The early months of the year had been occupied in efforts—as ever, unsuccessful—to find grounds on which a treaty of peace might be concluded; but all hope of agreement having been abandoned by the middle of April, Essex at that date advanced towards Reading, with the intention of besieging that town.

His army was composed of about 16,000 foot and 3,000 horse, and every care was taken to secure the supply of all kinds of provisions and stores from London; thus under the management of Major-General Skippon, an old soldier of the best type, the besiegers daily gained ground. The garrison numbered only about 3,300 of all arms, and were badly furnished with munitions of war, having less than forty barrels of powder. About a week after the commencement of the siege, the governor, Sir Arthur Aston, was wounded, and the command consequently devolved upon Colonel Fielding, the senior officer of the garrison.

From the earliest commencement of the siege the King strained every nerve to accomplish the relief of the town. Rupert was hastily recalled from Lichfield; but the necessities of the garrison not permitting sufficient delay to allow of his arrival, Charles sent out every man he could muster, under Lord Forth, his then commander-in-chief, with orders to raise the siege. By means of a convoy, which had fought its way in, the besieged had been previously informed that they should be relieved in a week.

The Royal forces marched by way of Wallingford to Caversham, where they attacked the besiegers, and were repulsed with loss. Much surprised that, at the time of their attack, no corresponding sortie was made by the garrison, communications were opened with the governor, who reported that he had been offered terms so favourable that he had decided to accept them. Though this decision was fully approved by the King at the time, Colonel Fielding was afterwards sentenced by court-martial to be beheaded for thus surrendering his command; he was, however, pardoned by the King, who was in truth not much grieved at a surrender which set free the garrison for service in the field; for by the terms, which were signed on the 26th of April, the entire force of the besieged was at liberty to march out with colours flying, and to proceed without hindrance to Oxford.

About this time also arrived a much-needed convoy of ammunition, sent by Newcastle from the north, of which the receipt so raised the spirits of the Royalists that those who, but a few days earlier, were ready to abandon Oxford, now talked of awaiting Essex and of offering him battle.

But the Parliamentary army was scarcely in a position to advance; for, partly on account of the weather, partly by reason of the marshy character of the ground around Reading, their men had suffered severely from fever and ague, and were now in no condition to move, far less to attack. Towards the end of May, some improvement having occurred in the health of his troops, Essex moved forward to Thame, about ten miles from Oxford; at this time the main body of the King's forces was about Abingdon. In these positions both armies remained, in an idleness which was varied only by frequent skirmishes between their mounted troops, until the middle of June, when an engagement occurred, small of itself, but of moment on account of the loss which the Parliament incurred in it by the death of one of its most remarkable members.

A certain Colonel Hurrey, or Urry, a Scot, being dissatisfied with his treatment by Essex, deserted from the Parliamentary army, and, for the purpose of ingratiating himself with his new comrades, gave full information to Rupert as to the quarters occupied by the cavalry of Essex, adding further that they kept but indifferent guard. Acting on this intelligence, the Prince made several attacks on the cantonments of the Roundheads, and finally determined to beat up their headquarters at Thame.

Leaving Oxford on the evening of the 16th of June, he marched through the night by a circuitous route until he had placed himself between his enemy and London; turning then towards Oxford, he swept through one village after another, carrying off prisoners and plunder.

As the day began to dawn, finding that he was followed by the cavalry of the Parliament, who were now at last fully roused, Rupert made his way to a bridge at which, on his advance, he had left a guard of infantry. As a narrow lane led to the bridge and he found that his pursuers were close upon him, the Prince determined to check their advance before committing his troops to the defile. A "fair plain," named Chalgrove Field, offered good ground for a cavalry action, and here accordingly at 8 a.m. on the 17th he took his stand.

The vanguard of the Parliamentary horse included in its number many of the principal officers of the army, who, in many cases only half armed, had hurried forward with-out waiting for their troops. These on arriving in front of the Cavaliers at once rushed to the attack, but being firmly met, were repulsed with loss and beaten back to their main body, which, under Essex himself, arrived only in time to see Rupert gallop across the bridge, his retreat being covered by musketeers, who lined the lane by which alone it could be approached.

Apart from its interest as a good example of skilful cavalry tactics, this skirmish has a name for all time, since in it, among the foremost in the charge, the great Hampden met with his death. Whether wounded by the fire of the enemy or, as another account has it, by the bursting of his own pistol which had been overloaded by a page,[1] he "rode off the field before the action was done, which he never used to do," and died of his wounds at his own house on the 24th of June.

Shortly after this action Essex, finding himself unable to undertake anything of importance against the King, owing to the continued ill-health of his troops, fell back with his army to St. Albans. Thence he himself proceeded to London, where he exerted every means to incline the Parliament to treat with the King, a mode of action which by no means increased the general's popularity with the majority of the people or with the army. It was at one time proposed that Waller should be put forward as his successor in the chief command, but the unfavourable results to the Parliamentary cause of events which now took place in the west, put an end to any plan of the kind, though Sir William, taking advantage of the waning popularity of Essex, obtained greater independence of command than had up to this time been allotted to him. From this date commenced the enmity between the two leaders, which during this and the succeeding year bore bitter fruit to the commonwealth, since each preferred the satisfaction of his private jealousy to the advantage of his cause and country.

It is difficult to conceive how any cause could be worse served than was that of the Parliament at this time by the two leaders of its armies, and we have here a good example of the truth of the principle, which lays down that service in a subordinate position, however excellent it may have been, can be no criterion of the fitness of a general for high command. It is true that other factors, besides incapacity, may have influenced the actions of Essex, but as regards Waller, there is not even this fact by which to account for the almost invariable failure of his plans. If we follow him to his campaign in the west, we shall see how he was at fault, not only in the details of his strategy, but also in the mere handling of troops on the field of battle.

In the early part of May, 1643, the Earl of Stamford, on the

---

1. Who, having been ordered to reload the pistol daily, did so indeed, but neglected to daily draw the previous charge.

abrogation of the private peace between Devon and Cornwall, had invaded the latter county with an army far superior to that which followed the leaders of the Royalists, but, having detached the larger part of his cavalry to Bodmin for the purpose of seizing the person of the high-sheriff, his camp at Stratton was on May 16th attacked in their absence, and most gallantly carried by the Cornish troops under Sir Bevil Grenville.

On the news of this success Charles despatched the Marquis of Hertford and Prince Maurice, with a strong force of cavalry, to assist "the Army of Cornwall," as it was now called; these troops he could easily spare, since Oxford was now (in June) no longer threatened by Essex, while they were much needed in the west, for Waller, who was at this time quartered at Bath, had lately received reinforcements from London, in addition to such increase of his strength as resulted from the rallying of the fugitives from Stratton.

The Royalists, advancing through Devon and Somerset, seized Wells, and, having been successful in a cavalry skirmish at Chewton, pushed on after a rest of a few days to Bradford in Wiltshire, within a short distance of Bath.

Small actions became now of daily occurrence, and in these, a new regiment, raised by Sir Arthur Hazelrigg, greatly distinguished itself; being armed in complete steel the men composing it received the nickname of the "Lobsters," and were said by the Cavaliers to be the first of the Parliamentary horse who could stand against them.

Hertford was so confident of success, that he determined to force on a battle, and, with this object, marched past Bath to Marshfield, as if with the intention to move on Oxford, which was indeed his design so soon as he should have succeeded in defeating Waller. The latter, who had received special orders to stop any such movement, at once followed him, and, on the 5th of July, having taken up a strongly intrenched position at Lansdown, awaited there the attack of the Royalists. In order to draw them on to the assault, which he did not doubt his ability to repulse, he sent forward at first a weak body of horse; this was quickly driven in, upon which he attacked with his whole strength of cavalry and dragoons. The charge of these troops, especially that of Hazelrigg's *cuirassiers*, was for a time completely successful, but they were at length repulsed by an attack from a mixed force of cavalry and infantry under Sir Nicolas Slanning.

The Cornish foot now clamoured loudly for "leave to fetch off the guns," and their leaders, yielding to this spirit of daring, so often the precursor and the cause of victory, prepared to assault the very strong position of the Parliamentary general.

The brow of the hill on which Waller's forces were posted was lined along their front with breastworks, while each flank of the line rested on a wood, which was held by a large force of musketeers. The King's forces, having detached two considerable bodies of troops against these woods, advanced towards the front of the position, and, after having been charged by the hostile horse, which inflicted upon them a serious check, by a supreme effort under the leadership of Sir Bevil Grenville, threw back the mounted troops and stormed the breastworks, which they gallantly carried.

This success dearly purchased by the loss of Grenville, who was killed by a blow with a pole-axe, was at once followed up by an advance of the whole of the Royalist line, and the woods having been by this time cleared of their defenders, the crest of the hill was crowned and the breastworks occupied by the Cavaliers. The Parliamentary army was however not yet beaten, for, sullenly drawing back, it took up a new position behind a stone wall on the level top of the hill, and in this attitude remained facing the enemy until nightfall.

Neither side had any reserve of fresh troops with which to bring the battle to a decisive issue, and Waller, after having about midnight made a semblance of an attack on his lost position, fell back before daylight on Bath.

This engagement is a notable example of a "soldier's battle," won as it was by sheer hard fighting, without so much skill to direct as could either choose a point on which to attack, or make use of the victory when gained. In this respect it resembles every action in the early part of the Civil Wars, for it is not until the entrance of Fairfax and Cromwell into power of command that we shall find, as the result of a battle, aught but a doubtful though costly victory, even in cases where either party could be said to be distinctly victorious.

The Royalists fell back on Marshfield, having suffered, in addition to the loss of Sir Bevil Grenville, a further calamity by the serious injury of Sir Ralph Hopton, who was, on the morning after the battle, much hurt by the accidental explosion of some barrels of gunpowder.

On the receipt of reinforcements from the King it was decided that the army of Cornwall should march on Oxford, and it accordingly moved to Chippenham, whither Waller, who had joined to his force a considerable portion of the garrison of Bristol, hastened after it; finding it there in a very strong position, he hesitated to attack, whereupon Prince Maurice continued his march on Devizes.

Waller's cavalry, well armed and well mounted, were as much superior to the weary and brokendown horse of the Royal army, as his infantry were inferior to those of the King, and for this reason it was determined by the leaders of the Cavaliers, that they would not attempt to move the foot to Oxford, since their way thither lay over open ground well suited to the action of the enemy's squadrons, but that, while the horse should march as quickly as possible to the King, the infantry should hold a position at Devizes and await reinforcements.

The march to Oxford (thirty miles) was executed by Prince Maurice, in the night of the 9th of July, and the following day saw Waller with all his army assembled around the town of Devizes, which was entirely open to attack. On the 11th Waller ordered an assault, which was repulsed by the besieged, to whom, feeling certain of ultimate victory, he then offered terms of capitulation; these the Royalists, whose object it was to gain time for the arrival of relief, feigned to be prepared to accept, and negotiations had been but just broken off, when Lord Wilmot appeared within a few miles of the town, with every horse and man that could be spared from Oxford.

The Parliamentary army at once drew off from the siege, and took up a position on Roundway Down, about two miles from Devizes, where, posted between the King's horse and his infantry, they prepared to give battle. Waller, however, without reason, abandoned his defensive attitude, and, "out of pure gayety," drawing off his horse from his foot, charged uphill with the whole of the former against Wilmot's squadrons. The result was disastrous; defeated in their first charge, the Roundhead troopers were with difficulty rallied and again advanced, only to be again thrown back; Hazelrigg's *cuirassiers* were routed, and troop after troop dispersed, so that in half-an-hour after the commencement of the action Wilmot's horsemen had left no formed body of the Parliamentary cavalry on the field; carried away by their panic all had fled, suffering more loss, the chronicler relates, by the fall of horse and man owing to the broken ground, than from the swords of the pursuers.

The infantry of the Parliament still stood firm, but the garrison of Devizes, who at first refused to believe the good news, now came up from the town, and Waller's foot, their "hearts failing them," were all either killed or made prisoners. That general himself fled to Bristol and thence to London, leaving the former city in great terror, since a large proportion of its garrison had been lost on Roundway Down.

The ill feeling between Essex and Waller rose to a greater height after this defeat of the latter, who accused the Lord-General of not doing his best to aid him, and had some followers in that belief; but the credit of the Earl was still too high to suffer much from the charges laid against him by his lately defeated rival, who averred that Essex, posted at that time at Thame, could and should have prevented or intercepted that advance of Wilmot from Oxford on Devizes, which caused the ruin of his army.

Of the Royal forces Wilmot returned to Oxford, while the Cornishmen, having taken Bath, commenced on the 24th of July the siege of Bristol. On the 27th, after some portion of the outworks had been carried by assault, that city was surrendered by Nathaniel Fiennes, the governor; an act for which, though eventually pardoned by Essex, he was by court-martial condemned to die.

Of all the valley of the Severn, almost we might say of all the west of England, the only point which now remained in the hands of the Parliament was the city of Gloucester. Could that be won, Worcester, Shrewsbury, and the country as far north as Lancashire might be supplied through the lately captured seaport of Bristol, which last, on the revival thus caused of its trade, would "bring in a notable revenue to the King." All the forces also in Wales could then be drawn out into the field army, and Charles might thus pit the western half of England against the eastern, with every hope of success.

On the other hand it was urged that much time would be required for the siege of a city of such importance, and that so great a delay would enable the Parliament to make good the recent losses of its army, while, should the King advance at once on London, nothing now stood between him and the capital but the dispirited and diseased force which Essex had lately withdrawn from Thame.

A message from Colonel Massey, the Governor of Gloucester, which seemed to promise a readiness to serve the King, turned the scale, and it was decided to march on that city, not with any intention to undertake a lengthened siege, but in the hope that it might be immediately surrendered. On the 10th of August the Royal army arrived at Gloucester, which was at once summoned. Within the two hours laid down as a limit for the consideration of the terms, came out from the city "two citizens, with lean, pale, sharp and bad visages," who signified clearly that "We, the inhabitants of Gloucester, are resolved to keep this city."

Moved by the opinion of experts in his army, that the siege could not last more than ten days, the King commenced the attack in due form. Thus passed the days of precious opportunity, of which moreover the Parliament did not fail to make use.

Leaving the King and his main army thus employed, we must

turn our attention to other parts of the kingdom, where events were occurring remarkable, not so much for themselves, as for the men, Fairfax and Cromwell, who guided them.

The Earl of Newcastle had in the early part of May possessed himself of the towns of Sheffield and Rotherham, and Lord Fairfax, being cooped up in the barren country about Leeds, found his forces in absolute want; on the night of the 20th of May he sent out a body of about 1,500 men, under his son Sir Thomas, who, moving on Wakefield, where they arrived at 4 a.m. on the 21st, stormed the town with small loss to themselves, though of the enemy they took 1,500 prisoners and four guns. But in spite of this success Fairfax felt himself unable to cope with the overwhelming strength of the Royalists, and, in the same letter in which he reports his last action, begs that Cromwell may be at once sent to his assistance.

Oliver, who was now a colonel, had been "up and down in Lincolnshire in the Parliamentary service," and in May advanced on Newark in the hope of drawing off some of the Royal troops from Fairfax. At Grantham he defeated a large body of cavalry under Cavendish (who was killed in the action), but was not in sufficient strength to attempt anything of moment against the garrison. This was the first engagement which brought Cromwell's name prominently before the public.

Towards the end of June the Earl of Newcastle advanced on Bradford, and on his way was met by Fairfax on Atherton (or Allerton) Moor, at which place, on the 30th, a battle was fought in which, though his foot were at first successful, Fairfax was utterly routed, owing to a determined charge by some of the Earl's cavalry. The Parliamentary forces fled to Leeds, whither the Earl was about to pursue them when he heard of Hotham's seizure at Hull, upon which news he at once marched on that town. On learning his destination Lord Fairfax and his son, by forced marches and at great personal risk, pushed on into Hull, of which the former was made governor.

Yorkshire being thus now almost entirely in his power, Newcastle, who about this time was created a marquis, prepared to attack the Associated Counties, and with this object marched on Gainsborough, then held by Lord Willoughby of Parham, which he closely besieged.

Cromwell, who was at once recalled to Willoughby's relief, had after the action at Grantham moved towards Nottingham in the hope of being able to cut off the march of the Queen's force to Oxford, whither she had gone from Yorkshire in the early part of June; in this he was unsuccessful, for Her Majesty without difficulty joined the King at Kineton, whither the latter had moved from Oxford for the purpose of meeting her. On hearing of Willoughby's danger, Cromwell at once marched to his assistance and, capturing on his way the town of Stamford and Burleigh House, on the 28th of July forced a passage into Gainsborough with a convoy. On attempting however to advance out of the town for the purpose of driving off the besiegers, Oliver found himself in the presence of the whole army of Newcastle, and was therefore obliged to fall back by a hasty, though skilful retreat on Huntingdon.

During the month of August Gainsborough and Lincoln were surrendered to the King's forces, and the eastern counties were saved from invasion only by the burning desire of Newcastle to possess himself of Hull, of which on the 2nd of September he commenced the siege.

The affairs of the Parliamentary cause were at this time in a condition of almost hopeless difficulty, for, apart from the actual losses which they had sustained in men and territory, a large party had grown up who, despairing of success or desirous of making good terms for themselves, demanded peace with no doubtful voice. Chief among these was the General Essex, though even he did not proceed to such extremities as did other members of the House of Lords, who did not scruple to abandon the principles for which they had struggled, and who fled to Oxford to make their peace while there was yet time. Their reception, it may be added, was not such as to encourage others to follow their example.

But the House of Commons, supported by the City of London, resolutely refused to listen to any suggestions for proposals for peace, and prepared to fight out the contest to the end.

The eyes of the nation were now turned upon the siege of Gloucester, which, without well knowing why, men grew to regard as the test-point of success in the war. To trust much to its resistance seemed indeed but a forlorn hope, for the total strength of the garrison was only 1,400 men, and their supply of powder did not exceed fifty barrels, while the line of defensive works was long out of all proportion to the force available to man it; there was further a party in the city, which was desirous of an immediate submission to the King.

Operations were commenced by the besiegers, who numbered, in horse and foot, about 8,000 men, with the object of cutting off the supply of water which drove the corn-mills; that for drinking purposes, being furnished by the Severn, was, fortunately for the defenders, out of their power. Batteries were thrown up, and a constant fire was directed on the city from guns and mortars of, for that day, very large calibre, but the besieged repaired the breaches as quickly as they were made, while several sallies were undertaken with entire success; at the end therefore of twenty-six days of siege, little or no impression had been made upon the defences.

The Parliament had in the meantime not been idle; the army of Essex was recruited with volunteers and pressed men; all shops were by their order shut until Gloucester should be relieved, with the object that no ordinary business might interfere with a matter of such importance; and the crowning result of their exertions was obtained, when, on the 21st of August, a force was prepared sufficient to ensure, under skilful direction, the relief of the beleaguered city.

On the 24th Essex mustered 10,000 men on Hounslow Heath, and on the 26th commenced his march by Colnbrook and Beaconsfield. On receipt of the news of his advance, Prince Rupert was detached with a force of cavalry from the besieging army, with orders to delay the march of the Roundheads by all possible means, "and it is recorded that scarcely a day passed on which an attack was not made on some part of the Parliamentary columns. On the 1st of September Essex received at Brackley Heath a reinforcement of a brigade of the London trained-bands; on the 4th, near Stow-in-the-Wold, he skirmished for many miles together with 4,000 of the Prince's cavalry, while on the 5th he arrived within sight of the city of Gloucester, and, from the Prestbury Hills, saw the huts of the King's camp in flames, their occupants having abandoned the siege on his approach.

On the 8th of September Essex entered Gloucester, where he was received with great rejoicings; on the 10th he marched to Tewkesbury, where he remained five days, with the object of covering from attack the foraging parties, which were sent out to revictual Gloucester; thence, after making a feint towards Worcester, he suddenly, by a forced march, swooped upon a Royal magazine of stores at Cirencester, obtaining there a large supply of provisions, of which his troops were in the utmost need. From this point he commenced his return march on London, which he conducted by way of Cricklade and Swindon, thus directing his route through a country less suited to the action of the Royal cavalry than that by which he had advanced.

But this care did not much avail him, for Rupert, following close in rear of the Parliamentary army, fell upon the rearguard in Aldbourn Chase with such gallantry, that he drove it in confusion on the main body, and, when it had there rallied on superior strength, by a second charge threw it again into disorder. Being thus delayed, Essex did not arrive at Hungerford until the evening of the 18th of September, by which date the King was in position at Newbury, between him and London.

Charles, after retiring from Gloucester, had taken up his post at Evesham, being deceived by the original direction of Essex's march (on Tewkesbury), and had proposed, at this point, should the Parliamentary general use the same road to return as he had already used to advance, to cut his line of retreat on London. The sudden and unexpected movement of the Earl on Cirencester disarranged this plan, but, thanks to the delay caused by the persistent attacks of Rupert, Charles was still able by dint of forced marches (which, however, seriously diminished his strength) to interpose at Newbury between Essex and his base.

The King was thus master of the situation; he had it in his power to refuse or to give battle, while Essex, in order to secure his road on London, was compelled to attack an enemy who was posted in a strong position. The Parliamentary army, cut from the source from which it derived both provisions and recruits, could find safety only in victory, while defeat implied the immediate advance of the King on panic-stricken London. A turning movement round the enemy's flank was, in those days of bad roads, an impossibility, and would in any age have been the acme of rashness, while a retreat, considering the relative positions in, which the two armies stood, could have no object and no safe end.

Thus the strategical attitude of the King was scarcely capable of improvement, while his tactical position, extending as it did across a range of hills, was against the mode of attack of those times exceptionally strong, especially since each flank rested on a marshy valley. Every circumstance pointed to the assumption of the defensive as the wisest policy, but owing to the gallant but unskilful leading of the Royal cavalry, the King's army in point of fact attacked during the whole of the day, and thus surrendered to their adversaries the entire advantage which they had purchased by a large expenditure of labour and lives.

On the 19th of September Essex marched from Hungerford on Newbury, but, finding the King's army in possession of the hills to the south of the latter town, of which fact, owing to his weakness in cavalry, he seems to have been previously unaware, he bivouacked at a distance of two miles from his adversary. At break of day on the 20th he continued his march, and, finding a hill (of which in contemporary accounts the name is given as Bigg's Hill), which he considered to be of essential importance to him, already occupied by the enemy, he attacked it in person at the head of his own regiment and two brigades of infantry, and drove from it the advanced posts of the King's troops.

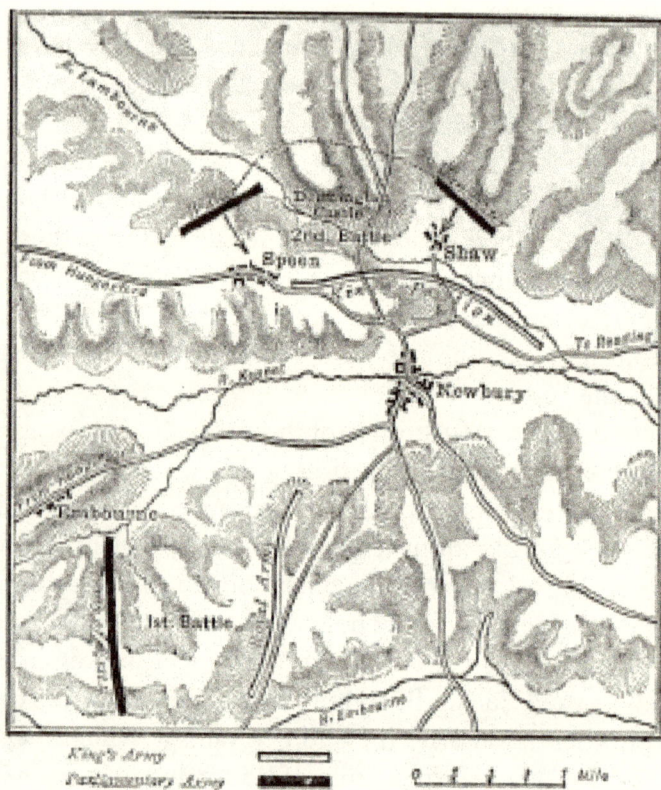

NEWBURY AND THE COUNTRY ROUND,
WHERE THE TWO BATTLES OF NEWBURY WERE FOUGHT,
SEPTEMBER 20TH, 1643, AND OCTOBER 27TH, 1644

The main position of the Cavaliers was upon a spur of the range of hills which divides the valley of the Kennet from that of the Embourne, and was in its nature purely defensive. The ground in front of the centre and left of the Royal army was broken heath land, presenting by the steepness of its slope considerable difficulty to the rapid advance of an assailant, an advantage of great value in those days when, owing to the poor character of the fire of musketry, no force could be driven from its ground except by an actual charge to close quarters. On. the right of the King's line, which extended almost into the valley of the Kennet, the ground was enclosed and in places marshy; for this reason the action in this part of the field was of a more desultory and less decisive character than that of the left and centre.

Essex having taken up his position on the captured hill, was immediately attacked by the Royal cavalry, who thus vitally changed the character of the action, while the King's foot, still standing on the defensive, took no part in the earlier phases of the battle. The artillery of the Cavaliers, having been placed with a view to the defence of the main position, was of little or no use in support of this irregular attack, while it is reported that that of the Parliamentary army "did very great execution."

Essex's cavalry, led by Sir Philip Stapleton, the commander of his bodyguard, repulsed several charges of the Royalists' horse, but being at length outnumbered and outflanked, they were beaten back behind their own line.

This temporary success of the Cavaliers led to a phase of battle, which, natural as it seems to us now, was then a matter of wonder; for the Roundhead horse, flying before their pursuers, found shelter and leisure to reform in rear of the infantry squares, which stood "as a bulwark and a rampire." We have seen before, and we shall see again in this war how, when a battle had been practically decided by the flight of the cavalry of the one or the other party, the infantry was, as a rule, broken up and cut to pieces by the combined attacks of the enemy's horse and foot; such was no longer the case here, for the trained-bands of London who, so said the Cavaliers, knew nothing of war "beyond the easy practice of their positions in the artillery garden," standing shoulder to shoulder, threw back the best blood of England from the front of their pikes.

On the right in the meanwhile Skippon had not been idle; he observed a movement of the King's left wing to their left, which apparently was made with the object of cutting off the march of Essex's train, then moving along the valley of the Embourne; leaving therefore a portion of his force to act as escort to the guns, he pushed forward with the remainder to make a counter-stroke; the Cavaliers upon this, slightly changing the direction of their advance, made an attack on the extreme right of the Parliamentary line, which was repulsed by a brigade of infantry under Lord Robartes, with the assistance of four field guns.

The centre being at this time hard pressed, Essex called up a fresh regiment to the relief of his two brigades, who had been fighting since daybreak, but this was made of no such stuff as the others, was at once "overcharged" and was extricated from its danger only by a new attack by the London trained-bands.

Night fell, but the battle still continued; at about 10 p.m. the Royalists, having at last brought their guns into a good position, opened a heavy fire on the line of the Parliamentary troops, but Skippon pushing forward his artillery in turn, appears to have enfiladed the King's left, and to have stopped any progress in that direction. Yet a little later another but weaker attack on the Parliamentary right was easily repulsed by 300 musketeers, and the engagement came to an end.

During the night the Royal forces threw back their left, which retired into the town of Newbury, and thus, greatly to his surprise, gave free passage to Essex, who had fully expected to fight again on the following day. He at once took advantage of his permission to depart, and marching early in the morning, arrived at Reading on the 22nd, having been pressed during the whole distance by Prince Rupert, who, with a strong force of cavalry and 1,000 foot, continually harassed the rear of the

Roundhead column.

From Reading Essex moved slowly on London, where he himself arrived about the 25th, his army being quartered in Windsor, while Waller's force lay about Staines. Reading was at once occupied by the Royalists, who also left a garrison in Donnington Castle, near Newbury; the King then withdrew his army to Oxford, and went into winter quarters.

The neglect or refusal of Waller to assist Essex in his hour of need, as he might easily have done from his post at Staines, by no means improved the relations between the two Parliamentary generals, but the House of Commons, foreseeing the danger of any quarrel which might thence arise, insisted upon and arranged a meeting, in which "Sir William was all submission and humility, and His Excellency all grace and courtesy." Yet was the rancour not lessened on either side.

The Parliament claimed that while their loss amounted to but 500 men, that of the King's army was at least 2,000; the truth of this statement is fairly open to doubt, as indeed are all accounts of casualties on either side during the war; the loss of the King's army included, as might be supposed, more men of family than that of the Parliament, and every man of learning or refinement, whichever cause he might favour, mourned the death of Lucius Gary Lord Falkland, a scholar and a gentleman in the highest sense of the words.

We must here for a while leave the progress of the war, in order to notice an incident which had more effect than any battle on its course and end. The Parliament, finding itself hard pressed in the field by the army of the King, had during the year debated the desirability of concluding an alliance with Scotland, and, having decided this question in the affirmative, received a favourable response from the sister country, coupled however er with the condition that England should join in a Solemn League and Covenant, to forward the reformation of religion, to extirpate Popery, to preserve the King's person and to punish malignants; the latter was a term which included all those who refused to sign the Covenant itself.

Accordingly, on the 25th of September, this document was formally signed by the principal members of the House of Commons, and the Scots in return promised their aid towards the prosecution of the war, a promise which was followed by the raising of an army under the Earl of Leven.

But the arms of Scotland, evil though the opposition of that country was to prove to the King, did but little injury to his cause in comparison to that which he himself inflicted on it by an ill-judged effort at a counter-stroke. For in order to balance the accession of power which the alliance with Scotland brought to the Parliament, Charles was so unwise, men then said so guilty, as to conclude a peace with the Irish rebels, with the intent that thus those of his forces which had been employed against them, might be set free to join his army in England.

No act of the King, not the levying of ship-money, not the crowd of monopolies which enriched the court and impoverished the people, neither the extravagance of Buckingham, the tyranny of Strafford nor the prelacy of Laud, not even the attempted arrest of the five members, raised such a storm of indignation and hatred throughout the kingdom, as did this determination of the King to withdraw (as men said), for the purpose of subduing his subjects, the force which had been raised to avenge the blood of 100,000 Protestant martyrs.

We, looking at the course of events at such a distance as softens both lights and shadows, fail probably to realise how deep and how fierce was this feeling of resentment in the breasts of Puritans, who saw the avengers of blood called back from their righteous work of slaying the Irish (foreign and therefore savage, Roman Catholic and therefore diabolical), and directed by the orders of a Protestant King to turn their weapons against God's saints on earth.

To us the "riposte" of Charles appears to have been a fair one. The Parliament had applied for aid to a country which, in spite of his father's reign and his own, was still to the minds of most Englishmen foreign; might he not with equal, or with better right, recall his troops from a task which did not immediately press for completion, and use them against those who dared to invite the stranger to invade their Fatherland? So to us, but to the England of the time this act was nauseous, was exasperating to the highest degree, while to the cause of the King it was fatal; for, from this moment, the condition of the Parliamentary party began to mend.

We must now return to the consideration of events in the eastern counties, where Lord Manchester had taken the command of a force composed of various detachments, which served under the respective orders of Lord Willoughby of Parham, Colonel Cromwell, and Sir Thomas Fairfax. The latter had lately, with twenty troops of horse, crossed the Humber from Hull, where his father was now besieged by the Marquis of Newcastle.

The siege was carried on by the Royalists with no less than 15,000 men, but Lord Fairfax had, by cutting the dykes, laid all the surrounding country under water, and had thus secured the town against an assault. A sally on the 11th of October, at first repulsed by the besiegers, was at last completely successful, and in it the garrison carried off a large gun belonging to the enemy; despairing of his object, the Marquis on the following day raised the siege.

On the 11th of October another victory for the Parliamentary cause was gained at Horncastle, where the Earl of Manchester defeated a detachment of Newcastle's army, which had been reinforced, a contest being obviously inevitable and near at hand, with all available cavalry from the garrisons of Lincoln, Newark, and Gainsborough.

On the 10th the Royalist force, being united while Manchester's troops were still scattered, had driven in the outposts of the latter, forcing him to abandon the town of Horncastle and to take up a position on Bolingbroke Hill. During the whole night the Parliamentary squadrons were gathering to the rendezvous, and the morning found them in strength equal to that of the enemy. The dragoons of either side first engaged, but, ere the fire of their muskets had produced much effect, the Roundhead horse, led by Cromwell and Fairfax, dashed at their foe; they swept through the Royalist dragoons, by whose fire Cromwell's horse was killed, and charging the front line of the hostile cavalry, bore them back on the second line and the reserve.

The remainder of Manchester's troops, seeing the advantage which had thus been gained, poured in upon the confused Cavaliers, who fled pell-mell, leaving their dismounted dragoons to the mercy of the enemy. What mercy they received may be gathered from the statement, that the Parliamentary forces "had the execution of them for five miles," killed 500 and took 800 prisoners.

Cromwell in this action had a very narrow escape of being killed, for his horse in its fall held him down, and, when he at last extricated himself from the pressure, he was again borne to the ground by a blow from a Cavalier; rising a second time, Oliver mounted a horse which one of his men had caught, and pressed on after the enemy. Lincolnshire was thus relieved, for Lincoln and Gainsborough fell into the hands of the Parliament before the end of the year, and preparations were now energetically made for the reconquest of Yorkshire.

In the southern counties, Waller, after some few small successes in Surrey, was appointed Major-General of the Associated Counties of Hampshire, Sussex, Surrey, and Kent, and the Earl of Essex having been forced by the importunities of Parliament to grant him greater powers and independence of command, he was able to reduce every part of these counties into obedience to the Houses, with the single exception of Basing House, the seat of the Marquis of Winchester, which defied all efforts for its capture.

On the King's side, the principal event which occurred during the latter part of 1643 was the landing in Wales of a considerable number of the soldiers of the army of Ireland. Prince Maurice, who commanded in the west, had in September captured Exeter; in October Dartmouth was surrendered to him, while during the remainder of the year he was engaged in the siege of Plymouth.

The balance of victory during the year was undoubtedly in

favour of the King, who, though he had not gained any very decided advantage, had yet in many instances inflicted great losses on the Parliament, in men, arms, and horses. That his successes had never more than a temporary effect was due in part to the absence of any distinct plan for his campaign, in consequence of which defect his movements in the theatre of war and in the battlefield were equally devoid of object; while when, as at Newbury, he obtained a distinct advantage of position, he was unable to make full use of it, owing to the want of discipline which was the curse of his army, and which was in great measure due to the unavoidable disproportion which frequently existed between the social and military rank of individuals.

In the army of the Parliament, on the other hand, with but few exceptions, each man took his status by his rank as a soldier alone, since, as a rule, no one had any position by birth or favour. In another respect, however, the Cavaliers were more fortunate than their opponents, since in the Royal army all, whatever their personal quarrels might be, were at one with regard to the object of the struggle against the Houses; while the soldiers of the latter were severely weighted by the various political opinions of their leaders, of whom many were for private reasons unwilling that either their own party or that of the King should obtain complete success. Should the former win the day, they would assuredly fall under the rule of men whom they regarded as their social inferiors, whose every hope was a blow to the privileges which the leaders loved; while, should the King prevail, their very heads sat loose upon their shoulders.

Such were the Earls of Essex and Manchester, while Waller, who was a mere soldier, had so little personal weight, that he was not even able to maintain discipline in his command. But a new school was soon to arise, of which Fairfax and Cromwell were types, composed of men who intended to crush the King, and who regarded the war as a means to this end, and not as a source of livelihood or as a field for intrigue. They were still for the most part in the junior ranks of the army, but the time was near when opportunity was to show of what stuff they were made, and their desert was to place them in their rightful positions as leaders of the Nation in arms.

This advance was contemporaneous with that of a new power, the spirit of Independency, which before long brought about a military crisis, in its turn the forerunner of a political revolution.

The Independents as strongly objected to the rigid trammels of Presbyterianism, as did the Presbyterians to the rule of Episcopacy, holding themselves, as their name implied, free from the chains of all dogma and of all forms of worship. Each man among them claimed the right to judge for himself in matters of religion, and from this assumption of liberty in such matters grew a similar demand with reference to things political. The freedom thus given to personal opinion proved at once the strength and the weakness of this party, for while it attracted thinking men of various sects to their banner, it also made certain the eventual resolution of the incoherent body into its constituent particles, when once the force which compelled them to coalesce should be withdrawn.

Tolerant of everything except Royalty and Popery, the Independents, when once the former had been extinguished by the execution of the King, and the latter rendered impossible by the feeling of the country, had no other foes to fight, and therefore no bond to hold them together; impatient of all control, each man of them then became the high-priest of his peculiar form of religion, in which in many cases he was the only believer, and the powerful party of the Independents thus, immediately after it had attained the acme of its power, fell apart into a multitude of insignificant and obscure sects.

In 1643 the party was daily growing in strength, and, having among its members many men of great ability, while the Presbyterians had been weakened by the deaths of Hampden and Pym, secured at first a hearing and then applause for their declaration that the time was now come for the abolition of all half-measures, and that England was to be saved at any cost, be it by the death of the King or of any other.

A further complication of the politics of the time was caused by the fact that the Scots, rigid Presbyterians as they were, had been called to the assistance of the Parliament at the very moment when the Independents, of whom Cromwell may be held as the head, were fast coming into prominence; and we shall find the key to many after riddles in the fact that Oliver, in common with the majority of his co-religionists, at once hated and despised the Scots, whom he regarded as pedantic formalists, governed by their ministers even in matters military. But in speaking of this we are anticipating the future; for in 1643 Presbyterian and Independent were arrayed side by side against the King and Prelacy.

# CHAPTER 3

# 1644

Towards the end of the year 1643 Sir Ralph Hopton (who had lately been created Lord Hopton), the Governor of Bristol for the King, having received invitations from some of the principal inhabitants of Hampshire and Sussex, was ordered to advance into those counties, with the object of preventing any movement on the part of Waller which might tend to disturb the siege of Plymouth, at that time beset by Maurice. Hopton moved by Salisbury on Winchester with a force about 3,000 foot and 1,500 horse, at which Waller at once retired to Farnham, and went himself to London to ask for aid.

Hopton, having received reinforcements under Sir Jacob Astley, moved on Arundel Castle, which surrendered on the third day of the siege; but Waller having returned from London with an addition to his strength of two City regiments of foot, and with 1,000 horse from the army of Essex, Hopton was compelled to fall back on Winchester, since he had received special orders, that in no case was he to allow Waller to pass him by and go into the west. The latter, after surprising a regiment of the Royalist cavalry at Alton and driving all outlying parties into Winchester, marched on Arundel Castle, which he retook in a few days.

Further reinforcements from the King having been received by Hopton, he moved on Farnham, where were Waller's headquarters, and on the 29th of March the two armies, each consisting of about 5,000 foot and 3,000 horse, met at Alresford.

Waller commenced the action with a charge of cavalry, which the Royalist horse received so ill, that the threat of a second made them wheel about and fly before it was delivered, their officers being left to shift for themselves. The King's foot, however, stood so firmly that the Parliamentary troops could not break their squares; this alone prevented the utter rout of Hopton's force. At nightfall that general drew off his men to Reading, while Waller on the following day hastened to Winchester, in the hope of receiving the surrender of the Castle; being disappointed in this, he wantonly sacked the city, after which he retired towards London.

The principal actions of the year 1644 took place in two distinct theatres of war, at a considerable distance from each other, and must on this account, as also by reason of the entire independence of the movements which accompanied them, be separately described, though many of the events of the two campaigns occurred simultaneously.

## 1. THE WAR IN THE NORTH

At the close of the year 1643 Newcastle was in possession of the whole of England to the north of the Humber, with the single exception of the town of Hull, in which Lord Fairfax was held fast; while Sir Thomas, being driven from the county of York, had united his strength with the forces of the Eastern Association in Lincolnshire. The arrival of the Scottish army, which entered England on the 19th of January, with a total of 18,000 foot and 3,500 horse, entirely changed the aspect of affairs.

On the receipt of the news of this invasion the Marquis moved at once to the north, and on the 2nd of February arrived at the town of Newcastle, before which the Scots came on the following day. After a few skirmishes of no importance, Leven, considering it unlikely that he would be able to take the town, which was defended by a large garrison, marched round it, and on the 4th of March entered Sunderland.

On the 6th of that month the Marquis, having been reinforced from Durham, pushed towards the Scots, but, as neither

side much desired to fight, no battle took place, and he continued his movement on Durham. Here Newcastle remained, the
Scots being in close proximity to him and frequent skirmishes
taking place between them, until in the early part of April he
was recalled to York by the unwelcome success of Lord Fairfax.

But before entering into the details of the exploits of the father, it is necessary to relate those of the son. In order to do this
we must first go back to the November of 1643, at which date
a body of troops from Ireland, set free by the King's treaty with
the rebels, landed at Mostyn in Flintshire. Under Lord Byron
this force on the 4th of December captured Hawarden Castle,
after which, driving back Sir William Brereton, they, in the beginning of January,

1644, laid siege to Nantwich. Sir Thomas Fairfax was sent
from the eastern counties to Brereton's assistance; on the 12th of
January the former arrived at Manchester, whence after a short
delay for the purpose of collecting additional troops, he effected
a junction with Brereton, and on the 21st marched on Nantwich, with about 2,500 foot and 800 horse.

Having, after some resistance, driven in the enemy's advanced troops, Fairfax found their main strength posted at Acton
Church, and, hearing that Lord Byron with the cavalry would
be compelled to make a long round before he could cross a
small river which separated him from the remainder of his force,
determined to attack the church ere he could come up. Being,
however, much delayed in his advance, Fairfax failed in this object, and therefore moved on the town in the hope of drawing
fresh troops from it.

As he retired, the Royalists fell upon the rear of his army and,
when these turned to resist the attack, made a new onslaught
on them from the other side. Fairfax at once turned again upon
them, beat them off with the aid of the townspeople, and following up his advantage, fought his way to the church at Acton,
surrounded it, and took all in it prisoners "as in a trap."

Of the captured on this occasion, the most memorable in
history, though but a colonel at the time, was George Monk,

who had, at the invitation of the King, passed with troops from Ireland to his assistance. Monk was sent up to London, and, after having spent two or three years as a prisoner in the Tower, took service in the Parliamentary army, where we shall meet with him again.

After this success, Sir Thomas Fairfax marched into Lancashire, where he undertook the siege of Latham House, the seat of the Earl of Derby; thence he was called by a letter, dated March the 5th, from the Committee of War in London, which ordered him to march across the West Riding of Yorkshire and to join his father, with the object that their amalgamated forces should in some way take advantage of the absence of Newcastle in the north.

The Marquis had, on his departure, left Colonel Bellasis as Governor of York, who, hearing of the intended junction of the father and son, moved to Selby for the purpose of interposing between them; in this he completely failed, and Lord Fairfax, in command of the united force, marched on Selby, which on the 11th of March he stormed, utterly defeating the Royalists, and making Colonel Bellasis himself a prisoner.

Newcastle at once hastily retired from his advanced position at Durham, fell back to York, and laboured only to secure that city from attack. The field being thus left open for their movements, the Scots advanced at their leisure, and, on the 17th of April, at Wetherby, completed their junction with the Parliamentary army. At an interview which took place between Leven and Lord Fairfax, it was decided to unite their forces at Tadcaster on the 20th, and to push on together to the siege of York.

This was accordingly done, but, as it was found that the total strength at their disposal was not sufficient to surround the city, while the amount of Newcastle's force (14,000 men), and his possession of a bridge over the Ouse, which enabled him to strike on either bank of that river, made it impossible for them to divide their armies, it was determined to call Manchester, who commanded the Associated Counties, to their assistance.

In order to trace the progress of the latter, we must now

go back a little in point of time. The Parliamentary party in Lincolnshire, having been roused to action and assisted by the Eastern Association, had, by the end of 1643, gained the upper hand in that county, and, commencing offensive operations about the beginning of March, 1644, closed in around Newark and besieged it.

In order to preserve this post, which was important as a connecting link between Oxford and York, Prince Rupert, who at this time lay on the Upper Severn, was ordered to relieve it. Marching with all haste, and collecting forces on his way, the Prince was at Wolverhampton on the 10th of March, and on the 19th, with 7,000 men at Bingham, eight miles from Newark.

On the 21st he attacked Sir John Meldrum, who had been left in command by Lord Willoughby of Parham. The left wing of the Parliamentary army fought well, but the right fled without a blow, and the entire force was eventually driven over a bridge of boats on to an island in the centre of the river Trent, whence their retreat, though threatened by a sortie of the garrison of Newark, might be carried out by means of a bridge to the further bank. But during the night six companies, who had been placed to guard this bridge, fled across it and broke it down, and Meldrum was thus compelled to purchase terms with the surrender of all his firearms.

Rupert was, after this success, called into Lancashire to the aid of the Earl of Derby, who was besieged in Latham House; him he relieved, but failed to find any such support in that county as the Earl had led him to expect.

Manchester, being thus left unopposed, on the 3rd of May carried Lincoln by storm, Cromwell being detached to keep off a force under Goring which was advancing to its relief. On the 15th of May Manchester was appointed by the Parliament General of the Associated Counties, Cromwell at the same date being made lieutenant-general of his horse, while orders were sent to them to join the army of the Scots so soon as the latter should enter Yorkshire.

In obedience to these commands Manchester marched on

York, and on the 3rd of June joined the forces of the besiegers. The siege, which up to this time had been little more than a blockade, now completely changed its character, for batteries were thrown up against the city, while daily attacks were made upon it by one or other of the allied forces. During the siege Newcastle found means to send a letter to the King, in which he undertook to hold out for six weeks or two months, but begged that ere that time expired some means might be taken to relieve him.

Upon receipt of this news Charles ordered Rupert to march to the aid of York, proposing himself, with such troops as he could collect, to take the field alone in the absence of the Prince. The latter, pursuing his advantages in Lancashire, had on the 28th of May taken Bolton by storm, but on the 11th of June, after the capture of Liverpool (a great gain to the King's cause, as giving him a port by which to communicate with Ireland), he marched at full speed on York.

Newcastle in the meanwhile, in order to gain time, asked for terms, which were offered only to be refused. On the 30th of June the besiegers heard of the near approach of the Prince, who was reported to be then at Knaresborough or Boroughbridge, at a distance of from twelve to fourteen miles from York, with a force of 20,000 men.

It was at once determined to raise the siege, and accordingly, on the morning of the 1st of July, the allied commanders drew off all their forces, and took up a position on Marston Moor, about five miles to the west of York, where they awaited battle. But it was neither Rupert's duty nor his wish to fight on this occasion, and he therefore, holding the passages of the Nidd, which covered his right, with detached parties of cavalry, marched across the enemy's front to the confines of the city.

At the meeting which ensued between Rupert and Newcastle, the latter urged that no present action was desirable, since he was daily expecting reinforcements, while the enemy, distracted by quarrels between the three generals, would in a few days divide their forces, in which case the Scots might even return to their own country. But Rupert refused to listen to one whom he probably despised as "a very fine gentleman, amorous in Poetry and Musick," and replied that he had an "absolute and positive command" from the King to fight the enemy, this being the colour it pleased him to put upon the King's order, which, after directing the relief of York, continued, "where being joined with the Marquis of Newcastle's army, there was hope they might fight the enemy."

Newcastle, who had "a particular reverence for the person of the King," responded that he was ready to obey His Highness in all things as though His Majesty was there present, and accordingly the army of the Prince and the garrison marched together from York, and on the afternoon of the 2nd of July came in front of the position of their adversaries.

The Parliamentary army and the Scots, who had passed the night on the moor, were about to move to Tadcaster, in order to prevent any movement of Rupert to the south, when at 9 a.m. they saw the Prince with a vanguard of 5,000 cavalry advancing over Marston Moor. The allied forces at once turned to fight, and recalled such of their troops as had already started on their march. Not being able to regain possession of the moor, the three leaders drew up their men on the rising ground between Long Marston and Tockwith, facing towards the north.

The order of battle was similar to that of Edgehill, the cavalry being placed on the flanks, while the centre was formed of the infantry with their battalion guns. Sir Thomas Fairfax commanded the right wing of horse, consisting of about 80 troops (4,000 men), added to which were a part of the Scottish horse, while Cromwell led the left, which was composed of the cavalry of the Associated Counties and three regiments of Scottish horse, in all about 70 troops (3,000 men); on the extreme left, since Rupert's lines overlapped that of the allies, were posted the Scottish dragoons.

Of the infantry, which were in two divisions, Lord Fairfax commanded the right, composed of his own foot, with two Scottish brigades as a reserve, while Leven on the left led two

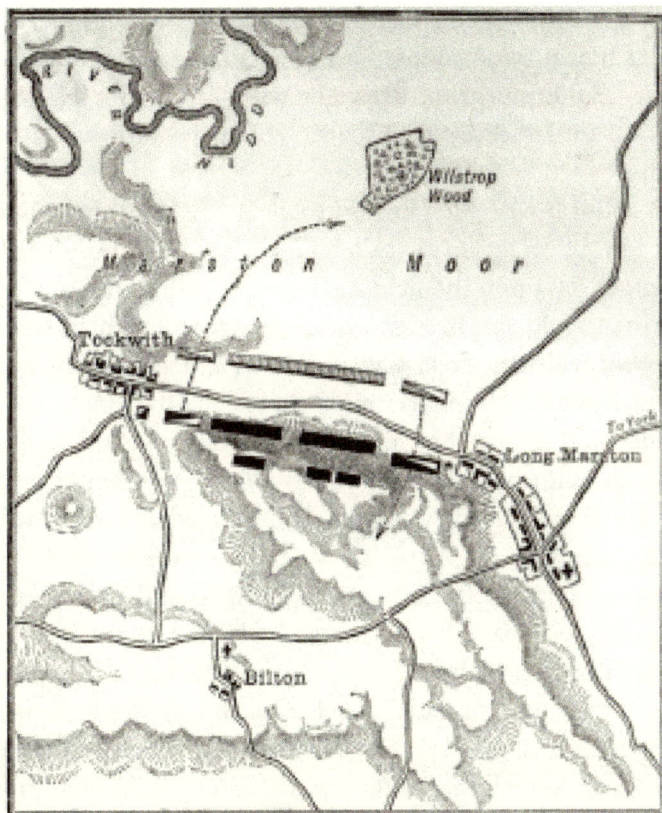

RISING GROUND BETWEEN LONG MARSTON AND TOCKWITH,
WHERE THE BATTLE OF MARSTON MOOR WAS FOUGHT,
JULY 2ND, 1644

brigades of the Earl of Manchester's infantry and six regiments of Scots, having one of Manchester's brigades as a reserve. The whole force, which was about equal to that of Rupert, amounted to some 14,000 foot and 9,000 horse and dragoons, while the line was one mile and a half in length.

The Royal army adopted a similar formation; Rupert commanded 5,000 horse on the right wing, while the left was led by Lucas and Hurrey, the infantry of the centre being under Goring.

At about 3 p.m. the guns on each side opened fire, and continued in action for nearly two hours, after which time a "general silence" fell upon the field, each army waiting to see what the other would do. For between the lines of battle, which were but a very short distance apart, were a ditch and a bank, the passage of which would almost certainly throw an attacking force into disorder, and would thus give an opportunity for the defenders to charge with perhaps fatal effect. During another two hours this pause continued, and men began to say that there would be no fight that day.

But at 7 p.m. the Parliamentary left, horse and foot, advancing at a quick pace, passed the bank and fell on. Cromwell's cavalry, though hard pressed by the Prince, who attacked Oliver's special division in front and flank, cut its way through the enemy, and drove them back to Wilstrop Wood, where, mingling with the foot, which Manchester's infantry had forced from their ground, they for the most part fled by the rear of their own left in the direction of York.

The Royalist left, under Hurrey, met the charge of Fairfax, and beat back the horse of the Parliamentary right wing, though Sir Thomas himself with a few followers, burst through them and joined Cromwell's horse in rear of the Prince's line. Keeping their order after the first shock, they turned next upon the infantry, of which the new levies and the Scots broke up before them, and flying rearwards, hampered the defence of the reserves, with the result that the whole of the right wing and centre of the allied armies were routed and fled to the south, giving out all was lost. Even Leven himself rode off to Leeds, and knew nothing of the outcome of the battle, until he was brought back on the following morning.

Matters looked ill for the Parliamentary party, until Cromwell's cavalry, returning to the charge, surrounded and cut to pieces the remainder of the Royalist infantry, who "scorned to fly." The forces of the adversaries were now mingled in confusion, from which, after a time, two large bodies disengaged themselves, arid it then appeared that the positions of so much as remained of the armies had become exactly reversed. Lucas and Hurrey with their cavaliers stood where had been the Roundhead right, while Cromwell occupied the ground opposed to them, where the Prince's left had been posted. Rallying all whom they could to their side, the leaders again charged with unabated courage, but by 10 p.m. the remainder of the Royalist army was in full flight to York, having lost 1,500 prisoners and the whole of their artillery.

Those employed to bury the dead reported that they found 4,150 slain; of these the Parliament acknowledged the loss of only 300. Thus ended the greatest and most important battle of the war, whether we gauge it by the number of combatants, by the losses of the vanquished, or by the result of the victory, for, from the 2nd of July, 1644, the north of England was for ever lost to the King.

Cromwell and Fairfax, to whom principally the victory was due, were both wounded; the former in the neck, possibly by the accidental discharge of a pistol by one of his own men; the latter on the head and face, he being unhorsed and narrowly escaping capture.

Newcastle, having secret information that Rupert had no intention to wait to be besieged in York, declared his own decision to leave England, and, quitting the city on the morning after the battle, sailed from Scarborough to Hamburg, where he arrived on the 8th of July, to return no more to his native country until after the Restoration. The Prince, also on the 3rd, marched from York to the northward, and, collecting what forces he could, passed unmolested into Lancashire, and so to Chester, where we may for the present leave him.

The fate of the city of York was not long in doubt. The siege was resumed on the 4th, and carried on with so much energy, that Sir Thomas Glenham, who had been left as Governor, surrendered on the 15th. On the 16th, the garrison, 1,000 strong, marched under his command to Carlisle, which he afterwards nobly defended.

The three leaders of the allied armies, having thus attained the object of their junction, now agreed to separate their forces. Fairfax, with his headquarters at York, was to guard that county and Lancashire; the Scots passed to the north to the town of Newcastle; while Manchester, whom we shall shortly meet again, retired into the eastern counties, for the purpose of recruiting his forces.

Amidst the list of aimless marches and counter-marches, of desultory fights and skirmishes, which up to this time have made up the story of the Civil War, this campaign attracts our attention as being the first of which criticism is possible; for where there is no plan, as in the earlier phases of the contest, military history becomes nothing but a catalogue of objectless slaughter, and war, losing its character as an art, is merely a series of sanguinary brawls.

The aim of this campaign, from the point of view of the Parliament, was the possession of Yorkshire, the key of the north, and the assurance of such possession could be gained only by the capture of the city of York. The plan by which this result was to be obtained had for its basis the junction of three armies, of which one was on the spot, while the two others were respectively to the north and south of the objective.

In the seventeenth century, when communications were execrable, and when the power of moving troops was in its infancy, we cannot expect to find any very skilful strategy, and accordingly in this campaign each force came to the rendezvous on the day which best suited its own convenience, while no effort was made to prepare the way for their joint action until the junction had actually taken place.

Though opportunities, which would be assuredly seized in modern war, were thus allowed to pass unheeded, yet the junction itself, and the handling of the three armies in combination, were a remarkable advance on anything which had up to this time been attempted in England. Of whatever faults of omission they may, according to our ideas, have been guilty, the leaders fully succeeded in their one great and necessary duty, in that they completed their concentration before the enemy could strike.

The second phase of the campaign opens with Rupert's march; his object, to enter York, was obtained without difficulty, owing partly to the want of mobility of his adversaries (a failing common to all armies at that period), and partly to the skilful manner in which he covered his right with the river Nidd. He thus succeeded in marching across the enemy's front, and effected a junction with Newcastle in their actual presence; a counterstroke was by this fairly given to the previous movements of the Parliamentary party.

But, as was customary in the case of every action of the Royalists, the Prince's advance was too late; he should, as he might well have done, have collected in March a force as large as that which fought at Marston Moor, and with it, in conjunction with Newcastle, should have crushed the Scots, while Fairfax might have been contained by a moderate detachment. In place of this the early part of the year was wasted in the capture or relief of comparatively unimportant points, whose fate, as the history of war has frequently shown, would have, without doubt, followed the fortunes of the field armies.

Throughout the whole of this war, until the stars of Fairfax and Cromwell rise, we shall find the same inability on each side to grasp the situation, and to judge of the decisive point on which the blow should be delivered. As a rule the armies wandered about blindly, until they came in contact; upon their meeting followed a battle, which was entirely destitute of any tactical plan, and was remarkable only for hard hitting. After this action one of two cases occurred; either the victors (if any decision could be made as to who had won the day), pursued the vanquished with gradually decreasing zeal, or both armies retired to repair their losses or to wait for fine weather.

The third era of the campaign opens with the two armies in presence, the one facing to the north, the other in and around York. The English portion of the Parliamentary force in this position covered its base, which may be assumed to have been for Fairfax the south-west corner of Yorkshire, for Manchester the eastern counties, and for both in case of need the City of London; but the Scots were by Rupert's march completely cut away from their country, and actually faced their line of retreat. But in those days of indirect supply and of unlimited plundering armies were not so sensitive as they are now in regard to their communications, while owing to their small size they were more easily fed than a modern force would be; again, the provision of ammunition, which next to food is the most vital necessity of an army of the present day, was not then of so great importance, since, owing to the slow rate of fire, the expenditure even in a lengthened battle was but small.

We find accordingly that the Scots, even before the engagement, were prepared to accompany their allies to the southward, without any scruples as to abandoning their natural base, from which indeed it is probable that they drew neither men, money, nor supplies. The Parliamentary position for battle was thus founded on logical principles; but it is impossible to say the same of Prince Rupert's attitude, for he formed his troops in such a manner, that the line of retreat of the whole (to York) was in prolongation of his line of battle, and thus invited disaster in case of a reverse.

As the natural result of such a disposition, we have seen how his right wing, when beaten, dispersed in rear of his left, since Fairfax, after charging through the latter, came directly upon the pursuers of the former; for the same reason the Royal infantry could not retire, and were absolutely destroyed as they stood, so absolutely, that of the 20,000 men with whom the Prince began the battle, he had on the following day not 4,000 by his side.

Of pursuit, such as we shall find in the later actions of the war, there was little or none, and that probably for the reason that the fugitives found ready shelter behind the walls of York. But it is certainly a blot upon the success of the Parliamentary leaders, that they should have allowed Rupert to escape with his diminished following; for this mistake within the year the Parliament had a heavy price to pay. The desertion of York by the Prince and Newcastle is beneath criticism, and was probably due rather to the personal characters of the two leaders than to any idea of military necessity.

Thus in the middle of July, 1644, we leave the northern counties in the undisputed possession of the enemies of the King, for he retained in them but a few garrisons, of which Carlisle and Newcastle, the most important, were shortly after reduced. The surrender of Newcastle was specially desired by the citizens of London, who were at this time suffering severely from the dearth of coal.

## 2. THE CAMPAIGN AGAINST THE MAIN ARMY OF THE KING

About the end of March, 1644, an ordinance of the Houses fixed the strength of Essex's army for the ensuing year at 7,500 foot, 3,000 horse, and a train of artillery. That of Waller was at the same time ordered to consist of 3,000 foot, 1,200 horse, and 500 dragoons, who were to be levied in the southern counties. The King's force amounted to about 10,000 men, and was, at the commencement of the campaigning season, quartered around Oxford.

The plan for the campaign, as laid down by the Parliament, was as follows: each of their armies was to be in every respect distinct from the other, though Essex was to remain in supreme command. If the King should continue at Oxford, the two armies were conjointly to undertake the siege of that city, which required a long line of works in order to enclose it, while the difficulty of so doing was increased by the fact that the besieging force must of necessity be divided into two parts by the Thames. Should, however, the King march, as was expected, towards the north, Essex was to follow him, while Waller was directed to proceed into the west, for the purpose of repressing Maurice and Hopton.

On the King's part it was determined, by the advice of Rupert, to hold Oxford, Reading, Wallingford, Abingdon, and Banbury on the defensive, and to send every man who could be spared from those garrisons to join Prince Maurice in the west; but this plan, which indeed was contingent on the movements of Essex and Waller, was considerably modified in execution, for, after advancing to Newbury, where he waited until the middle of May, with the object of ascertaining the plans of the enemy, Charles moved to Reading, whence, having demolished the defences of that town, and added the garrison (2,500 old soldiers) to his infantry, he returned to Oxford.

At this time, Essex was at Windsor, and Waller in North Hampshire, each endeavouring, by all possible means, to recruit his numbers to full strength. In May both armies marched on Oxford. On the 23rd, Essex was at Reading, while on the 25th, his advanced cavalry, after occupying Abingdon, passed Oxford by the Worcester Road. Waller, having mustered over 10,000 men at Farnham, joined Essex on the 26th about Abingdon, which place, against Charles's orders, had been abandoned by the Royalists.

The bulk of the King's army lay in Woodstock, and in the adjacent villages to the north of the city, and the further movements of the Parliamentary generals were directed with the object of closing round these cantonments, which were shut in on either side by the Isis and the Cherwell. With this intention, Essex crossed the Thames at Sandford Ferry, and, extending his force round the city, endeavoured to pass the Cherwell at Gosford.

In this attempt he was, on the 1st of June, repulsed, but, on the 2nd, Waller having in the meantime sent 5,000 over the Isis at Newbridge "in the boats called punts," the Royalists abandoned their works and fell back, leaving the bridge at Gosford open for the general's advance.

The King's horse was now at Woodstock, and his foot at Woolvercot; he himself, returning to Oxford, gave orders for a sortie in the direction of Abingdon, and under cover of this, which drew the enemy's attention to the south, left the city about 9 p.m. on the 3rd of June, with his eldest son and a few noblemen, and, meeting shortly after with his escort of 3,000 foot and 4,000 horse, marched with them and a train of sixty or seventy carriages to Handborough, where he arrived at daybreak; thence continuing his march to Burford he reached Evesham on the 5th. Here he had intended to rest, but, fearing that the enemy might cross the Avon at Stratford, and push in between himself and Worcester, he moved at once to that city, which he entered on the 6th, having broken down the bridge at Pershore behind him.

Since after the King's departure the standard remained flying in Oxford, while on the 4th a body of troops was again pushed out towards Abingdon, Essex discovered nothing of his flight but Waller, having received notice of it from friends of the Parliament in the county, despatched some cavalry to fellow Charles. These made prisoners at Burford of a few of his stragglers, but do not appear to have found the main body. Essex, on receipt of the news, marched by Woodstock to Chipping Norton, where he arrived on the 5th, on which day Waller was at Stow-in-the-Wold in Gloucestershire.

Since the King had thus moved from Oxford, one of the cases provided for by the orders of the Parliament had now arisen, and the question of the direction of march of the two armies had to be resolved; on this point occurred a most serious quarrel between the leaders. Essex, at a council of the officers of both armies, stated it as his will that Waller, who had the lighter ordnance and the smaller train, should follow the march of the King, while he himself would pass on into the west against Hopton and Maurice.

To this Waller objected that, in the case of the separation of the armies, it had been distinctly laid down by the Parliament, that he was to go into the west, and Essex to follow the King.

But to such words Essex refused to listen, and, as his commanding officer, gave him positive orders to abide by the plan which had been promulgated in the council. Waller, enraged at this treatment, appealed to the Parliament, who, feeling that the true reason of the action of the Earl was his dislike to fight against the King in person, sent direct orders to the Lord General to follow the instructions which they had given him, and to send Waller into the west.

These orders found Essex at Salisbury on the way to the relief of Lyme Regis, which was besieged by Maurice and defended by Blake, and on his returning an answer to the Houses, to the effect that his action had been founded on military reasons, he was permitted to continue his march.

The armies of Waller and Essex being thus employed, the Parliament raised a new force, under Major-General Browne, a citizen of London, for the purpose of keeping in check the King's garrisons in the valley of the Thames, such as Wallingford, Oxford, and Greenland House near Henley, and also, if possible, of reducing Basing House and Banbury.

It will be well to follow first the fortunes of Waller's army. He, thinking that the King, who had marched in the direction of Shrewsbury, intended to make for that town, moved on the 13th of June to Bromsgrove; but Charles had no such plan, and had so led his troops, with the object of keeping the Severn between him and his enemy, as also on account of his great desire to avoid being besieged in Worcester. Since Waller had advanced so far to the north, and was daily receiving reinforcements from Staffordshire, the King determined to double back and to slip past him to Oxford.

On the 15th accordingly he pushed some horse to the west, as if he intended to move on Shrewsbury; Waller fell into the trap, and pressed forward to intercept his march, upon which the King retired at full speed to Worcester, was on the 16th at Evesham, on the 18th at Witney, and by the 21st had returned to his former position at Woodstock. Waller at once perceived that all pursuit would be useless, and having drawn to himself such troops as Massey could be induced to spare from Gloucester,[1] returned leisurely towards Chipping Norton by way of Stow-on-the-Wold.

The King, hearing of his approach, and having collected all available forces (5,500 foot and 4,000 horse), moved by Banbury, and arrived at Culworth on the 27th, at which date Waller was at Hanwell with 8,000 men; on the following day the two armies stood face to face on either side of the Cherwell, Waller on the defensive, the King eager to fight.

The position of the Parliamentary troops being too strong to allow of a successful attack on it, Charles endeavoured to draw them from it by advancing on the 29th of June, as if with the intention of entering farther into Northamptonshire.

The Royal army marched in three divisions, a vanguard, a main body, and a rearguard, the latter consisting of 1,000 infantry and two brigades of cavalry, while in order to cover the left flank of the column, a party of dragoons was sent to hold Cropredy Bridge. Information having been received by the vanguard that a body of reinforcements for Waller was crossing their line of march, the two leading fractions of the army, with the permission of the King, who was with the main body, increased their pace in the hope of cutting it off. The rear, who had heard nothing of any such advance, still moved on at the same rate as before; from this it followed that in a short time a considerable interval divided the rearguard from the remainder of the army.

Waller, who was waiting for an opportunity to strike, having seen the vanguard and the main body pass, imagined, since there were no other troops in sight, that the whole force had filed by. He at once determined to attack that which he believed to be the rear of the column, and for this purpose, driving back the dragoons from Cropredy Bridge, he threw across the Cherwell a detachment of 1,500 horse and 1,000 foot under Middleton; the mounted portion of this body pressing on left the foot to follow. The latter having been surprised on the march by the leading squadrons of the King's rearguard, were at once charged

---

1. These were not many, as Massey was a partisan of Essex.

and dispersed, while the other parts of the Royal force, having turned about, drove back Middleton's cavalry upon the victorious rear-guard; these again charging, cut the enemy from their line of retreat by Cropredy Bridge, until Waller, pushing down the Tower Hamlets trained bands, at last made way for the remnants of the ill-fated detachment.

It is worthwhile to note the statements as to casualties of either side, in order to learn how little dependence can be placed in any roll of losses. The Royalists claimed to have killed 150, and to have taken 193 prisoners, and eleven guns, while they themselves had lost but two officers and fourteen men. On the other hand, the Parliamentary army denied that of their men more than twenty-three men were killed, but acknowledged the loss of 100 prisoners, against which they set 100 Cavaliers killed and sixty made prisoners.

It being only 3 p.m. when the action ended, the King made a half-hearted effort to attack Waller's position, but, being repulsed at Cropredy Bridge, and being thus unable to cross the river, he remained in front of Waller during two days, after which he drew off and lost touch of the Parliamentary force. The latter marched on the 2nd of July to Towcester, where it met Browne's troops, who had advanced to its assistance; but as he soon after returned to his charge of the Royal garrisons, while Waller's City battalions for the most part found their way home, neither of them for the moment exercised any influence on the war.

The King, being thus freed from opposition, determined at once to march into the west against the Earl of Essex, and, having sent orders to Hopton to draw all the men he could from Monmouthshire and Wales, moved by way of Cirencester to Bath, where he arrived on the 15th of July. Shortly after leaving Oxford Charles heard of the defeat of Rupert at Marston Moor.

We must now return to Essex, who, passing Salisbury, was on the 15th of June at Dorchester, and on the 19th at Weymouth. Hearing of his advance, Maurice had, on the 16th, raised the siege of Lyme Regis, which small and unimportant town had, since the 20th of April, bravely sustained his attacks. The Prince, retiring by Honiton, was himself at Exeter on the 18th, but had then sent a part of his force to Bristol to join Hopton.

About this time, Essex, who had signed his last letter to the Parliament as their "innocent though suspected servant," received a letter from them in return, in which he was told that the Houses approved neither of his actions nor of his letters, but recommended him to use his best endeavours towards reducing the west.

The Independents were, in truth, becoming daily stronger in the House of Commons, and this letter was but one of many signs of the increasing power of the party which meant war to be war, and not a, military promenade. It may fairly be doubted whether Essex's heart had ever really been in the cause, while the manners and the designs both of the Parliament and of the army were not such as would be likely, on further acquaintance, to please the great lord, who, by accident a seeming democrat, was by birth and breeding an aristocrat, though no courtier.

On the 26th of June, Essex was at Chard, where he received a message from the Queen (who had in the beginning of the year left Oxford for Exeter, where on the 16th she had been confined of the Princess Henrietta), asking for a free passage to go to Bath; this Essex refused, upon which the Queen, as soon as she was in a condition to travel, sailed from Falmouth on the 14th of July and arrived safely at Brest, her ships being "fresh tallowed" to enable them to sail faster than those which Warwick, the Parliamentary admiral, sent after them.

Essex arrived at Tiverton on the 5th of July. Towards the middle of that month, hearing of the King's advance into the west, he proposed to turn back and engage him before he should be able to unite his forces with those of Maurice. In this wise project he was overruled by Lord Robartes, a general in his army, who, with others, assured him that, if he would but continue his march into Cornwall, he would secure that county for the Parliament, prevent the King from passing out of Devonshire, and thus detain him until a fresh force from London might attack him in rear.

Essex, angry though he was at the supposed preference of the Parliament for Manchester's army rather than for his own, and astonished with reason at the neglect of Waller to follow the King, yet could not believe that he would be left to face alone the whole of the Royal army; he therefore, though against his own conviction, yet without needing much persuasion, agreed to the plan proposed by Robartes, and continued to advance westward after the Prince.

On the 18th of July, after making a feint to march against Charles, the Earl moved from Tiverton towards Plymouth, and on the 26th entered Cornwall and took Launceston. On the same day the King was at Exeter, and thence following Essex fairly held him in a trap. The Lord General on the 29th captured Lostwithiel, and also the haven at Fowey, of which the latter was eventually of the very greatest use to him. He thence sent letters to the Parliament praying for aid, in answer to which Middleton was sent with 2,500 horse and dragoons; he, however, was not only too weak, but too late, to be of any use to the Roundhead army.

On the 6th of August, the King, whose headquarters were at Liskeard, as those of Essex were at Lostwithiel, sent a letter to the Earl, which on the 8th and 9th was followed by others from the officers of the Royalist army, all entreating him to join their cause and promising him honours and rewards should he do so; to these Essex answered but a few words in which he refused to betray the trust reposed in him by the Parliament. For this answer he received the thanks of both Houses, a compliment which in no way delayed his fate.

The King, having moved his headquarters to Boconnock, a house of Lord Mohun, drew his line closer and closer around Essex, who could neither escape nor force Charles to fight, and who now held nothing but Lostwithiel and Fowey. Sir Richard Grenville, advancing with the Cornish troops from Bodmin, pressed on the Parliamentary army from Lanhydrock, while the King seized all the passages of the river between Lostwithiel and

Fowey, as also a fort which guarded the mouth of the harbour at the latter place.

Finding that his quarters were daily being narrowed, and having no longer subsistence for his cavalry, while constant skirmishes along the river made him fear lest he should be cut off from the sea, Essex gave orders to his horse to break through the enemy's lines, and on the same night, that of the 31st of August, drew back the whole of his infantry into Fowey.

One regiment of cavalry only was retained; the others, under Sir William Balfour, marched at about 3 a.m. through the Royal army, passing within pistol-shot of a cottage where a special guard had, on the information brought by two deserters of the intended escape, been placed to intercept their retreat. Goring, who had succeeded Wilmot in the command of the King's horse, was at a drinking bout when he received the news of their march, and, choosing utterly to discredit it, allowed Balfour to ride away with no greater loss than 100 men; nor was Sir William in any way further troubled during the whole of his long march to London. Such was Goring's favour with the King that, since all men knew that he was most to blame, no one was ever punished for this most disgraceful neglect.

On the 1st of September, Essex, finding his case hopeless, deserted his infantry, and taking ship, sailed from Fowey to Plymouth; he wrote from the latter place to Skippon, whom he had left in command, to the effect that "Nothing but fear of slavery and to be triumpht on, should have made us have gone." No words are needed to characterise this action of the Earl; it stands condemned by his own excuse, and, if ever a soldier deserved to be shot, Essex was that man. Fortunately we can say that there is but one other instance of such behaviour in the military history of England,[2] and in this case there is good reason to suppose that the deserter was not sane at the time.

No such plea can be urged for Essex, and by this cowardice he forfeits any claim which ne ever possessed to the name of soldier; but he was not punished; he was even permitted to retain

---

2. Namely in Nepaul, in the year 1816

the command of that army which he had deserted in its hour of need, though it is true that, owing to other events, he never again led it into action.

Very different was the action of old Skippon, who, assembling his officers at a council of war after the flight of the general, made such a speech to them as deserves to be recorded.

"Gentlemen," he said, "you see our general and some chief officers have thought fit to leave us, and our horse are got away; we are left alone upon our defence; that which I propose to you is this, that we, having the same courage as our horse had, and the same God to assist us, may make the same trial of our fortunes, and endeavour to make our way through our enemies as they have done, and account it better to die with honour and faithfulness, than to live dishonourable."

But it was of no use; the army dispirited would not fight, and the brave old man, through no fault of his own, was compelled, on the 2nd of September, 1644, to surrender his artillery, arms, and ammunition to the forces of the King. The men, having embarked at Plymouth, were in the course of the month landed at Portsmouth, where Essex resumed the command, reclothing and rearming them with supplies sent from London.

It is difficult to understand why Charles did not take full advantage of his situation, and, having the Parliamentary foot at his mercy, did not insist upon the acceptance of harder terms. An explanation may perhaps be found in the fact that, while he had no place in which to keep and guard them as captives, that custom of war had not yet become general, which allows a victor to bind his prisoners not to serve again either during a war or for some given term. As a result of his leniency, we shall, before the year ends, find many of this infantry again in the field.

The Parliament, on the receipt of the news of this disaster, wrote to Essex to assure him of their continued regard, and to inform him of the intended advance of Manchester and Waller on Dorchester, as also of the dispatch of arms and clothes to equip his troops when they should arrive at Portsmouth.

After the completion of the surrender, the King moved to the eastward. He was on the 10th of September at Plymouth, which he attempted to carry by assault, but, having been repulsed in several attacks, he passed on to Exeter and thence to Sturminster in Dorsetshire, where he was on the 9th of October. Part of his army under Grenville was in the meantime carrying on the siege of Plymouth, while Goring had forced the surrender of Barnstaple and Ilfracombe. On the 15th of October Charles was at Salisbury, and on the 18th at Andover.

Waller and Middleton, who had effected their junction, retired before him, in order to avoid an engagement until they should have met the army of the Earl of Manchester, and also that of Essex. This junction took place on the 21st of October at Basing, the King being at that date at Whitchurch. in Hampshire.

On the 22nd, the King, covering his march with parties of cavalry, drew off his infantry from Kingsclere, and moved to Newbury. The forces of the Parliament, advancing first on Reading, changed direction towards New bury, and a battle thus became inevitable. Essex, on the nominal ground of illness, was not present with the army, which was therefore under the command of Waller and Manchester; it amounted altogether to about 10,000 men, of which 8,000 were cavalry. The King's strength had been seriously impaired by the dispatch of three regiments of horse, under the Earl of Northampton, to the relief of Banbury Castle, for though this service was efficiently performed, the detachment did not return in time to take part in the battle.

Charles, having determined to stand upon the defensive, in order to gain time for the arrival of Northampton or of Rupert, who was marching to him with 3,000 horse, took up a position on the hill to the south of the Lambourne, which stream covered his front. The latter was also protected by the fire of Donnington Castle, which, but a month before, had repulsed Manchester from its walls. Here the King threw up earthworks, providing with especial care for the defence of the approaches to Newbury town, the village of Shaw being very strongly held. The line of defence extended towards the right (east) as far as the junction of the Lambourne and the Kennet; while the left, which rested on the village of Speen, was covered by works which could sweep the open down with their fire.

The plan of attack of the Parliamentary generals was as follows: Waller, with the army of Essex, part of Manchester's cavalry, and most of his own force, was to make a circuitous inarch, out of reach of the fire of Donnington Castle, and was to attack the King's left at Speen, while Manchester, with the remainder of the army, should assault Shaw, in order to gain an entrance into Newbury, or in any case to draw away some portion of the enemy from the scene of Waller's attack.

The horse of the turning column under Balfour and Waller and the foot under Skippon started at daybreak on the 27th of October, yet even thus it was nearly 3 p.m. before they were formed in order of attack. The King's left, which was commanded by Prince Maurice, was taken by surprise, not imagining that so strong a post would be assaulted at so late an hour; they, however, rallied to their front, but were, after about three hours of hard fighting, driven from their lines and from the village of Speen, at which place Essex's troops retook six of the guns which they had lost in Cornwall.

It had been arranged that, on hearing the guns of Waller's column in action, Manchester should attack Shaw and a fortified house, which the Royalists held on the south side of the bridge which crosses the Lambourne; but in place of so doing, he assaulted Shaw at daybreak with 1,000 men, and, driving the surprised Cavaliers across the river, pressed on until his progress was stopped by the fire from the house above mentioned. A sally from this post pushed back the Parliamentary attack with severe loss, and, though Manchester in the afternoon, on hearing the guns at Speen, again assaulted the bridge, he did so in small strength and without success.

On the high ground about Speen the engagement now took

the form of a cavalry action, in which neither party had obtained any decided success when the fall of night put an end to the battle.

During the night the King's forces, having drawn out of Newbury, placed their guns, ammunition, and wounded in Donnington Castle; after which, abandoning the town, they marched between the two fractions of the enemy's army without receiving any interruption from either, and proceeded to Wallingford.

Each party as usual claimed the victory: the Parliament on the ground that their attack had dislodged the King from his position; the Royalists on account of an asserted minority of loss incurred in the action. It is perhaps most just to either side to say, that no victory was obtained and no defeat suffered, since though the King thought fit to retire, there was in truth no necessity for him to do so; while with regard to the proportion of loss of either army, it may be assumed as an axiom that when, as was the case on this occasion, a battle is not followed by a pursuit, the greater part of the casualties will be furnished by the force which attacks, in this instance the Parliamentary troops. Judging by the light of subsequent events, it may be considered probable that Charles, anticipating the coming of Rupert and his reinforcements, had no wish to bring matters to an immediate issue; while one at least of the Parliamentary leaders did not desire to force the King's hand, or to cripple him beyond recovery.

On the departure of Charles, Manchester and Waller at once occupied Newbury, and sent Colonel Hurrey, for the second time a deserter, to the Earl of Brentford, who lay wounded at Donnington, to demand the surrender of the castle; this being refused they marched on Oxford, but finding the road so bad that all advance was difficult, returned to Newbury, where they arrived on the 6th of November.

The Royal army awaited at Oxford the junction of Rupert and the return of Northampton; when these had taken place, and the Prince had been declared General *vice* Brentford, it pushed forward to Wallingford, and thence to Donnington Castle, which was relieved without a blow.

The King, having drawn his artillery from the castle, offered battle, but the Parliamentary leaders decided at a council of war that it was not advisable to fight; a similar council in the Royal army having come to the same conclusion, Charles, after pushing a small force over the Lambourne against the Roundhead position, now nearly the same as that which he himself had held a fortnight earlier, drew off to Wallingford with drums beating and trumpets sounding. Despatching a detachment to relieve Basing House, Charles marched with his troops to Oxford, and on the 23rd of November went into winter quarters in and around that city.

The Parliamentary army, weary with war and disgusted with their leaders, fell back on Reading, and took up winter quarters between that place and Farnham.

Thus ended the campaign of 1644.

Before entering into a relation of the events of the winter, it will be well to review shortly the relative positions of the two contending parties. Newcastle having been stormed by the Scots in October, the Parliament had at the end of the year possession of the whole of the north, Chester and Newark being the most advanced garrisons of the King in that direction. The latter had, however, much increased his power in the west, towards which the rule of the Houses extended but little beyond the boundary of Surrey and Hampshire.

The eastern counties, as ever, held with London against the King, while the midlands had changed but in a small degree from their attitude of the previous year. On the whole, in spite of the surrender of the army of Essex, the advantage of the year of fighting remained with the Parliament, since the decided victory of Marston Moor, and the consequent gain of the north, far outweighed any and every success which Charles could claim.

The King had now but one army, properly so called, and this, which in December, 1644, numbered about 11,000 men, was made up of the remnants of the various forces which had fought and suffered for him. The Parliament in a similar manner in the following year collected its troops under one head and sent forth a single army to battle. But how great a difference in constitution was there between the two forces; that of the Parliament was selected from their super-abundance, that of the King was scraped together. from far and near, and, as we shall find at a later date, made up some part of its deficiency from the rejected overplus of the former.

Again, owing to the prolonged nature of the war, the want of money at this time afflicted the King as much as did the dearth of men, for his adherents, most of whom drew their income from land, had, now that their tenants were soldiers and their meadows fields of battle, no rents to offer for the Royal service.

On the other hand, the supporters of Parliament, men who lived by commerce, having no fear of danger by sea, since the fleet was in the hands of their rulers, lost little, perhaps in some respects even gained, by the existence of war, and could afford further subsidies to obtain their end. Thus the fortunes of the King were fading, and it became more and more certain as time went on, that he would never recover by the sword that kingdom which he regarded as given to him by God.

But there yet remained the hope of negotiation, and in this Charles put his trust, knowing well that there were some among the ranks of the Parliament who, though they had at first armed against him as a tyrant, now trembled with fear at the storm which they had raised, and regarded with greater dread than any one King could inspire that legion of rulers which called itself the House of Commons.

Encouraged by his hopes in such men, Charles, during the period of inaction which was coincident with the coming of winter, sought to reopen negotiations with his foes. But all agreement was impossible between the two parties, who started from totally opposite premises, and moved thence in directions which diverged, and no more space need be given to this abortive effort towards a treaty, than will suffice to mention that the Commissioners appointed by either side to discuss the question met at Uxbridge on the 29th of January, 1645, and separated on the 22nd of February, without having found it possible to agree on any one point.

The scope of this work will not permit of the narration of the smaller actions which distracted the country, but did not affect the progress of the war, and many brave deeds must be left unrecorded, among which there are few so deserving of renown as is the ride of Colonel Gage from Oxford to the relief of Basing House.[3] The skirmishes of Middleton during his effort to relieve Essex in Cornwall, the exploits of Massey around Gloucester, the "excursions and alarms" of Fairfax and the Scots in Yorkshire, as also the sorties from Newark and other garrisons, must be all left unnoticed, as they were in fact immaterial to the issue of the war.

But one act, though not strictly military in its beginning, must be mentioned at some length, since by its result it proved itself to be the most fatal arm which the hand of Parliament could prepare against the King, and, in time, against itself. To the former it brought imprisonment and death, to the latter disgrace and annihilation. The "Self-denying Ordinance" stands almost alone in history in the remarkable disproportion between the simplicity of its principle and the complexity of its causes and effects, even though we confine our examination of the latter to those only which immediately preceded or followed its adoption.

Introduced in the early part of December, 1644, it had not passed both Houses until the beginning of April, 1645, for which reason, among others, it is proposed to reserve its discussion until the succeeding chapter, pausing here only to draw attention to the fact that it was between the above dates that efforts had been made to come to an agreement with the King; a treaty with Charles being the counter-stroke with which the Presbyterians proposed to answer the blow, which, as they knew well, the Independents were preparing against them.

---

3. *Clarendon.* vol. 2, part 2, edition of 1717, page 527.

## CHAPTER 4

# 1645

The conduct of the war by the Parliamentary leaders had, up to the commencement of this year, given satisfaction to very few of their party; opportunities had been neglected, victories had been but half won, while defeats, though they had not been disastrous, had been far too numerous. The contest had thus lingered on, and now, after nearly three years of hostilities, men found that peace, with the freedom from service and taxation which should accompany it, was practically as distant and as improbable as ever. In proportion as men had at first plunged headlong into the sea of war, in the hope, almost in the assurance, that after a short struggle they should draw thence the pearl of their liberty, they now, as that hope dwindled and became uncertain, were inclined to give hard judgment on those who had first led them, but who now seemed to have deserted their charge.

To many of the foremost adherents of the Parliament, the war was at its commencement but an acute form of court intrigue, by which they proposed to oust their rivals from their positions, and even up to the period at which we have now arrived, very few had dared to suggest the abdication or the deposal of the King; for this civil war was unlike all those which had preceded it, in that there was no counter-claimant to the throne. Such being the case, the above section of the party were naturally careful not to offend too deeply that King whom they intended to replace upon the throne, as soon as he had been convinced by misfortune of the error of his ways.

But there were others, more especially in the army, who feeling in themselves the power, as they had the will, to rule, were not well pleased by the thought that, when peace had been made to the liking of their military or social superiors, they, by whose swords such a peace had been rendered possible, must be content to sink back into obscurity, happy indeed if they escaped punishment at the hands of those who had suffered so much by them.

These men were not content to take as the reward of their labours such a modicum of satisfaction, as might be derived from seeing the Garter at the knee of Essex, or from the elevation of Manchester to a marquisate, while to such an end, as they suspected, events were turning, since those who were their generals preferred to threaten rather than to strike, and fought only a mock combat with (so to speak) blunted swords, against that army which in many a Roundhead's belief was composed exclusively of men of Belial.

In the eyes of such soldiers as these, mostly Independents and indebted for voice to Cromwell and Ireton, their leaders had turned back after putting their hands to the plough, and were thus a doubting and backsliding people, deserving no longer to be trusted or obeyed by the elect. Again, these very leaders were for the most part Presbyterians, and as such absolutely intolerant of variation from their religious ritual and dogma, while the Independents, desiring liberty in all, thought "Presbyter," in the words of Milton, to be *merely Priest writ large.*

The time had now come also when the army, as is natural to any army which has pride in itself as such, desired to be led by men chosen for what they had done in the field, not for what they had said in the Houses, while the entire nation, weary of the shilly-shallying, of the alternate battles and negotiations, neither of which seemed ever to have any result, and of the variations from frenzy to apathy, with an occasional change to a feeble loyalty, felt that the army was in the right, and that, if any good end was to be obtained, the beginning of that end must be a sweeping alteration in the organisation of the Parliamentary forces. Doubtful men must be set aside, those neutral in heart must be made incapable of evil, and the full power of the sword of England must be placed in some hand, which would use the weapon to strike and not to guard only.

The grievance of the nation and of the army found a voice in the Grand Committee, into which on the 9th of December, 1644, the House of Commons resolved itself. There Cromwell spoke, as did another, much to the purpose, while after a long debate the Committee passed the following resolution: "That no member of either House of Parliament shall during the war enjoy or execute any office of command military or civil, and that an ordinance be brought into that purpose."

By this Act in effect every Peer was disqualified from employment, and all the principal leaders of the army were thus at once dismissed; but there was more in it than this, for since a Peer could not by any means cease to be a member of his House, he was of necessity debarred from command for all future time, while a member of the House of Commons could, if he were permitted to do so, resign his seat and so preserve his office. We shall however find that this Act, like many others, having served its purpose was allowed to become a dead letter.

The ordinance, after another long debate, passed the Commons on December the 19th, 1644, but was on the 13th of January, 1645, thrown out by the Lords, who fully realised its scope. The Commons nothing daunted pressed on their scheme for the "New Model": of the army, which was to be selected from the old forces, and was to be officered by men in whom entire confidence could be placed,

The new model was organised as follows:

| | |
|---|---|
| 10 Regiments of Cavalry of 600 men | 6,000 |
| 10 Companies of Dragoons of 100 men | 1,000 |
| 10 Regiments of Infantry of 1,400 men | 14,000 |
| Total | 21,000 men. |

All officers were to be nominated by Sir Thomas Fairfax, the new General, and (as was insisted upon by the Lords, with the object of excluding the more fanatical Independents) every officer was to sign the covenant within twenty days of his appointment.

The cost of this force was estimated at £539,460 *per annum*, about £1,600,000 of our money.

On the 24th of March, 1645, the ordinance was again read in the Commons, and finally passed that House on the 31st March. Sir Thomas Fairfax having been appointed commander-in-chief by a vote of both Houses on the 1st of April, Essex, Manchester and others of the Lords resigned their commissions on the 2nd, and all reason for resistance being thus removed, the ordinance passed the Lords on the 13th of April, 1645.

The name of Cromwell was of course, with those of other members of the Commons, omitted from the original list of the New Model army, but with a significance which could not have escaped remark, the appointment of lieutenant-general was left vacant, while none doubted by whom that vacancy would be filled.

Sir Thomas Fairfax, the new Lord General, the eldest son of Ferdinand Lord Fairfax, was born in 1611, and was therefore at this period in his thirty-fourth year. He was in person tall and well made, but his constitution was not strong, and he was much subject to illness, caused partially by hardships endured on active service in Holland during the earlier years of his life. The expression of his face was sad and unintellectual; he stammered in his speech, which was in consequence slow, and was timid and reserved in his manner. He was not as a rule quick to act, but a decision once made was with him irrevocable, and, though easily led, he had much character of his own.

In battle only he seemed really to live, and under fire or in the rush of a cavalry charge, changed entirely in disposition as in the expression of his face. Slow though clear in council, he was in battle "as one distracted and furious," though not so much so but that he governed all things well. His personal bravery was remarkable even among brave men, and his modesty was such that all loved as they admired him. He was not a genius, except in war. and his enemies said of him that, unless in actual battle he was a weak and foolish man; but, as we know, after the Restoration, at which time only his enemies dared to speak, virtue was accounted folly, and the wisdom of the serpent the only wisdom. In religion he was a Presbyterian of the strictest type, and was in this respect much influenced by his wife, the daughter of Lord Vere of Tilbury.

Such was the man who, on the 1st of April, 1645, was made the leader of the Parliamentary cause, an appointment mainly due, as may be supposed, to the influence of Cromwell, who was not as yet himself in the position to aspire to the supreme command.

Before proceeding to the narration of the actions of the new army, it is necessary to draw attention to those which took place during the months of January, February, and March, which preceded its formation.

Of these the principal were: a defeat inflicted on Rupert at Abingdon by Browne, who was still employed in blockading the posts around Oxford; the success of Langhorne (or Langhorne), a Parliamentary general, in South Wales, where he captured Cardigan; and the appointment of Waller to the chief command in the west, where Grenville was engaged on the siege of Plymouth.

Sir William, having been joined by Cromwell, advanced to Weymouth, but, on his endeavour to press on to Plymouth, was driven back by Goring. The Scottish army, having with the assistance of Fairfax forced the King's party from the northern counties, began in February to move southward, and in March joined Brereton about Chester.

But little was done in the field, until on the 3rd of April Fairfax proceeded to Windsor, at which place he had ordered the army to rendezvous, for the purpose of taking up his command. With the assistance of Skippon, who was much beloved by the soldiers, the new general, who was personally unknown to many of his troops, succeeded in reducing the regiments which were ordered to be disbanded, and in re-organising those which were to be retained, without arousing that spirit of mutiny, which had but a short time before shown itself among Waller's men. Essex's life-guard, who had done such good service under Sir Philip Stapleton, were disbanded, but were afterwards enlisted under new officers to serve as a bodyguard to Fairfax.

The whole of the month of April was spent in the organisation of the New Model, and Cromwell, who, leaving Waller, had by this time drawn towards Oxford, coming, as was said, for the purpose of taking leave of Fairfax on his retirement from the army, had the honour of fighting the first action of importance of the new year.

It came about as follows: Massey, who was still the active Governor of Gloucester, set out towards the end of April from that city, and marched to Ledbury with about 400 horse and 500 foot; at that point he was on the 22nd surprised by Rupert, who broke with great fury from all sides into the town. Massey, in no way dismayed, caused his infantry to retire across country, while he himself with the cavalry covered them as a rear-guard, upon which Rupert, finding that in the pursuit he lost as many men as his enemy, fell back on Worcester.

The King had at first proposed, on the suggestion of Rupert and of Sir Marmaduke Langdale, a north-country leader, to begin the year by marching into the north, with the object of defeating the Scots before the organisation of the New Model should be completed; but Goring, who was jealous of the renown of the Prince, coming from Taunton, which he left besieged by his foot and artillery, urged Charles rather to march into the west, which was all his own, and there to raise an army which might compete with that of the Parliament. This being agreed upon, Goring returned to the siege and Rupert was directed to send 2,000 horse to join the King at Oxford, and to act as his escort on his march into the west.

Orders were at once sent by the Parliament to Fairfax to cause the advance of this force to be intercepted, and Cromwell was specially named, as the commander most capable of executing this commission. Oliver, having been reinforced, marched into Oxfordshire, and at Islip Bridge encountered four regiments of the King's cavalry, whom he completely defeated, capturing about 200 prisoners, 500 horses, and the Queen's standard. Pressing the pursuit he came to Bletchingdon House, which, though defended by infantry as well as by horse, surrendered without an effort to Cromwell's cavalry, who, in order to intimidate the garrison, called loudly as they advanced to their foot, of whom they had none, to fall on. For this error or act of cowardice the Governor, Colonel Windebank, was afterwards shot by sentence of a council of war.

From Bletchingdon Cromwell marched by Witney and Rampton-in-the-Bush, at each of which places he cut to pieces a body of the enemy's troops, and took in all an additional 250 prisoners; he was however repulsed from an attempted attack on Faringdon, which he made on his way back to the general.

By the end of April the new army was ready for action, and Fairfax was at once directed to march to the relief of Taunton, which under Colonel (afterwards Admiral) Blake was by this time hard pressed.

Before entering into a narration of the important events which followed the advance of Fairfax, it will be well to review shortly the relative positions at the beginning of May, of the parties of the King and of the Parliament. The latter had practically possession of the following counties, *viz.*:

Bedford, Cambridge, Cumberland, Derby, Durham, Essex, Gloucester, Hertford, Huntingdon, Kent, Lancashire, Lincoln, Middlesex, Norfolk, Northampton, Northumberland, Nottingham, Rutland, Suffolk, Surrey, Sussex, Warwick, Westmoreland and Yorkshire; in all twenty-four.

The King was paramount in nine counties, in addition to almost the whole of Wales, *viz.*:

Cornwall, Devon, Hereford, Monmouth, Oxford, Shropshire, Somerset, Wilts and Worcester.

Berks, Buckingham, Cheshire, Dorset, Hampshire, Leicester

and Stafford, in all seven counties, were partially in the hands of either party.

The field armies of the King were as follows:

1. The army of the west under Lord Goring, consisting of about 14,000 men.

2. The Royal army commanded by Prince Rupert, amounting to about 7,500 men.

3. The cavalry of the various garrisons, which could be called out in case of need.

Against these the Parliament put into field:

1. The New Model army under Fairfax, 21,000 men.

2. Such regiments (about seven) as had been neither disbanded nor united to the New Model; these were under Massey at Gloucester.

3. Some small bodies of troops in Wales, in Shropshire, and in three or four other counties.

Thus at the commencement of the campaign, omitting the Scottish army (who after Marston Moor did nothing more in the field), the forces of the opponents were about equal, but the Parliament had at starting the great advantage, that their force was concentrated and under one head, whereas the two parts of the Royal army, owing to the dissensions of their leaders, were with difficulty induced to act in unison.

The best plan for the campaign of Fairfax, as indeed at a later period it was worked out, was therefore plainly this, to defeat one army of the King in the absence of the other, and then to turn upon and destroy the latter in its turn.

But the public voice, as before in the case of Gloucester, loudly demanded the relief of Taunton, and on the 29th of April an order was sent by the Commons to the general that the army should march to the West with that object. Accordingly, Fairfax leaving Cromwell and Browne before Oxford with 4,000 men, marched on the 30th from Windsor to Beading.

On the 2nd of May, at Newbury, a meeting took place between Fairfax and Cromwell; but information having been received from a prisoner captured that night, that Goring intended to beat up Oliver's quarters, the latter hastily returned to his command. Goring before his arrival had already carried Radcot Bridge, and Cromwell, having sent some horse across the Isis to reconnoitre, the Royalist cavalry drove them back with some loss.

Being reinforced, the Roundheads again advanced, only to be again forced to retire by the overwhelming strength of their enemy, while the further passage of reinforcements was checked by Lord Wentworth, who held the bridge. Goring had thus possession of the river, but on the following day, Cromwell having crossed at Newbridge on his flank, he quitted his position and hastened back to his main army at Taunton.

On the 7th of May Fairfax, being then at Blandford, received an order to detach a brigade to the relief at Taunton, and to march himself on Oxford. This change of plan was caused by the receipt of information that the King, taking advantage of the movement of the army of the Parliament to the west, was drawing out of his headquarters, with the view of taking the field, and had with this object called Rupert to his side. Orders were at the same time received by Cromwell and Browne to follow the King wherever he might go, and to hamper his movements in order to gain time for the advance of Fairfax.

In obedience to this order, on the 8th of May 4,000 foot, and from 1,800 to 2,000 horse, were detached under Colonel Welden from the main Parliamentary army; these marched directly on Taunton, and being mistaken by the enemy for the advanced guard of the entire force, succeeded on the 11th of May in relieving that town.

This mistake of the loyalists had been favoured by the movements of Fairfax, who had with this intention marched at first on Dorchester, but had, after proceeding a few miles, turned abruptly to the east, and thus left the detached brigade to continue its march alone. The besiegers having retired on the approach of Welden, he, after entering Taunton, fell back on Chard, but was a little later, on the arrival of Goring with 3,000 horse, driven into Taunton, and thus besieged in the very place which he had come to relieve. Fairfax, in the meanwhile, marching on an average twelve miles a day, reached Newbury on the 14th of May, Here we must for a time leave him in order to follow the movements of the King.

Charles, taking advantage of the original direction of the march of Fairfax, left Oxford on the 7th, taking with him 7,000 or 8,000 men under Rupert; Goring being detached, as previously mentioned, to Taunton almost immediately after the force had started. The King moved by easy marches by way of Droitwich, Newport, and Market Drayton, to the relief of Chester, which was at that time besieged by Sir William Brereton. On the arrival of the Royal army within twenty miles of the city the siege was abandoned, and the Parliamentary forces retired into Lancashire. Charles then changed the direction of his advance, and proceeded through Staffordshire into Leicestershire, where he, on the 29th of May, commenced the siege of Leicester, this being intended as a counterstroke to the siege of Oxford, which had then been beset by Fairfax.

At this point we must for awhile break the narrative of military events, in order to draw attention to an act of the Parliament, of which the results, perhaps unforeseen, were very important. On the 10th of May an order was made by both Houses that Lieutenant-General Cromwell "should be dispensed with for his personal attendance at the House, and continue his service and command in the army for forty days longer, notwithstanding the Self-denying Ordinance."

This order has been frequently noticed, as indeed considering its effects was certain; but it appears to be the general belief that Cromwell was the sole exception among the members to the action of the Self-denying Ordinance. This was by no means the case, for we find that on the 12th of May Brereton and two others were also confirmed in their authority for the same period; and it might not be impossible to find additional cases in which the same permission was given.

On the march of the King from Oxford, Cromwell and Browne, according to their orders, followed his army,, but soon finding that their strength was too small to cope with the increasing forces of Charles, reported to that effect, and were recalled. A party of about 2,500 horse, detached from Cromwell's brigade, was however sent to the north under Colonel Vermuyden to join the Scots, who would, it was expected, hinder the further advance of the Royal army.

The reason why this force was thus detached from the troops under Cromwell's command is worthy of notice. The Scots entertained for Cromwell very strong dislike and distrust; feelings which were amply returned by the latter, with a large admixture of contempt. In order to learn the cause of this variance, which was in the future to bear bitter fruit to the Scots, we must look back for awhile into the year 1644.

At the end of November in that year Cromwell, who was lieutenant-general of Manchester's army, was engaged in bringing before the House his report of the behaviour of his general at Newbury, and in this report, as also in other speeches, did not spare Essex, the commander-in-chief.

The latter was warned by the Lord Chancellor of Scotland, at a meeting at the house of the Lord General, that Cromwell if not destroyed would certainly oust him from his position; that he was an "incendiary" between the two kingdoms, and that unless he were removed from power the existing friendship between the two nations would undoubtedly soon come to an end, "For," said the Chancellor, "you ken vary weele that Lieutenant-General Cromwell is no friend of ours." For the above reasons, as the spokesman of the Scottish Commissioners, he urged that Cromwell should be proceeded against in order to "clip his wings from soaring to the prejudice of our cause."

But nothing was done in pursuance of this proposition, a report of which was almost certainly carried to Oliver, and which no doubt had its effect on his after proceedings with the Scots.

The original cause of this quarrel cannot be discovered, but we should probably not be far wrong if we placed the date of it in the previous July, about the time of the battle of Marston Moor, and we may perhaps assume that it arose from the friction which was certain to follow from the close contact of the bigoted Presbyterianism of the Scots, with the broad and liberal theology of the Independents.

The behaviour of the Scots in the battle itself may in some degree account for the contempt with which the great soldier afterwards regarded them, and it is possible (though this can be nothing but surmise) that the death of young Oliver, Cromwell's eldest surviving son, who is generally supposed to have fallen about this time, may have afforded good reason for his father's hatred of the allies of the Parliament.

Whatever may have been the originating cause of the disagreement, the fact remains that Cromwell, on account of the known ill-feeling between them, was not ordered to join the Scots, but fell back to Fairfax, whom he found, on the 22nd of May, engaged in the siege of Oxford, an undertaking which the general then felt to be as hopeless as we now know it to have been. After a few skirmishes with the garrison, Fairfax received orders to raise the siege and to inarch against the King, who on the 1st of June carried Leicester by storm. So little real was the siege of Oxford, that the artillery intended for that service did not arrive until the day before the abandonment of the enterprise.

The reason for this sudden change of plan on the part of the Parliament is to be found in the movements of the Scots, who, contrary to the hope and the expectation of the Commons, fell back into Westmoreland before the advance of the King. Colonel Vermuyden at once rejoined Fairfax with his cavalry, and the whole army prepared to "attend" Charles's march. Upon the idea that the King from Leicester might move upon the Eastern Association Cromwell was sent, with an escort of but four troops, to organise the defence of the Isle of Ely; but Charles had at first headed for Oxford; on hearing however that the siege of that city had been raised, he marched into Northamptonshire, and was about the 10th of June at Daventry.

It is pitiable to observe how even now, after nearly three years of war, the King's generals marched and counter-marched their troops without plan or object; they appear at first sight to have learnt nothing by the practice of war, but we shall probably be nearer to the truth if we attribute this seeming vacillation to the multitude of counsellors, in whom, in spite of Solomon's dictum, there is in war no wisdom, but rather the confusion of imbecility.

The Court, as ever, was a maze of intrigue, in which every man strove not to surpass but to supplant his neighbour, while as has been before mentioned, social precedence being the sole measure of military rank, there were in the Royal army too many equals and no one supreme; for the King was compelled to turn his attention rather to compose the quarrels of his own leaders, than to frustrate the plans of those of the enemy.

Fairfax, having marched from Oxford on June the 5th, was on the 8th near Newport-Pagnell, whence he wrote to the House to ask that Cromwell might be retained in its service; the answer being favourable, Fairfax on the 11th sent a letter to him, in which he appointed him lieutenant-general of the horse; Cromwell on receiving it marched at once, with 3,000 cavalry whom he had raised in the eastern counties, to rejoin the army, which on the above date was at Northampton. Orders were also despatched by Fairfax to various Parliamentary garrisons, directing the Governors to come at once to him with what strength they could; while Skippon, as before the sergeant-major-general of the army, was instructed to organise it in brigades.

The King, having thrown supplies, swept up by his foraging parties from Leicestershire and Northamptonshire, into Oxford, was still at this date at Daventry, but on hearing of the retreat of the Scots, proposed to move with his army to the relief of Scarborough and Pontefract Castles, which still held out against Lord Fairfax.

On the 12th the Parliamentary army marched to Kislingbury, advancing directly on the position which the King occupied on Burrough Hill, near Daventry; a reconnoitring party of cavalry pushed forward to beat up the quarters of the Cavaliers, and found, as they reported, all in disorder, the horses at grass and the King hunting.

During the night Charles hastily broke up his camp and fell back on Market Harborough. Fairfax followed at once, and on the evening of the 13th was at Guilsborough; the van of the Royal army being then at Harborough, and the rear at Naseby. Early on the morning of the 13th Cromwell with his cavalry joined from the eastern counties.

It is interesting to note how, while the Royalists were entirely without information as to the movements of their enemy, every step of the army of the Parliament was guided and guarded by the action of detachments of cavalry. For example: during this day Harrison was sent with a body of horse to Daventry, in order to learn more details of the strength of the King; while Ireton with a strong force moved on the flank of Charles's columns, watching everything and ready to strike if opportunity should offer. In speaking of these things we almost seem to be considering the respective action of the French and German armies during the days which preceded the battle of Gravelotte.

Towards evening on the 13th, Ireton's forces fell upon the rear of the King's columns in Naseby village, and drove it in confusion before him; on the receipt of the news of this engagement, Charles in the middle of the night assembled a council of war at the quarters of Prince Rupert, where it was decided that the Royal army should offer battle, and abandon the previous plan of retiring on Leicester and Newark for the purpose of gaining reinforcements; it was even deemed advisable to march to meet the advance of Fairfax.

Accordingly, in the early morning of Saturday the 14th of June, the Royal army was drawn up in a strong position to the south of Market Harborough facing southward; the centre of the line was as usual composed of infantry, of which there were four regiments in the first line, and three in the second, while in rear of these stood the reserve consisting of the King's and Prince Rupert's regiments; this infantry was under Lord Astley, and was formed as was customary at that time by regiments, each with a central body of pikemen and two wings of musketeers. Its strength is given by Clarendon at 3,300 men, but other accounts value the nine regiments at about 5,500 soldiers.

The right wing was composed of about 2,500 cavalry under Rupert, while the left, which was equal in strength, was led by Sir Marmaduke Langdale, and was made up of the Northern and the Newark Horse.

The King's army being thus drawn up ready for action, a force of cavalry was sent to the front about 8 a.m. to discover the enemy's position and intentions. With the carelessness which by this time had become characteristic of the Royal army, this reconnaissance was pushed only three or four miles towards Naseby, and the scout-master on his return having reported that he could find nothing of the enemy, Rupert with his usual precipitation dashed forward with his horse, to overtake and scatter the force, which he supposed to be retreating.

When he had advanced some little way, small parties of the Roundheads were seen; these in all probability were but advanced scouts of Ireton's force, and at the sight of the Royal cavalry they naturally fell back on their supports. Rupert, now confirmed in his belief of the retreat of Fairfax, sent back a message that the whole of the King's force should move forward at once, and should make haste to arrive at the point where he stood. At this order the line was set in motion, and leaving its excellent position, the King's army advanced "as well as might be" towards Naseby.

All who have read Kinglake's account of the battle of the Alma will remember how the English line, advancing to the attack over about a mile and a half of ground, became disordered and disorganised; if such was the condition of a highly trained army in the nineteenth century, what may we not conceive to have been the result of an advance, over about the same distance, of the half-trained levies of King Charles?

Shaken by their march out of the stiff formation in which men fought in those days, the Royal army was hurried into action by the impatient ardour of Rupert "before the cannon was turned, or the ground made choice of upon which they were to fight."

To return to the Parliamentary troops. At 3 a.m. on the morning of the 14th of June, Fairfax moved from Guilsborough on Naseby, with the intention of harassing the rear of the King's army with his cavalry, in order so to delay its march that his foot might have time to come up and inflict a decisive blow. By 5 a.m. he reached Naseby, and passing on, came at daylight in sight of masses of the Royal horse, who were shortly after followed by the main army of the King.

Fairfax at once determined to accept battle, and took up a defensive position along the brow of a low hill to the north-west of Naseby, where was a hedge which flanked the front of his line. In order to conceal his numbers and formation from the Cavaliers, he drew up his troops about a hundred yards in rear of the crest, and there stood awaiting the attack.

The following was the order of battle of the Parliamentary army:

The cavalry of the right wing, consisting of six regiments, was commanded by Cromwell, who formed his force in three lines, composed respectively of five, four, and three bodies of about 300 men each, so placed that the intervals in each line were covered by the troops of the line in rear; half of Rossiter's regiment was *echeloned* in rear of the right flank, which was exposed to attack.

The cavalry of the left wing, five regiments, with one troop and the dragoons of the Associated Counties, was under the command of Ireton, who formed it in two lines, the first of three regiments, the second of two, while the dragoons lined the hedge and guarded the left flank from attack.

The infantry in the centre, commanded by Skippon, were formed in one line with a reserve; the first line, naming the regiments from the right, was composed of Fairfax's, Montague's, Pickering's, Waller's, and Skippon's battalions, while the reserve included the regiments of Pride, Hammond, and Rainsborough.

The baggage of the army, under a guard of musketeers, was parked on the hill which lies close to the north-west corner of Naseby village.

On the approach of the Royal army Fairfax advanced his line to the crest of the hill, and sent forward, as was then the custom, a small body of about 300 men (termed a forlorn hope), which passed down the slope towards the enemy; these were quickly driven in, and the battle began almost simultaneously along the whole line.

The best contemporary account of the battle of Naseby divides the action under four heads, which we propose to examine in turn.

1. THE CONTEST BETWEEN THE PARLIAMENTARY LEFT AND THE KING'S RIGHT.

Ireton, on seeing the approach of Rupert's force, advanced to the crest of the hill, where, finding that the Cavaliers in his front had halted, he did the same; but on their resuming their forward movement he sounded the "charge," and attacked them in *echelon* right in front. A fierce hand-to-hand fight now took place, and the extreme right of his line being galled by the fire of some of the King's infantry, Ireton led a half-regiment of his force against the square whence the fire proceeded; in this charge he was wounded in the thigh and the face, and, having his horse shot under him, was made prisoner, but afterwards escaped in the confusion of the battle.

Of his cavalry, the front line broke that of the enemy opposed to them, but not being well supported by their comrades, were in their turn driven back by the Royal reserves, who, pushing on, routed the whole of the Roundhead left wing, and drove them pell-mell into and through the village of Naseby.

Returning from the pursuit, Rupert wasted most valuable time in a fruitless attack on the camp of the Parliamentary army, from which he was gallantly repulsed; the opportunity to rally thus offered to the defeated horse of Ireton was not lost, for four

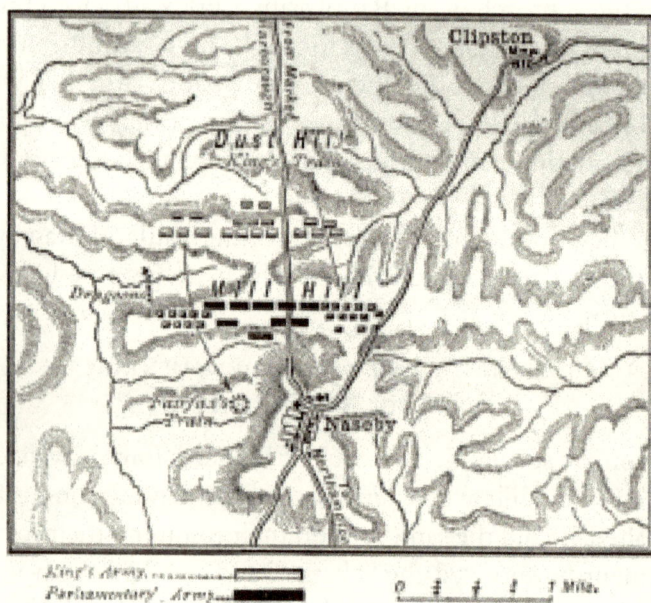

MILL HILL, NEAR NASEBY,
WHERE THE BATTLE OF NASEBY WAS FOUGHT,
JUNE 14TH, 1645

regiments of them reformed in sufficient time to press on the rear of the Prince as he at last fell back to join the King.

This charge of Rupert's cavalry was entirely isolated, and, as far as its effect on the battle was concerned, might have been a totally independent skirmish; but this was as a rule the case in the days of which we write, for each arm then fought as it were "for its own hand," and the combined movements of mounted and dismounted troops were things as yet undreamt of. But nothing can excuse the attack on the camp, which, we must believe, was actuated only by the hope of plunder, and heavy was the penalty paid by the King for the ignorance among his adherents of the axiom, that the first object of a battle is to defeat the enemy; since, that done, minor advantages follow as a matter of course.

### 2. THE ACTION OF THE CENTRES OF THE TWO ARMIES

Here also the advantage in the battle was at first to the King, for attacking in strength the left of the Parliamentary foot, which we may conceive to have been partially shaken by the charge of a portion of Rupert's horse, the Royal infantry drove back every regiment of the front line, with the exception of that which stood on the right. The broken troops fled in disorder behind the regiments which were in reserve; but the latter, advancing against their enemy, forced them over the crest and down the hill to their former position. Skippon was at this time dangerously wounded by a shot in the side; but the stout old man refused to quit the field, and remained at his post until the battle had been won.

### 3. THE CHARGE OF THE RIGHT WING OF THE PARLIAMENT UNDER CROMWELL.

This force advanced in *echelon*, the right thrown back; but it may be doubted whether this formation was not principally due to the nature of the ground, which was full of rabbit-holes and covered with furze, and much delayed the attack. Whalley, leading the front line, was completely successful, and Cromwell, though he met with a stout resistance, turning both flanks of his adversaries drove without a check through Langdale's cavalry, and forced those who yet remained on the field to take refuge behind the King's reserves; the remainder "fled farther and faster than became them."

We must now note how different is the action of a true leader from that of a mere soldier. Cromwell, unlike Rupert, in the place of pursuing with his entire force, detached two regiments to observe and to hold in check the cavalry which he had defeated, and turned back with the remainder of his troops to a new task. The King's right was victorious, but out of reach; his left was shattered, but his centre still stood firm," and unless this could be broken before the return of the Prince he might yet win the day. Against the centre of the Royalist line were therefore turned all the efforts of the Parliamentary troops.

In front, the regiments of Hammond, Rainsborough, and Pride, with the reorganised remnants of the broken front line of the Roundheads, pressed upon the enemy's infantry, which soon gave way, with the exception of one gallant square that held its ground, though charged in front, in rear, and on both flanks. At length Fairfax himself led up his own regiment of foot, who attacked it with the butt-ends of their muskets, while the horse charged it at the same time; thus pressed, the brave battalion at length broke, and with it the last of the King's infantry and artillery were captured or destroyed.

Charles in the meantime had endeavoured to rally his beaten cavalry, and was proposing to lead in person his guards upon the enemy, when the mistaken loyalty of the Earl of Carnwath, who turned the King's horse from the battle, joined to the confusion created by a wrong word of command, caused a panic, from which but few could be rallied even by the individual exertions of the King.

At this moment Rupert returned from his chase of the Parliamentary left wing, but his troopers, as ever, could not be rallied or formed for a second charge; and when Fairfax advanced, after a short pause to reform his infantry, with a force of all arms against the King's remnant of cavalry, the Cavaliers swung round and fled from the field.

The pursuit continued to within two miles of Leicester (about fourteen miles), and as the battle had been the hardest fought of all in the war, so were the losses of the defeated party exceptionally great, while their disorder and disorganisation were irremediable: 5,000 prisoners, and 8,000 arms, with more than 100 colours, were the trophies of the action, the last in which Charles was in person engaged, and the true death-blow to his cause.

Of even greater importance than the above was the capture of the King's cabinet of private papers, which included many letters to and from the Queen. These were printed by the orders of the two Houses, and served by their contents to assure the rise of the Independents, since oven the most moderate Presbyterians could not deny but that Charles had been playing a double game, appearing to desire alliance with and to promise favour to them, at the very moment that he was asking aid from the Catholic Powers, and declaring his intention to befriend those who held to the Roman faith.

The Parliamentary army after the battle marched to Market Harborough, while the King fled on through Leicester to Ashby-de-la-Zouch; thence he pursued his way by Lichfield, through Worcestershire, to Hereford, in the hope that he might be able to raise a new army in Wales; at Hereford Rupert left him for the purpose of taking command of the city of Bristol.

At the termination of this phase of the campaign we may perhaps pause, in order to say a few words as to its general character. Attention must first be drawn to the waste of time and of labour caused by the orders of the Parliament, by which Fairfax was forced to march, first to the west and then north-east, for the purpose of undertaking a siege which at that time could have but one result, absolute failure.

The escape of the King from Oxford gave the general the excuse which he needed, and he then, as no doubt he had longed to do at first, marched directly on the Royal army, seeing with a true soldier's eye that, so long as that remained in the field unbroken, no real success could be possible; and that, that once defeated, all sieges became matters of certainty, and the surrender of each fortress a mere question of time.

Of the strategy and tactics of the campaign there is not much to be said, for we can scarcely dignify with the former name the very simple plan of interposing an army between the King and Oxford, and by advancing to force him either to accept battle, or to undertake a retreat of which the direction would lead him upon the Scots; while the manner of conducting the battle itself consisted as usual of a series of frontal attacks by the several arms, followed in the case of success by isolated combats of small mixed bodies against such fractions of the enemy as might yet hold their ground. It may be said that up to the time of the battle of Naseby, all the contests of the war had been "soldiers' battles," in that they had all been won by sheer hard fighting, without much assistance from any plan of attack, or, except in the last, by any decided attempt to increase the value of the victory by a very determined pursuit; but much of this want of plan was undoubtedly due to the quality of the troops, who could fight but could not manoeuvre.

The character of the battles of Naseby and of Marston Moor stands out entirely distinct from that of any other combat in the war, in the fierceness of their conduct and in the crushing nature of their results; and we may fairly judge that they took this character from those of Fairfax and Cromwell, the leaders of the victorious armies. Indeed, to the student of war it seems as though each commander, in our own times as well as in those of our forefathers, had a "style" of his own in battle, and that a man skilled in reading between the lines in military history could well gather from anonymous details of an action the name of the general who gained it.

Thus, Wellington could never have conceived an Austerlitz, while Bazaine had it not in his nature to produce even a poor copy of the campaign of 1814; of Napoleon alone can it be said that nothing was impossible to him, since he was capable of all.

The difference between the troops of Fairfax or Cromwell

and those of Essex or Waller is noticed by Clarendon, in a passage where he mentions that those of the two latter generals could never be brought, as could the others, to rally after a charge, whether successful or the reverse; a failing which he also states to have been characteristic of the King's troops.

From this time forward we shall find all the military operations of the Parliamentary army marked by a directness and thoroughness which were before unseen in this war, and to whatever causes we may attribute the weak handling of Essex, Waller, and Manchester, there can be no doubt but that the New Model army, under its great leaders, knew well what it meant to do and did it.

Of all England, since the north had been lost at Marston Moor and the midlands at Naseby, there remained now to the King, in addition to a few isolated garrisons, only the west, where Prince Charles held the nominal command of an army which was in reality directed by Hopton and Goring. Leaving the King in Wales, and calling the Scots towards the south to occupy the valley of the Severn, and thus to cut Charles from England, to the west accordingly Fairfax bent his way.

He had before the battle of Naseby, through the treachery of a spy, become possessed of some letters from Goring to the King, in which the former stated that, when he had taken Taunton (in some three weeks), he would march northwards to aid the main Royal army. Had Charles received these letters, he would probably have refused to risk a battle before Goring's arrival; to Fairfax they spoke loudly of the danger of Taunton, and of the necessity for its relief.

But Leicester was near at hand, and was in trepidation on account of the issue of the battle; to Leicester therefore he first turned his attention, and having beleaguered it, secured its surrender on the 18th of June by the threat of a bombardment. From Leicester Fairfax marched by Warwick (22nd of June), Lechlade (26th), Marlborough (29th), over Salisbury Plain[1] (July

---

1. "Being drawn up that morning to a rendezvous at a place called Stonage." (*Anglia Rediviva*, p. 55.)

the 1st).

At Salisbury, whither some officers and men went at a distance from the main column, the Parliamentary forces first met the "club-men," of whom before long they were to have considerable experience.

The so-called "club-men" or "club-risers" were members of associations formed among the agricultural population of Dorsetshire, Wiltshire, Somersetshire, and parts of the neighbouring counties, under the leadership of local personages; they professed themselves to be neutral in the war, and to desire only the cessation of hostilities and the prohibition of plunder, but were commonly suspected of favouring the Royal cause, insomuch that Fairfax was of opinion that, should his army be worsted in an engagement with Goring, these bands would fall upon the fugitives and destroy them.

As however to his advance they offered no opposition, of which indeed they were incapable, he, on July the 3rd at Dorchester, consented to receive a petition from them; but found himself compelled to refuse their desires, among which were the cessation of the war, with a promise of a renewal of the efforts to bring about a treaty of peace, and the possession of all garrisons in Wilts and Dorset; to which was also added a demand for reparation for some little loss which Massey, who with 3,000 men was striving to assist Taunton, had shortly before inflicted upon them.

On the night of the 15th of July, at Beaminster, Fairfax received authentic information that Goring, having heard of his advance, had raised the siege of Taunton. The general at once pushed forward some cavalry under Fleetwood in pursuit, while, after a very long and very hot march to Crewkerne, the infantry, hearing that this force had been engaged with the rear of the enemy, hurried on towards Petherton, where the Royalists held the bridge, in the hope of bringing them to battle. The defence of the passage was however abandoned on the approach of the Parliamentary forces, of which the outposts during the 6th occupied the line Petherton-Martock.

On the afternoon of that day information was received that the main body of the enemy lay at Long Sutton, and that the bridge over the Yeo at Yeovil had been broken down, while those at Load, Ilchester, and Langport were held in force.

The army having paraded at 6 a.m. on the 7th, the general made a reconnaissance of the river-line, and decided that it was too strong to allow of a successful frontal attack; he therefore determined to observe the three above-named bridges with detachments, and to force a passage at Yeovil, on the left flank of the enemy, where, since the bridge was considered impassable, the defence had been entrusted to a party of horse.

On the advance of Fairfax this force retired, and the bridge having been repaired, all was ready for the passage, when early on the morning of the 8th it became known that the Royalists, finding that the flank of their line had been thus turned, had abandoned their position, and had fallen back on Langport. On the receipt of this news Fairfax, withdrawing from Yeovil, marched along the south side of the river to Ilchester, which he occupied. Information now arrived that Goring, hoping to find Taunton undefended, proposed to make a dash at that town; to counteract this movement, Massey was sent with a large force to observe his actions.

If the above manoeuvres be followed on the map, it will be noticed that the strategy of Fairfax was excellent; he avoided an engagement with his enemy in a position where the latter wished to fight, and would have fought at great advantage; and nobly aided by the energy of his men, who had suffered greatly from the heat and the length of the marches, turned them out of this position without firing a shot.

On the 9th the army moved to Long Sutton, while the cavalry, who, under Massey, had been pushed close up to the enemy's position, fought a small but successful action with the Royal horse. On the following day Goring, finding that his expected reinforcements did not arrive, drew off his guns and baggage towards Bridgewater, and proposed to cover this movement by holding the passage of the river about one mile to the east of

Langport. Fairfax, on discovering this intention of the enemy, formed his army in order of battle, and after a preliminary fire of artillery, sent forward his infantry against the "pass";[2] these running from hedge to hedge secured the passage.

The King's horse at once threatened to charge, at which the Parliamentary cavalry, in the most gallant manner, pressed on up a narrow lane, attacked, and broke their adversaries; the pursuit was for a moment checked, to allow of the arrival of greater strength, but being again taken up, was continued, with one short pause caused by an effort of the Royalists to make a stand on particularly favourable ground on Aller Moor, to within two miles of Bridgewater, with the result that 1,400 prisoners and 1,200 horses were captured. Fairfax on the same day pushed on to Middlezoy, and the following day to Chedzoy, where he had an interview with some of the leaders of the club-men, who since his success had grown more friendly.

A reconnaissance of the town of Bridgewater, carried out by Fairfax and Cromwell, showed it to be a place of great strength, defended by a wet tidal ditch thirty feet in width, with good fortifications armed with forty guns, and with a garrison of about 1,400 men. After a series of councils of war, it was at last decided that, since the town was too important to be neglected, while a siege by approaches would give time for the King to recruit his army, it should be attempted by storm on Monday, the 22nd of July. Accordingly the storming-faggots, which the assailants carried for the double purpose of covering themselves and of filling up the ditch, were prepared, as were also long ladders which might serve as bridges; all being ready on the Sunday night, the storming parties moved to their posts as soon as it was dark, and waited for the three shots which were to be the signal for attack.

Six regiments under Massey were ordered to assault the Devonshire side of the town, while the eastern face was to be attacked by seven others. At 2 a.m. on the 22nd the latter fell on, the former merely threatening the enemy, and thus preventing

2. Presumably a ford or a bridge.

them from reinforcing the point of the true attack. The storming parties quickly forced the passage of the ditch and rampart, and fighting their way to the gate lowered the drawbridge, over which dashed the forlorn-hope of horse; in those days, strange as we should think it now, an ordinary feature of a storm. These quickly cleared the streets, and pressed in as far as a second gate, which led to the inner town. Repeated summonses from Fairfax failing to induce the Governor to surrender, fire was reopened on the town, with the result that it yielded at 8 a.m. on the 23rd.

The capture of Bridgewater, apart from its moral effect, was of great service to the cause of the Parliament, who now held a line of fortified posts, including Taunton, Langport, and Lyme Regis, by which the Royalist counties of Devon and Cornwall were cut off from communication with the rest of England.

At a council of war assembled on the 25th it was determined to advance into the west against Goring, whose troops lay at this time at Torrington, he himself being at Barnstaple with Prince Charles; but after one march Fairfax, doubting the wisdom of a further advance until Rupert had been driven from Bristol, retraced his steps with the intention of taking Bath and Sherborne Castle, the possession of which two points might serve to cut off the Prince from Goring and Devonshire.

On the 28th, accordingly, the army marched to Wells, having detached a small force to observe and report upon Sherborne Castle. On the 29th a party of horse and dragoons having been sent to Bath under Colonel Rich, the latter summoned the city, which refused to surrender. Upon this the dragoons dismounting crept over the drawbridge in the dusk of the evening, drove the defenders from the loopholes, fired the gate, and most gallantly forced an entrance. The governor at once surrendered; and thus Bath was won. Having placed a garrison of two regiments of foot in the city, the army on August 1st marched as far as Queen's Camel, in the direction of Sherborne.

Information having been received of an intended meeting at Shaftesbury of the club-men of Wilts, Dorset, and Somerset, a party of horse under Colonel Fleetwood was despatched to seize the ringleaders, of whom he secured about fifty; these were at once imprisoned, pending an opportunity to send them to London for trial.

The effects of this action was immediate, for on the following day 10,000 men of the three counties rose with the intention of releasing their leaders. Cromwell (whose tenure of command, prolonged in June for three months, had been now renewed for four additional months) set out on the 4th of August with a body of horse towards Shaftesbury, in order to convince or to coerce the insurgents, as might be most easy or most advisable.

The first party which he met, upon his assurance that their goods should be protected, and that justice should be done on all marauders, broke up and returned quietly to their homes; but, upon a hill (styled "Hambleton Hill, near Shrawton," probably Hamilton Hill, near Blandford), where was "an old Romane work deeply trenched," he found a body of 4,000 men, who refused three messages of peace, and even fired on the messenger. These Cromwell determined at once to dislodge, and his first attack in front having been repulsed, owing to the narrowness of the track by which it was necessary to ascend the hill, he sent Desborough with a regiment to attack the club-men in rear. After a long and difficult climb the cavalry reached the top of the hill, charged the mob and dispersed them with but little loss, taking the leaders prisoners.

On the following day, August 5th, Cromwell with his party returned to Sherborne, against which the siege was pressed with energy. Though bombarded with heavy guns and attacked with mines, for which latter purpose miners were brought from the Mendip hills, the Castle, under Sir Lewis Dives, held out gallantly until the 15th, on which day, after the outworks had been carried, the garrison, about 400 men, surrendered at discretion.

A council of war was now called for the purpose of deciding upon the next step in the campaign, whether to go west after Goring, or to attack Rupert in Bristol. It was finally determined to undertake the latter, for the following reasons: the Prince had then so large a force under his command that, in addition to finding a sufficient garrison for the city, he could put 3,000 horse and foot into the field; it was dangerous to leave so great a strength in rear of the army, especially since Bristol might at any moment become a rallying-point for the club-men of the adjacent counties; and finally the great advantage which would accrue to the Parliamentary cause by the capture of a city of such importance.

Accordingly, on the 18th, Fairfax started from Sherborne, and marching by way of Castle Gary, Shepton Mallet, and Chew, pushed forward from the latter place on the 21st to Bedminster with a party of horse, desiring both to reconnoitre the city and to prevent a reported movement on the part of Rupert, who, it was said, intended to break out of Bristol to the west, and thus to effect a junction with Goring. There was probably little truth in this rumour, since any combined action of these two leaders would have been impossible, considering their mutual dislike and distrust.

On the 22nd the army moved to Keynsham, and on the 23rd a part of it advanced to Stapleton, in Gloucestershire; on the latter day the system of posts which was to shut in the city on the west was completed, and by the 25th Bristol was entirely surrounded; on the same day Massey with a force of cavalry was despatched to Taunton, to cover the siege from any attempt which Goring might make to interfere with it. Sorties took place from Bristol on the 23rd, 24th, 26th, and 27th, as also on the 1st of September, but they were all repulsed with loss. On the 2nd of September it was determined to storm the city, for any further delay might be dangerous, since the Scottish army had raised the siege of Hereford and were retiring by Warwick to the north.

The cause of this movement was the success of Montrose in Scotland, for Leven, on hearing of the result of the battle of Kilsythe, had sent Lesley with a strong force into Scotland to drive back the Marquis. It was considered possible that the King, being thus relieved might pass to Oxford, and having there collected troops, might endeavour to join Goring, who for his part, as was known by intercepted letters, undertook to relieve Bristol in three weeks.

The assault having been determined on, there was nothing to delay its execution, all things having been prepared to that end since the first commencement of the siege, and after a summons which was sent in on the 4th, the final answer to which was delayed by Rupert until the night of the 9th, an order was issued that the storm should take place at 2 a.m. on the 10th of September.

The dispositions for the attack were as follows: Welden, with the troops which first relieved and then defended Taunton, was to assault the city from the Somersetshire side; from Gloucestershire two attacks were to be made, one by Montague, Pickering, and Sir Hardress Waller upon the works to the east of the city between the Avon and the Frome, while the second, under Rainsborough and Hammond, was to storm the northern face, their efforts being particularly directed against Prior's Hill, on which stood a strong fort.

The fortunes of these assaults varied much. Welden's failed utterly on account of the strength of the defences on the side which he was ordered to attack. Montague, Pickering and Waller made good a lodgement, and being seconded by Desborough with the horse, fought their way into the city, which was then set on fire by the enemy. Rainsborough's attack on the fort on Prior's Hill was at first checked, but after three hours of fighting Hammond with some of his troops, having broken another portion of the Royalist line of defences, took the fort in reverse, carried it, and "immediately put almost all the men in it to the sword."

Thus before noon nearly the whole of the defences on the east side of Bristol were in the hands of the Parliamentary party, and as Rupert shortly after asked for terms, articles were proposed which by 7 p.m. had been agreed on by both sides. By these Bristol was surrendered at 1 p.m. on the 11th of September. On that day Prince Rupert and his troops marched out and

136

proceeded under escort to Oxford.

It may be well at this point to narrate the movements of Charles after the Battle of Naseby. Wandering in Wales until the early part of August, he had then passed through that principality round the flank of the Scottish army, and had thus arrived at Ludlow in Shropshire. He there formed the idea of joining Montrose, who was at that time carrying on a fairly successful war in Scotland with the Presbyterian party (of which Argyll was the leader), and with this object marched by Nottinghamshire to Doncaster, where he was met by many of the Royalists of Yorkshire; but on the alarm of the approach of Lesley who, as has been before mentioned, was moving to the north for the purpose of opposing Montrose, this force dispersed, and Charles fell back to Newark, whence before the end of August he went to Oxford.

From that city, after a rest of only two days, he passed to Raglan Castle, with the object of raising troops to relieve Hereford, then besieged by the Scottish army, and when this city had been freed by their departure, he turned his every thought to the succour of Bristol. But before any sufficient body of troops could be prepared, the news came of Rupert's surrender, upon which the King, broken-hearted, recalled all the Prince's commissions, and from Hereford wrote to him a letter in which he spoke of the loss of Bristol as "the greatest trial of my constancy that has yet befallen me."

Here for the present we must leave Charles, and return to the progress of events in the west.

Goring being now successfully cooped up in Devon and Cornwall, it was decided that the Parliamentary army, while holding the chain of posts which kept him in, should send out detachments to reduce the various garrisons which hampered their communication with London; at the same time Colonels Poyntz and Rossiter were ordered to follow the King, and to prevent him from raising a fresh force.

Berkeley Castle and the castle at Devizes were the first points to claim attention, as they were the nearest to the army; the reduction of the former was entrusted to Rainsborough, who was detached with three regiments for that purpose, while Cromwell with four regiments marched for the latter.

The castle at Devizes which commanded the great western road, was a place of considerable strength by nature, and its defensive power had been much augmented by art, extensive earthworks having been thrown up about it; the siege commenced on the 20th of September, but to Cromwell's summons the Governor returned only the answer: "Win it and wear it!" This bravado was, however, not the forerunner of a long defence, for on the 23rd the Castle surrendered; on the same day a detachment from Oliver's force under Colonel Pickering took possession of Laycock House, a post in that neighbourhood of some strength. Rainsborough had like success, for Berkeley Castle, the outworks having been carried by storm, was surrendered on the 26th.

These tasks having been performed, it was determined to complete the work by reducing Winchester and Basing House, which commanded the road from London; this was the more necessary since the army was by this time in great need of money, which could be sent by that route only. Cromwell was accordingly, with the same brigade reinforced with three regiments of horse, despatched on this duty, while the main army, which on the 18th of September was at Devizes, turned westwards by Warminster, Shaftesbury, Dorchester, and Beaminster, and so came on the 6th of October to Chard.

Cromwell, having arrived at Winchester on the 28th of September, received on that night the submission of the governor of the castle, and thence, in a few days, moved on to Basing House, the seat of the Marquis of Winchester. This strong post (of which the ruins are still standing near Basingstoke) had up to this time laughed at all attempts to force or starve it into surrender; but its time was now come, for at 6 a.m. on the 14th of October it was carried by storm. It was, after its capture, by the advice of Cromwell, dismantled and rendered untenable, since on account of its great size it required to hold it a garrison of at least 800 men.

This duty being done, Cromwell returned towards the west, capturing on his way Langford House near Salisbury. In the meantime Fairfax had advanced through Honiton, and by the 17th of October, having occupied Tiverton, had driven Goring back behind the Exe. On the 19th, Tiverton Castle, the chain of the drawbridge having been accidentally cut by a round-shot, was stormed with a rush and occupied. It was now determined, in consideration of the time of year and of the great exertions which the troops had made, to attempt no more action in the field, but to commence a rigid blockade of Exeter, in which were about 5,000 men.

Accordingly, during the remainder of the year 1645, the Parliamentary troops contented themselves with holding the country around Exeter, while Goring, for similar reasons, took up his winter quarters, the horse being posted at Okehampton and the foot about Launceston; the Royalist leader's were however not idle, for throughout the winter strenuous efforts were made to raise a strong force from among the Cornishmen.

At this point we may therefore leave Fairfax and return to the action of the King, whom we left at Hereford. On the 20th of September, having heard that Chester was in danger from an attack of a Parliamentary force under Colonel Jones, Charles with 5,000 horse passed northwards to its relief. Poyntz who, as has been before mentioned, had received orders to follow the Royal army, pressed hastily after them, and on the 24th attacked them on Rowton Heath, about two miles from Chester; the Cavaliers charged at first with such resolution that they routed the Roundhead horse, but a detachment of 800 men, coming up from the besieging force which lay around Chester, fell upon the rear of the Royalists with entire success; after a severe struggle the King's party fled in utter disorder into Wales, with the loss of about 1,000 prisoners.

After collecting some few men in Denbighshire, the King avoiding Poyntz, who was waiting for reinforcements, pushed across England to Newark, which the Scots, who at this time lay at Durham, had, in spite of frequent orders to that effect from the Parliament, neglected to besiege. Indeed, since the Independents had gained ground over the Presbyterians, the relations between the Scots and the Parliament had become much strained, the former demanding constant supplies of money, while the latter gave nothing but orders.

From Newark Charles, in the vain hope of establishing communication with Montrose, despatched Lord Digby and Sir Marmaduke Langdale with a considerable force to Scotland; but these leaders, while attempting to fight their way through Yorkshire, where at first they met with some slight success, were about the 18th of October defeated by Poyntz, with the loss of 400 men. From the field of battle the Royalists fled into Westmoreland and endeavoured still to push on, but were a few weeks later discomfited and dispersed on Carlisle Sands, by a force which the Governor of Carlisle had sent out against them; the entire body being broken up, the leaders fled by sea to the Isle of Man.

The King, now nearly alone, escaped by night from Newark on receipt of the news that the siege of that place was about to be undertaken by Poyntz and the Scottish army, and arrived on the 6th of November at Oxford. Here on the 7th of December he was joined by Prince Rupert, to whom he had been previously to some degree reconciled, and under the command of the Prince a force of 1,500 men left the city on the 16th, with the object of relieving Chester; they were, however, beaten back before they had reached Warwick.

The King's cause had by this time become hopeless, for with the exception of Hopton's army, he had now no troops who could keep the field, while his garrisons were daily reduced in number. Hereford was in December carried by a stratagem, and even Wales, the stronghold and recruiting-ground of the Royalist party had, as regards its southern counties, been reduced by Langhorne into obedience to the Parliament.

Thus ended the year 1645, during which the war, which had dragged on its length for nearly three years without any result but the abundant shedding of blood, was in nine months brought to a crisis, decisive and favourable to their cause, by the action of the New Model; the leaders and soldiers of which, unlike those of the earlier armies, had set forth to themselves a clear object for their action, and, further, possessed the will to work out their intentions to the full end. In this year also we meet with the first signs of that military skill which was in later days to ensure the supremacy of Cromwell in the army, and through the army in the State.

## CHAPTER 5

# 1646, 1647, and 1648

If we compare the condition of the Royal party at the commencement of the year 1646, with that which it enjoyed in January, 1645, we shall be able to realise how terrible was the blow inflicted on their cause by the single defeat of Naseby; for indeed with the exception of this battle no action of the first importance had taken place during the year. Yet there now remained to the King but one army, that which was held fast in Devonshire by Fairfax; it is true that a body of from 1,500 to 2,000 cavalry still accompanied Charles in his wanderings, but these were little more than a bodyguard, and as we shall find were soon wasted in desultory fighting.

Of all England the King now possessed only Devon and Cornwall, for we cannot reckon as territory the land occupied by the few, though strong, garrisons which still held out for him in various parts, such as Newark, Chester, Oxford, Worcester, and the Castles of Raglan, Caernarvon, Conway, Donnington, Wallingford, and others. To that portion of his kingdom which was still his own he was unable to make his way, and was perforce compelled to permit the army which defended it to be crushed without an effort to aid.

At the commencement of the year 1646, the Civil War was thus practically over, and save by the help of foreign arms, no power at that time remained to Charles to continue the struggle with any, even the wildest, hope of ultimate success; this fact, which was patent to all, was not hidden from the King, and we shall accordingly find that during the year on which we have now entered, he was busily employed in the endeavour to obtain by mediation or intervention that position which he had risked on, and lost by, the sword.

It was more than suspected by the Independents that already there was a tendency on the part of the Scots to make advances to the King, who on his part was at this time offering all things to the Irish, the French, the Pope, to anyone indeed, who would accept promises as an equivalent return for aid in some form.

The policy of Charles was undoubtedly dishonest, but it was also unfortunate, and much of his vacillation, with its consequent apparent deception, may be justly set down to the weakness of his will, through which he surrendered himself to each of twenty advisers in turn, and following the advice of each for a while, recklessly threw over any plan, however far advanced, which appeared likely to clash with his latest hobby. He further believed that he had sufficient skill in the game of politics to play off one party against the other, and ventured even to apparently favour two opponents, of whom at that very moment he had fully determined to crush one.

Again he felt deeply in his heart, that his kingly office was of a character so majestic, that men neither could nor would dispense with it, and even at this time when his fortunes were at a very low ebb, he was unable or unwilling to realise that the Crown, worshipful as he held it, had no longer any weight as compared with the sword of the people. Charles still believed, and believed to his death, that such was the inherent grandeur of his office, that his acceptance of one or the other of two parties was sufficient to ensure the moral superiority of that side which he preferred, and to turn the scale of evenly balanced power in its favour.

He hoped to prove himself to be necessary to each, and to be wooed by all for their purposes, to gain which he intended that they should first serve his own; but in place of this he was used now as a puppet, and a little later as a scapegoat, and when no longer needed was erased as a superfluous zero. At this very moment, while beseeching help from every power on the Continent, he was engaged in the endeavour to arrange a treaty with the Scots, was making a series of proposals for peace to the Parliament, while in writing to Rupert he tells that Prince that in any case he will give no more than had already been refused at Uxbridge, in January, 1645.

But that the King's cause was lost was obvious to every eye, and the saddest portion of the story of this year is the gradual desertion of this unfortunate man by friends, dependants, and relatives, at the time when he was tasting the fruits of the greediness of the first, of the ambition of the second, and of the foolhardy rashness, of the third.

To return to the actions of the main army of the Parliament, which we left at the close of 1645 cantoned around Exeter, while Sir Richard Grenville in Cornwall and Hopton in Devonshire[1] still kept the field in the King's name. On the 8th of January after a council of war, which on the 5th decided to advance, Fairfax moved forward on Crediton, whence on the following day a brigade under Cromwell pushed on to Bovey Tracey, where lay some of the Royalist horse. Attacking at about 6 p.m.

Oliver surprised them, and captured all their horses and about fifty prisoners. The officers, who when Cromwell's cavalry burst into the town, were playing cards, on finding that the house in which they were had been beset by the Roundheads, flung the stakes out of the window among the men and, taking advantage of the delay which was caused by the scramble for the money, escaped through a backdoor, and so across the river.

On the 10th of January the Parliamentary army, driving the Cavaliers before them, occupied Ashburton, and there decided to move directly to the relief of Plymouth, in preference to fighting Hopton's force, which was in position on the northern edge of Dartmoor. On the 11th a further advance was made to Totness, whence a despatch was sent to Plymouth to assure the garrison of aid; from Totness strong parties of cavalry were sent out over the more towards Okehampton and Tavistock, and

---

1. Goring, seeing no chance of success, had sailed for France in November, 1645.

some of these having been mistaken by the besiegers for the vanguard of the main army, the siege was hurriedly abandoned by the Cavaliers, who fell back over the Tamar into Cornwall.

It was now determined that, since Plymouth had been thus relieved, no further advance should take place until after the capture of Dartmouth, since a sea-port was urgently needed, in order that the money and recruits sent from London by sea might be received by the army; Dartmouth was accordingly invested on the 12th of January, and after a pause of some days, needed for the preparation of ladders, etc., as also for the arrival and co-operation of the fleet, was stormed at 11 p.m. on the 18th with the loss of but one man killed.

On the capture of the town the outlying forts at once surrendered, as did also two men-of-war which were at the time in the harbour. The total number of guns captured was 103, while 800 to 1,000 prisoners were taken. These, with the exception of the officers and the gentlemen of the county, were all set free; and Fairfax, in addition, wisely gave a present of two shillings to every Cornishman to help him to his home.

Having by the relief of Plymouth obtained the object of his march, Fairfax now retired by Totness and Chudleigh towards Exeter, with the intention of continuing the siege of that city, which during his expedition to Dartmouth he had left carefully blockaded.

On the 29th of January news was received that a force of cavalry from Oxford had advanced as far as Corfe Castle, while the Royalist horse of Hopton's force, now under the command of Lord Wentworth, had pushed forward to Barnstaple, with the intention of effecting a junction with the former body. Upon the receipt of this information Fairfax moved forward to Tiverton, and sent out three regiments of cavalry to reconnoitre in North Devon; these last were however recalled on the 5th of February, when it had been discovered that the enemy's horse, after revictualling Dunster in Somersetshire, had retired on their infantry, pursued by such of the troops stationed in those parts (under Blake in Taunton) as had not been drawn off towards

Corfe Castle. The Royal troops who had attempted to surprise this latter post were with some difficulty driven back, and returned to Oxford.

On the 8th of February it was discovered that Hopton was again about to make an effort to break out, for having collected about 4,000 foot and some cavalry at Launceston, he marched thence into Devonshire, and was at this date on his road to Torrington, at which place he proposed to arrive on the 10th. About the same time some letters were also intercepted, in which Wentworth undertook to shortly relieve Exeter.

On the receipt of this information a council of war was assembled, in which on the 9th, it was determined to leave Sir Hardress Waller, with a detachment of troops (three regiments of foot and one of horse), to continue the siege of Exeter, while Fairfax and the remainder of the army (five regiments of horse and seven of foot) should march against Hopton. Accordingly, on the 10th the General moved to Crediton, where he heard that the enemy had 5,000 horse and 4,000 foot at Torrington, and expected a further reinforcement of 1,000 men from Barnstaple.

On the 14th Chumleigh was reached, and it was intended to arrive at Torrington on the following day; but the weather was so bad, and so much delay was caused by the action of the enemy in breaking down the bridges, that the engagement was deferred until the morrow, though many skirmishes took place during the day between the horse of the two parties.

At 4 a.m. on the 16th the drums beat the "assembly," and by 7 a.m. the whole army of the Parliament was formed in order of battle on the moor, about five miles from Torrington; by 5 p.m., after skirmishing all the day through the narrow lanes, the Parliamentary forces advanced to within a mile of the town, towards which, at 8 p.m., the enemy retired after some hard fighting in the fields and enclosures. Fairfax having decided that it would not be wise to venture an attack in the dark over unknown ground, halted his army, pushed forward the outposts in double the usual strength, and gave orders that the assault should be delayed until the following morning.

During the night a noise was heard in the town, which gave the idea that the enemy was retiring; in order to ascertain if this were really the case, six dragoons were ordered to creep up to the barricades of the Royalists and to fire over them. This fire was answered by a sharp volley, to which the Parliamentary advanced troops at once replied; the firing was immediately taken up along the whole line, and even the reserves were soon pushed into action.

Fairfax, observing the good spirit of the soldiers, ordered the attack to be supported by the whole force, and the firing thus became general; the Parliamentary foot crept on from hedge to hedge, and, after about two hours of hard struggling, drove the Cavaliers behind the barricades which guarded the approaches of the town. By fresh efforts, and not without serious loss, these defences were stormed, and the enemy, still fighting from house to house and from street to street, was at last forced out of Torrington.

This success had been scarcely gained, when eighty barrels of powder, which had been stored in the church, also unfortunately used as a place of confinement for 200 prisoners, were exploded by a man named Watts, who had received 30 in payment for this crime. The prisoners and their guards were all killed, and many houses in the town were destroyed, while the Royalists, led by Sir John Digby, strove to take advantage of the resulting confusion, and by a vigorous charge to redeem their defeat. But they were repulsed by the Parliamentary horse, who about 11 p.m., after a pause for the purpose of rallying their scattered troops, started in pursuit of the Cavaliers, of whose entire force only about 400 recrossed the Tamar into Cornwall.

Thus ended one of the most severe and gallant contests of the war. The Cornishmen proved themselves as ever soldiers of the best, while the loss of the Roundheads in officers and men was greater "than hath been in any storm since the army came forth." But from this day's work the Royal infantry never rallied, for the greater part of the Cornishmen dispersed to their homes, while the Devon men deserted in large numbers; Hopton had still, however, 5,000 horse on the west bank of the Tamar.

At a council of war held on the 20th of February, it was unanimously decided to march into Cornwall, and this for three reasons: to put an end to the field army of the King and to settle the west; to do this at once lest succour, already expected, might soon arrive from France; and because when once the force in the field had been routed, Barnstaple and Exeter, the only towns which yet held out for the King, would infallibly fall.

It was therefore determined to blockade these while the main army should pursue its march after Hopton; in February the Parliamentary forces moved, a part from Torrington to Holsworthy, and the remainder from their cantonments to Torrington, while a party of horse was sent on in front to force the passage of the Tamar. This cavalry encountered the enemy at a point near Stratton, and defeated them with the loss of 480 prisoners.

On the 25th the army marched by way of Tamerton to Launceston, a long and weary journey, it being midnight when the rear of the column was yet two miles from the town, which was held by 500 Royalist foot, who were however quickly driven out, though without much loss, owing to the darkness of the night. During the following day the tired troops rested in Launceston, where Fairfax again won golden opinions from the inhabitants by dismissing every Cornish prisoner with a present of twelve pence.

It became now a matter of the greatest solicitude to Fairfax that the enemy's horse should not, imitating the action of those of the army of Essex when in a similar situation, break out through the chain with which he bound them within Cornwall, since, if they could be retained in their present position, their surrender would be only a question of time. The precautions which he took to this end are not without interest.

Special orders were sent to Colonel Cook who, with Massey's horse, lay before Barnstaple, to be in readiness to strike at the flank of any party of the enemy which might pierce a line of posts which the General formed along the Tamar, of which river every passage was occupied by detachments of the cavalry of the Parliamentary rear-guard. He further sent forward in advance of the main army a troop of dragoons, which were posted at Camelford, where they might obtain the earliest possible information of any attempt of the Royalists to pass round his right flank.

All being thus prepared against any attempt on the part of Hopton to escape from Cornwall, Fairfax advanced in order of battle on Bodmin, whence, so great was his dread lest the Cavaliers by breaking his blockade should be able to prolong the war, he sent a special messenger to Whalley, who was watching Oxford, ordering him to move thence into Wiltshire, for the purpose of cutting off any troops who might succeed in passing the other lines.

The Parliamentary army, being somewhat delayed in their movements by the threatened attack of some parties of the Royalist cavalry, were on the night of the 1st of March at Blisland, where they, at 10 p.m., heard that the enemy had evacuated Bodmin. Thither on the 2nd they advanced, and there halted until the 7th, posts being placed at Wadebridge, Padstow, and Lostwithiel to form a new line against the escape of the Cavalier horse.

On the 4th it was known that Prince Charles had sailed for Scilly, and that Hopton's headquarters were at Truro, his main army being stationed between that town and the three points, St. Columb, Grampound, and Tregony, while the mass of his horse was at St. Dennis; against these every passage across Cornwall was carefully barred, while the country people were urged to barricade the lanes and watch the fords.

On the 4th also a ship from Ireland, which had 300 Irish on board, was captured at Padstow; in her were found letters to the effect that 6,000 Irish were ready to embark at once for England, while 4,000 more should follow them in May; the Cornish gentlemen who had come in to Fairfax expressed to him their very strong dislike to the landing of any "foreigners" for the

King's service, and inclined more decidedly to the Parliament on account of their hatred of such action on the part of the Royal generals.

On the 6th a summons to surrender was sent to Hopton, and on this day information was received that the long-expected effort to escape was to be made by the Royal cavalry. A strict watch was ordered to be kept by the whole of the Parliamentary army, and on the following day Fairfax moved on St. Columb, with the object of still further narrowing Hopton's quarters. On the same day, in order that the Royalist horse might have no rest, and might thus be unfit for a long and hurried march, Colonel Rich was sent with 1,000 cavalry and dragoons to beat up the enemy's quarters; Rich fell in with the enemy a few miles to the west of St. Columb, drove the outposts back on their reserves, and then charging the latter forced them from the field with the loss of 100 prisoners, and of 300 horses.

On the 8th Fairfax advanced to St. Stephens, St. Blazey, and other points near to Truro; in the evening an answer to the summons sent on the 6th arrived from Hopton, in which the Cavalier leader spoke of an intended treaty between the King and the Parliament, and of his readiness to be a party to it, offering further to appoint commissioners to discuss conditions of peace; it was however known by a prisoner, that the summons of Fairfax had been kept secret from the soldiers of the Royal army, while that general demanded not peace but surrender.

On the 9th a summons was sent by Fairfax, who in order to emphasise his message advanced on that day to Tregony and Probus; during this march it was found that so firmly were Hopton's troops assured of the existence of an armistice, that crying out "A Cessation! A Cessation!" they refused to engage their adversaries, though the latter pressing on denied altogether that there was any ground for their belief; when at last convinced that they were mistaken, the Royalist horse retired, "expressing much sorrow." With troops so dispirited, it was of course impossible to prolong the struggle, and Hopton, yielding to the circumstances, asked for a meeting at Tresillian, at which terms of surrender might be discussed. Fairfax agreed to this request, but demanded as a preliminary step to any negotiations, the abandonment of Truro by the Royalists; this condition was perforce accepted, and the town was occupied by the army of the Parliament on the 10th of March.

Offers of submission now flowed in on all sides; at mid-night on the 11th, the treaty was concluded, and between Sunday the 15th of March and Friday the 20th, the whole of Hopton's army was entirely disbanded. It had consisted of nine brigades, composed of twenty-seven regiments, of which about 3,000 men were cavalry. Thus was ended the great business of the year, for with Hopton's surrender the war came to a complete end, since no organised body of the King's troops now kept the field, though here and there in various parts of the country, isolated contests continued until almost the end of the year.

Of this campaign in Devonshire and Cornwall, it is not too much to say that its strategical plan would have reflected honour on any general, and that its conductor, whether Fairfax or Cromwell was the real chief, was a man of the first rank among skilful soldiers.

At the commencement of 1646 the Parliamentary army found itself so placed that their enemies were confined to a peninsula, across the neck of which stretched a line of posts, forbidding egress; to maintain this position, while gradually advancing, and thus narrowing the ground available for Hopton's forces, was the principal object of Fairfax, and this he succeeded in doing without a single check. It may be that according to our modern ideas his movements were slow; so slow that an active enemy might perhaps have forced his way through the line, by the simple plan of making a concentrated attack on one point after a feigned effort upon another; but we must remember that the marches of which we have spoken were made in bad weather, sometimes with snow on the ground, and over roads which in our day would scarcely be considered practicable for troops.

The skilful use of detachments, in front, in rear, and on the flanks, the full recognition of the value of an obstacle, and above all the example on the Yeo of the principle of manoeuvring an enemy out of a position which is too strong to be attacked in front, all prove a great advance in this campaign on the military power of the commanders during the previous years of the war. Here again we find that Fairfax, realising the superiority of his infantry over that of Hopton, trusted in it as a source of strength sufficient to more than neutralise the great advantages which the enemy possessed over him as regarded the number of cavalry at their command.

It will be well also to observe how the Royalist cavalry is continually annoyed, not with any hope of permanent success against it, since it was so superior in strength to that of the Parliament, but for the sole purpose of wearying the horses, in order that they might not be in a condition to carry their riders through the long and hard march, which would inevitably follow on any effort to escape.

The events of the twelve months which had nearly elapsed since the formation of the New Model may fairly be classed as "war," in contradistinction to those of the previous years, in which there was only "fighting," and from this time forward we may venture to look for a plan for each campaign, and for some sort of system in its execution.

To return to the King, who at the end of the year 1645 was at Oxford. He remained in this city during the earlier part of 1646, in personal security indeed, but so completely cut off from the rest of England, that he could neither give nor receive aid; his safety resembled that of a man who from an island sees all that he possesses swept away by an encircling flood, he himself being both powerless to help and beyond rescue.

His garrisons one by one fell into the hands of his enemies; Chester on the 3rd of February surrendered to its old foe Brereton; Ashby-de-la-Zouch a little later shared the same fate; while Whalley and Fleetwood were gradually drawing in the net around Oxford, a task in which, after the dispersal of Hopton's army, they were assisted by Browne.

On the 22nd of March occurred the last combat of the war, of which the result was so disastrous to the cause of the King, that even his personal surrender, deprived as he was of all hope or help, became merely a question of time. Sir Jacob Astley, having with difficulty raised a force of 3,000 men, proposed about the middle of March to join the King at Oxford, with this welcome reinforcement; on receipt of the news of his intended movement, Charles sent out a body of 1,500 soldiers to meet him and bring him in, but they failed altogether to find him, and knew nothing of his fortune until they received the information of his decisive defeat.

Colonel Morgan, who had command of the cavalry about Gloucester and Hereford, having heard of Astley's intended march, sent warning of it to Whalley and Fleetwood, and further drew from Brereton all the horse which the latter could spare; with these he pushed on after the Cavaliers. So fast did Morgan advance that he came in contact with the Royal troops before Brereton had succeeded in joining him; but though inferior in strength to Astley, he attacked him at once, and fought alone with him for four hours, with the object of delaying his advance until Brereton should come up.

Towards morning, for this engagement took place wholly at night, Sir William at last arrived, and the Parliamentary leaders, having completed their junction, charged together on the Cavaliers, and at about half-an-hour before daylight on the 22nd of March, completely routed them, taking 1,600 prisoners, 2,000 arms, and Sir John Astley himself. The latter, fully realising the decisive character of the victory, is reported to have said in conversation with his captors after the battle, "Now you have done your work, and may go and play, unless you fall out among yourselves."

During the remainder of the year 1646, there is little to record but the successive surrenders of the various Royal garrisons; Exeter having yielded on the 11th of April, Barnstaple followed its example on the 14th. The west being thus altogether in the hands of the Parliament, Fairfax moved his army eastwards, to join in the siege of Oxford, the headquarters of the

King, his present abode, and the centre of the Royalist strength. Cromwell, resigning his command, returned to London, for the purpose of making a report to the House of Commons of the doings of the campaign.

On the arrival of Fairfax at Newbury, on the 27th of April, he heard the news of the escape of the King from Oxford, which had taken place on the preceding day.

Charles, after offering propositions to Fairfax and the army, that they should, on his surrendering himself to them, conduct him to London, finding that these met with no favourable response, determined to evade the circle which was closing in around Oxford, and with this object, but without any distinct plan, fled with only two companions. Intending at first, it would appear, to go to London, where he seems to have expected to find friends, the King passed by Henley and Brentford to Harrow.

Abandoning that scheme he next turned to the north, through St. Albans, and was on the 28th at Market Harborough; thence he went to Stamford, thence again to Downham in Norfolk, where he lay hid until May the 4th. During this time he was endeavouring to find some means of passing into Scotland, with the intention of joining the army of Montrose; but on the 5th of May, having given over all hope of being able to effect this purpose, Charles presented himself, under the escort of a troop of cavalry which had been sent to meet him, at the headquarters of the Scottish army, which were at Kelham, near Newark.

On the 2nd of May Fairfax had completed his preparations for the siege of Oxford, of which, though it ultimately surrendered rather for political than for military reasons, it may be well to give a short sketch.

The situation of Oxford was, in the days when the range of firearms was very limited, one of great defensive strength. Standing at the junction of two rivers, the Isis and the Cherwell, the city from its position possessed one great advantage, in that the besieger, should he surround it, must of necessity find his army cut into three parts, upon either of which under ordinary circumstances the garrison might throw its concentrated forces.

But when, as was the case at this time, the country to the south of the junction of the two rivers had been inundated by shutting the locks, this advantage was lessened, since in proportion as the floods rendered the city unapproachable, so they equally limited the ground available for sorties to that which lay on the north front of the defences.

As might be expected from what has been just said, the main attack was from the north, on the ground between the Isis and the Cherwell. This was connected by a bridge at Marston with the Parliamentary headquarters, which were in a strong fort on Headington Hill, while from this latter point approaches appear to have been pushed forward to St. Clement's. The right of the main attack was defended by a fort on the Isis, while the outer edge of the inundations was watched by cavalry. Such troops as remained after this line had been provided for were employed to reduce the outlying posts which, standing around Oxford, alone rendered an active defence possible; of these were Faringdon, Radcot, Wallingford, and Borstal House. After providing for the blockade of each of these points, Fairfax despatched all other troops which could be spared to press the city of Worcester.

The siege of Oxford itself presents no very salient features, for being no doubt aware of the fate of the King, the Governor, Sir Thomas Glenham, accepted the proposals of Fairfax for a treaty, and on the 18th of May negotiations commenced; but they were not brought to a conclusion without a long delay, for the terms were not agreed on until the 20th of June. At noon on the 24th the garrison marched out, about 3,000 strong, leaving another 4,000 in the city, who were afterwards disbanded.

With Oxford surrendered Radcot and Faringdon, while Wallingford shortly after made terms. On the 19th of July— Worcester yielded to Whalley, and Newark having been surrendered early in May by order of the King, there then remained but a few castles which still held for the Royal cause. Among these the chief was Raglan Castle, which was defended with great courage until the 20th of August. Of all England and Wales the last post which was taken from the Royalists by the Parliamentary party was Harlech Castle, which did not fall into the hands of Colonel Mytton until March, 1647.

The Scots, having possession of the person of the King, moved to the north immediately after the capitulation of Newark, and arrived at Newcastle about the middle of May. Thus, the King being a prisoner and his army dispersed, ended the First Civil War.

But there were soon not wanting many symptoms that the cessation of war by no means implied a permanent peace. The Royalist party having been destroyed as a separate entity, was certain to cling for its own sake to one or other of the two prevailing factions, while, though it had been defeated, it was still of no little importance in number and in influence; and its existence could thus not be ignored without danger by either the Presbyterians or the Independents, between whom the commencement of a struggle could not be long delayed.

The City of London, the majority of the House of Commons, and so much as remained of the Upper House, were of the Presbyterian party; they, in addition to their own strength, relied upon the assistance of their co-religionists, the Scots. On the other hand, the New Model army, of which the success was so fresh and so decisive, was, with the majority of the country, on the side of the Independents. The person of the King, with the prestige gained by his presence, became a possession coveted by each party.

Of this Charles was fully aware; but overestimating his value to the Independents, he presumed too much on the supposed fact that he was absolutely indispensable to them. Fully believing that, defeated though he was, his very name was a tower of strength, he led on each party in turn to a crisis, only to abandon it as soon as a direct decision became requisite.

Strenuous efforts were at this time made by the Presbyterian party to obtain from Charles such terms of peace as might satisfy their religious and political opinions, and the Scots themselves vehemently urged him to accept the terms offered by their brethren; but the King, as usual planning when he should be acting, refused that which he considered he could not be forced to grant, and the Presbyterians, who had hoped by a timely reconciliation with him to have united with them the great mass of public feeling, found themselves checkmated by this unfortunate obstinacy.

The Scots were placed in a yet more difficult position, for they had in their hands a king whom their own authorities would not recognise, nor even admit into Scotland, except on condition that he took the Covenant, which Charles resolutely refused; at the same time they were invited, nay pressed, to quit England. The difficulty was at first evaded by a refusal to return to their own country, until the arrears due to them had been paid, while these were set at the huge sum of £1,000,000; this was. however, on discussion reduced to £500,000, and by the end of 1646 the Scots had been induced to accept £200,000 at once, with the promise of an equal sum to be paid at a future time.

These terms having been settled, the Scottish Parliament, anxious above all to keep on good terms with that of England, and to thus assist their brother Presbyterians against the increasing power of the Independents, voted the surrender of the King, who was accordingly given up in the early part of February, 1647, the Scottish army crossing the border on the 13th. In December, 1646, Skippon with a considerable force was sent to the north to serve, nominally as a convoy to the £200,000, but really as an escort to the King, while Fairfax with the main army moved into Northamptonshire to provide for the due execution of the treaty, and to receive the person of the King.

But before this, difficulties had begun to arise with regard to the army, which in the opinion of many in the Parliament should, now that its duties in war were over, be either disbanded or sent to Ireland, where alone hostilities still continued; but after long and tedious discussions the power of the Independents was sufficient to ensure the passing of a resolution at the end of July, 1646, that none of the forces of Fairfax should go to Ireland, to which destination all other troops were to be at once despatched.

In August it was decided that the troops which had served under Langhorne and Massey, and who had formed no part of the New Model, should be sent across the Channel; while on the 11th of that month an Act was passed, by which all troops not in Fairfax's army were to go to Ireland or be disbanded. On the 7th of October it was determined that the New Model should be paid and clothed for six months longer; while on the other hand, on the 21st Massey's force was dispersed under the conditions named above.

Two other matters of interest remain to be noticed as having occurred in the year 1646: the Earl of Essex died in September, and was buried with the highest military honours,, though his power in the State as in the army had passed away with the acceptance of the Self-denying Ordinance: while Monk, who had been made prisoner at Nantwich, having taken the Covenant, was released from the Tower and sent to Ireland.

With the beginning of the year 1647, the Presbyterian party renewed their efforts to rid themselves of the army, in whose existence they saw a perpetual threat. After numerous orders and ordinances, none of which were of any practical effect, a vote passed on the 8th of March, which renewed the Self-denying Ordinances, and ordered that all officers should take the Covenant, while the appointment of all governors of garrisons was to be in the hands of the Parliament.

On the 17th a petition from the City of London was presented by the Lord Mayor, praying that the army might be disbanded. This was at once answered by a petition from the army, demanding their rights as regarded arrears of pay and indemnity for all acts done during the war. This latter petition the House ordered Fairfax to suppress, and further appointed Hammond, Ireton, and Skippon to reside as Commissioners with the army. Upon this another meeting was called by the army, which decided to hold to their, former petition.

On the 20th of April it was reported that the army as a whole refused to go to Ireland, whereupon on the 27th it was ordered that the army should be disbanded "with all convenient speed." Upon this a vindication of the petition of the army was presented by three troopers, after a debate upon which Cromwell, Skippon, Ireton, and Fleetwood were ordered by the House to go down to the army, and assure them that their arrears should be paid. But the Parliament had no money with which to fulfil their promises, while the army steadily refused to be satisfied with words; abandoning the old system of a council of officers, the soldiers now chose committees or adjutators, who should debate upon the propositions of the Parliament.

On the 18th of May, the Commons striving again to carry matters with a high hand, voted that all forces which refused to go to Ireland should be disbanded, and further sent Fairfax to the army, in the hope of bringing it to reason. But the power of the General over the army had been lessened by the efforts of the Presbyterian party, of which he was a prominent member, to put down all religious sects, to punish preaching by any who were not ordained, and to arrange the government of the Church by Presbyters; accordingly the soldiers persisted in their dissatisfaction, in spite of a letter which Fairfax sent to every regiment, and which was favourably received by some few of the Presbyterian officers.

At the end of May Fairfax called a council of war at his headquarters at Bury St. Edmunds, at which he endeavoured to persuade the army to disband quietly; but Ireton and others drew up in return a paper for the general, in which they demanded a rendezvous of the whole army before disbandment, stating that, if this were not granted, the soldiers would without their officers hold such a meeting, in which case disorders must occur. The letter in which Fairfax announced this fact to the House so alarmed it, that it at once erased from the books the declaration against the army.

But it was now too late, for the army, determined to act, having taken the King from Holmby House, where he had been ordered to reside, came to a rendezvous at Triplow Heath, near

Cambridge, where on the 8th of June it was decided to advance on London. Upon the receipt of the news of this action, the House endeavoured to raise militia to protect the city, and sent an order to Fairfax not to come within fifteen miles of the capital.

On the 12th of June the army arrived at St. Albans, Fairfax saying that he had advanced so far before he had received the message of the House. On the 14th the militia and trained bands were called out of the city to form a guard for the Commons; at the same time an order was sent to Fairfax calling upon him to deliver up the King.

The army, now beginning to feel their true strength, demanded next the suspension of eleven of the members of the Presbyterian party who had been most hostile to them; among these were Sir Philip Stapleton (the commander of Essex's bodyguard), Sir William Waller, Hollis (who had led a regiment at Edgehill, and who was one of the five members demanded of the House by Charles at the commencement of the war), and Massey (the defender of Gloucester).

Thus had the victors already commenced to quarrel over the spoil. The army now sent in a long list of demands to the House, in which, abandoning the purely military questions to which up to this time they had confined their attention, they pressed for triennial parliaments and other political changes. This document was drawn up by Ireton, with the assistance of Cromwell and Lambert. In answer to this, the Commons on the 21st passed a vote agreeing to some of the demands of the army, but refusing others. The latter not being satisfied, after a further remonstrance, advanced to Berkhampstead, and on the 26th to Uxbridge.

As a sign of the manner in which political power was passing from the Parliament to the army, it is worthy of note that at about this time we have the first notices of addresses and petitions being made to the latter instead of to the former.

Alarmed at the near approach of the army, the Commons now began to threaten proceedings against the eleven proscribed members, who, having received timely notice of their danger, fled from the House. Having thus unseated their most prominent adversaries, and having caused some of the troops who favoured the Presbyterian party to be disbanded, the army satisfied retired to Wycombe.

On the 2nd of July the following were named Commissioners of the army to treat with the Parliament: Cromwell, Ireton, Fleetwood, Rainsborough, Harrison, Sir Hardress Waller, Rich, Lambert, and Hammond. In these we recognise the names of the principal leaders of the Independents. On the 3rd the headquarters moved to Reading, whence on the 8th they were transferred to Aylesbury, their distance from London serving as a measure of the degree of satisfaction which the army felt with the proceedings of Parliament.

But the truce was not to be of long duration, for the Commons, relying on the support of the city gave way to the demand of the latter, that the command of their militia should be in their own hands; while a mob of apprentices forced a not unwilling House to recall the eleven members. After this act, which took place on the 26th, both Houses adjourned to the 30th, and immediately after the adjournment many of the Independent members fled to the army, which on receipt of the news of the action of the Parliament moved at once on London.

The city, for its part, ordered the trained bands to man the fortifications around London, while so much as remained of the Commons passed votes in favour of resistance. Massey was appointed to command the militia, who were ordered to muster at St. James's. This they did on the 31st of July, on which day also the exiled members returned to the House, which passed a declaration to the effect that the militia of London was independent of the command of Fairfax.

The army in the meantime advanced directly on the capital; on the 2nd of August it was at Colnebrook, and on the 3rd held a rendezvous, 20,000 strong, on Hounslow Heath, the headquarters being on the same day at Isleworth. The preparations of the city and of .the Houses now collapsed with an almost ludicrous rapidity, for Fairfax, having learnt that the feelings of the inhabitants of Southwark were opposed to those of the citizens of London, ordered Rainsborough to inarch thither with a brigade, and to force his way into London from the south.

Accordingly at about 2 a.m. this force entered Southwark without opposition, and in a few hours received the surrender of the fort which guarded London Bridge. The city now gave way, yielded all forts on the south and west of the capital, while their representatives, at a meeting with Fairfax on the 5th of August at his headquarters at Hammersmith, professed their satisfaction at his proceedings.

On the following day the Speakers of both Houses and the members who had fled, returned to Westminster in procession, and at once annulled all Acts passed since the 2 6th of July. On the 7th of August the army, after marching through London for the purpose of overawing the citizens, bivouacked at Croydon; whence on the 11th they moved to Kingston, the King being then at Oatlands. The army, in order to complete the discomfiture of their opponents, demanded that those members of the House of Commons who were hostile to its pretensions, should be debarred from sitting in the House; upon this the eleven members fled, many of them across the seas.

Orders were issued that proceedings should be taken against the officers of the city militia, and that the fortifications which lay around London should be demolished; the Lord Mayor was also removed from office, while Vice-Admiral Batten, having permitted some of the proscribed members whom he captured at sea to escape, was replaced by Rainsborough, who, though now a colonel, had at one-time served at sea; of this latter change the after effects were considerable.

Affairs between the Parliament and the army now took the form of a series of addresses from the latter to the former, in which directions were given as to the changes desired by the soldiery. But matters were by this time, in the opinion of some of the leaders of the army, going too far, since Cromwell, Ireton, and others, who had intended to guide every movement of the troops, found that much of their power was gradually passing into the hands of the adjutators.

Behind all this confusion lay another mystery, for there can be no doubt but at this time negotiations were in progress between the foremost Independents and the King, which, had the latter possessed the power of inspiring or deserving trust, might have brought all difficulties to a good end. But Charles was, unfortunately, impressed with a belief in his power to manage men and to rule events, and thus proposing to himself to balance each party by another to his own ultimate advantage, undertook to conduct the threads of an intrigue in which he was, not as he imagined the head, but the instrument. Thus he was, at the very moment when he pretended to be listening to the proposals of Cromwell and Ireton, engaged in negotiations with the Scots, the Irish, the Cavaliers in England, the Parliament, and even with foreign Powers.

Insincerity could go no farther, and such chicanery could not be concealed. After a scene in which some very plain speaking passed between Ireton and the King, all hope of a composition with the army was lost to Charles, who, finding that such was the case, fled from them in November, only to fall, as had no doubt been previously arranged, into the hands of Colonel Hammond, who had in September, as if in anticipation of the event, been appointed Governor of the Isle of Wight.

The army at once broke into almost open mutiny, and at a rendezvous at Ware gave an opportunity for which not improbably some of its leaders had been waiting, for signs of insubordination becoming evident in the ranks, the ring-leaders were at once seized, and one of them was shot on the spot as a warning to the others. This mutiny, which was the first sign of the rising of the new sect of Levellers, was judiciously suppressed by a mixture of severity and mercy, and though in after times both they and the Fifth Monarchy men gave some further trouble, yet neither of these sects became at any time a real danger to the State.

The officers of the army, of whom Cromwell was the true head, since Fairfax on account of his Presbyterian tendencies lost ground daily, thus roughly asserted their power over their men; and having now both soldiery and Parliament at their command, proceeded to determine their course of conduct with regard to the King, who had so deceived them that it was impossible that they should ever trust him more.

On the 22nd of December a solemn fast was kept at Windsor, during which Cromwell, Ireton, and others prayed and preached. But worship was not the sole object of this meeting, for there is ground for strong presumption that it was at this gathering, or at some more private assembly at about the same time, that it was determined to obtain the ends of their party without reference to the King's will; a determination which was in all probability supplemented by the intention to bring about the death of the King, since the latter could be but useless to them after their new departure, while for those opposed to them he might be a valuable instrument. Thus in strife and confusion, after a very narrow escape from the renewal of civil war, ended the year 1647.

The result of the Council mentioned above is apparent in the first of the actions of the new year, for on the 3rd of January the Commons, obedient to the army, voted that no more addresses should be made to Charles, while on the 11th a declaration from the troops was presented to the House by Sir Hardress Waller, in which it was stated that, seeing "no further hopes of settlement or security" by the King, the army declared that it was resolved to settle the kingdom "without the King and against him." This declaration was approved by the Commons.

But this cordiality between the nominal and the real rulers of England was to be rudely interrupted, for already rumours had arisen of an intended invasion by the Scots, who, dreading the rise of the Independents and the consequent loss of power among the Presbyterians, had driven Argyll, the friend of Cromwell, from his position as the head of their Government, and in his place had set up the Duke of Hamilton who, though he had suffered many things at the hand of the King, was yet inclined rather to him than to the Parliamentary party.

There was yet more than this to give promise of coming danger, for the officers serving in South Wales under Langhorne were extremely dissatisfied, as indeed were all troops who were not included in the New Model; while the fleet, strongly protesting against the appointment of Rainsborough to command them, were on the eve of mutiny. Throughout all England the Presbyterians were roused against the dominating sectarians, and the country at large was weary of the rule of the army, who however were so strong in their unanimity, that but little hope of success could exist for their opponents.

Nevertheless, the Presbyterian members of the Commons did not cease from agitation, and were quick to seize any opportunity which might offer itself of effecting a reconciliation with the King, in which they saw their best chance of recovering the ascendency. With those who were thus inclined, under certain conditions not impossible of fulfilment, to favour Charles, joined such of the Cavaliers as had escaped imprisonment, and the result was a party which included men formerly so opposed to each other as Massey and Langdale, Langhorne and Glenham.

At the beginning of March matters came to a crisis, by the action of Poyer, a drunken but capable colonel, who refused to deliver Pembroke to a new governor appointed by the Parliament, and who finally declared for the King. Orders were at once sent for the disbandment of the forces which under Langhorne held South Wales, and of whose fidelity there were grave doubts, with no other result than to send them to Pembroke, where they joined Poyer in his revolt.

In the month of May the difficulty caused by the disaffection in Wales was further complicated by risings in the north, in Kent, and in Cornwall, which last was however promptly suppressed by Sir Hardress Waller. The Scots also, apparently intent on war, sent such a list of demands as the Parliament could not possibly grant, while the fleet in a, state of mutiny sent their new Admiral Rainsborough ashore, declared for the King, and set sail to Holland, where lay the Prince of Wales.

It was evident that matters were now growing serious, but

such men were at the head of affairs as were accustomed to act swiftly and boldly; the army was strong and confident in its strength, while the Parliament, though divided against itself, was yet as a body entirely opposed to the restoration of the King, except under such conditions as he refused to accept; and to crown all, Charles himself was a prisoner.

Under such circumstances, in May, 1648, began the Second Civil War.

# CHAPTER 6

# The Second Civil War
# 1648 and 1649

The action of this contest divides itself naturally into three parts, of which the scenes were distant, and the events, though in some cases contemporaneous, quite unconnected. It will therefore be well to divide the narrative in a similar manner, and relate in order

1. The Campaign in Kent and Essex.

2. The Campaign in South Wales.

3. The Campaign against the Scots and the Cavaliers under Langdale.

The affairs of the fleet scarcely fall within the compass of this work, and moreover its action, though troublesome to trade, produced little or no effect on the country, since the only enterprise of which the result would have been important, namely, an effort to carry away the King from the Isle of Wight, was not even attempted.

## 1. The Campaign in Kent and Essex

Though the people of Kent were generally inclined towards the King's party, and many of the gentry had every intention of exciting at the first opportunity a rising in that county, yet it had been determined to attempt nothing until the entrance of the Scottish army into England should have drawn off the principal forces of the Parliament towards the north.

But action was precipitated in a remarkable and almost ludicrous manner. One L'Estrange, a Norfolk gentleman, who had been imprisoned by the Parliament for his share in the late war, urged a young gentleman named Hales to declare for the King, saying that if he should succeed in restoring him he would gain great honour, and would further ensure his succession to a large estate, which was at this time in the possession of his grandfather.

Hales, being in addition influenced by his wife, "who was full of zeal for the King," readily consented to this romantic proposal, whereupon L'Estrange issued warrants in his own name (which was quite unknown in the county), calling upon all men to meet for the purpose of delivering the King from prison. Contrary to what might have been expected, large numbers obeyed this extraordinary call, and having been addressed in a wild speech by L'Estrange, agreed to march under Hales as their general.

A second meeting, at which even larger numbers attended, followed the first, and the insurrection daily grew in importance; but as the force which they had raised increased in size, both L'Estrange and Hales were found wanting in influence and in skill, and they, upon the assumption of the command by Lord Goring, fled together to Holland from the storm which they had raised.

On the first alarm of the invasion of England by the Scots, Fairfax had been directed to advance into the north to the assistance of Lambert, who had there but few troops under his command. As from his religious opinions the General was favourably inclined to the Scots, he was most averse to the performance of this duty, and was proportionately relieved when the outbreak of the insurrection in Kent enabled him to leave the former task to other hands.

Hearing that Goring had advanced to Blackheath, Fairfax with four regiments of horse and three of foot left London, and passing by Eltham marched on the 1st of June by Dartford on Gravesend, the insurgents retiring before him as far as the bridge over the Darent at the former place. Three hundred horse, of whom one hundred carried infantry soldiers behind them, were sent to clear the bridge. This was done with little difficulty, as the horse swimming the river turned the flanks of the defences of the bridge.

After having driven off the defenders, 1,600 in number, this small force pushed two or three miles beyond Gravesend without meeting with any opposition, and thence returned to the main army. The latter now moved on Maidstone, to which town the lesser body (about 2,000) of the insurgents had retired, the larger (about 7,000) having fallen back on Rochester.

At 7 p.m. on the 2nd of June orders were given to storm the former town, but the resistance offered was so determined that this was not effected until midnight, when the insurgents retreated with the loss of 200 killed and 400 prisoners. While the fight was in progress a large force from Rochester approached within two miles of Maidstone, but Fairfax having sent out against them three regiments of horse and one of foot, they remained idle during the engagement.

After the defeat of their friends at Maidstone the insurgents at Rochester began to disperse, many of them with Goring marching on London under the impression that the citizens, who at heart wished them well, would join them but finding no response to their call, while 500 cavalry sent by Fairfax caught them up on Blackheath, the Kentish men dispersed to their homes without further resistance. Goring and the leaders, with a few hundred followers, passed the Thames about Greenwich, crossing into Essex in lighters and boats.

The gentlemen of Essex, who had intended to join Goring in Kent, flocked to him as soon as he landed, and he very shortly found himself in command of a force of 4,000 men, including many officers of great ability and renown, such as Lord Capel, Sir Charles Lucas, and Sir Bernard Gascoigne. With these troops he seized Colchester, and at once proceeded to throw up fortifications around it.

Whalley, who commanded in Essex, had no force capable of

coping with the Royalists: but Kent being now almost pacified, Fairfax crossed the Thames at Gravesend in pursuit of Goring, leaving a few regiments on the southern side to obtain the surrender of Canterbury and of the castles which yet held out.

On landing in Essex he was joined by Whalley with 2,000 men, and about the 15th of June, having shut up the Cavaliers in Colchester, commenced the long and weary siege of that town by the capture of Mersea Island at the mouth of the Colne, thus cutting off the garrison from all hope of escape by, or succour from, the sea. The besieged used every effort to prepare for defence, and knowing the advantage which the possession of Mersea Island would give them, made two gallant attacks on it, which were however both repulsed; while some of the remaining ships of the Parliament came from Harwich to complete the blockade.

On the 24th of June the Suffolk forces, amounting to 2,000 foot and five troops of horse, joined the besiegers, and completed the line of investment to the east of Colchester.

In the beginning of July the artillery of the besiegers commenced to arrive and, in spite of constant and determined sallies, the besieged were gradually beaten back, while the investing force crept closer and closer to the town. Provisions soon began to fail, and the garrison were driven to eat horseflesh; before the end of July the supply of even that food fell low, while the inhabitants were starving. Goring ordered the suburbs to be burned, lest in them the besiegers might find cover and, in spite of the distress of his garrison, scornfully rejected a summons which Fairfax sent in on the 17th; on the 26th the supply of water having been cut off, the besieged could get none that was not muddy or contaminated with the bodies of dead animals.

On the 5th of August the daily allowance of bread to the Royalist soldiers was reduced to ten ounces for each man, and they then began to desert at the rate of twenty to thirty per diem. By the 19th all the dogs and cats and most of the horses in the town had been eaten, and women with starving children prayed on their knees to be allowed to pass through the besiegers' lines; but they were all pitilessly turned back, in order that so much misery might hasten the surrender of the town.

By the 21st the approaches were so close to the walls that besiegers and besieged laid aside their muskets and threw stones at each other, and at this date the inhabitants petitioned for leave to quit the town; this the general granted, with an exception as regarded the families of such men as remained to fight. Five hundred women having however left the gates, the soldiers of the Parliament refused to allow them to pass, and the defenders equally denying them re-admittance, they remained between the two forces without shelter or food.

Proposals made by Goring on the 25th of August were refused by Fairfax, but after an abortive effort to induce the garrison to fight their way out, the former surrendered on the 28th, on conditions which, while they offered quarter to the inferior officers and soldiers, promised nothing with regard to the lives of the superior officers.

On the completion of the surrender, Sir Charles Lucas and Sir George L'Isle were shot as an example, while Lords Goring, Capel, and Loughborough were sent as prisoners to London, where the second was beheaded in March, 1649. Thus ended this most ill-advised rising which, begun without an object, was carried through without hope, and ended as it could only end, in disaster and death.

Another effort, yet more senseless, in favour of the King, was made by the Earl of Holland in the early part of July, when that nobleman, with Lord Peterborough, the Duke of Buckingham and his brother Lord Francis Villiers, having collected about 500 horse, called on the country to rise with them for King Charles, their primary object being the relief of Colchester. The first gathering was at Kingston, as was also the last; for after being repulsed from an attack on Reigate, the Earl returned to the former town, and confidently awaited the junction of the City troops from London.

Rich's regiment was hastily called out of Kent to repress this rising, and a skirmish ensued near Kingston between the two parties, in which Holland was driven into and through the town, and thence fled, pursued by the Parliamentary horse towards Harrow. Here the pursuers were joined by a detachment of cavalry who had been summoned from Colchester, and at St. Neot's in Huntingdonshire the Earl with most of his officers was captured.

Buckingham escaped to the Netherlands, but Lord Francis died of a wound received in the skirmish, while Holland himself was beheaded in company with Capel in March, 1649. With the fall of Colchester every effort of the King's party in the south came to an end, and the Parliament employed the opportunity afforded by the absence of the main army with Cromwell in the north, in recalling the eleven members (or such of them as were within reach), and in endeavouring to arrange a treaty of peace with Charles, proceedings which on the return of the troops with their great leader were at once annulled.

## 2. The Campaign in South Wales

Major-General Langhorne, who had been foremost in the reduction of South Wales into obedience to the Parliament, was after the surrender of the King left in command in those parts, while under him were two colonels, Powell and Poyer. These being all three discontented with their treatment by the Parliament, agreed to declare for Charles on the arrival of the Scots, but owing to bad management and to some want of faith on the part of Prince Charles, to whom they had sent for support, they allowed their plans to be discovered before they were ready to take action in the field.

Poyer being Governor of Pembroke, the others, after having received orders to disband their troops, threw themselves into that town and castle, in the hope of being able to raise the country. In this they were only partially successful, but the forces of the Parliament in South Wales being few in number, were in various small actions disconcerted and defeated, while supplies were without difficulty drawn by the garrison from the whole neighbourhood around Pembroke.

On the 1st of May, the Parliamentary troops under Colonel Horton having suffered another defeat, Cromwell received orders from Fairfax to march into Wales with three regiments of foot and two of horse. This was in effect the first independent command which Cromwell had held, for when detached in 1645 on Winchester and Basing, lie had still been directly under the orders of Fairfax, whereas on this occasion, the distance between them being so great and the general being fully employed in Kent and Essex, Oliver was at liberty to use his troops as he should best please.

The lieutenant-general started from London on the 3rd or 4th of May, and on the march received information of the defeat of 8,000 of the Welsh troops under Langhorne by Horton, who had but 3,000 men. On or about the 14th Cromwell arrived at Chepstow, which some days earlier had been surprised by a party of Cavaliers; he sent a force under Colonel Pride against the town, which was stormed without difficulty, but no impression could be made on the castle in the absence of artillery.

Since the march of events in Wales would not permit him to make a long stay, Cromwell was content to send for guns from Bristol, and to leave a detachment before Chepstow, while he himself moved on to Pembroke. On the 20th of May news arrived in London that he had captured Caermarthen, and that Langhorne with his associates, quitting the open field, had withdrawn into Pembroke. Before the end of the month Chepstow was retaken, while early in June Tenby surrendered to the Parliamentary forces.

In June also Cromwell commenced the siege of Pembroke, against which he placed in battery six guns drawn from the Lion, a ship of war which lay in Milford Haven. About the middle of the same month, a breach having been made, an assault was attempted, which was however repulsed with loss; but shortly after, the Parliamentary troops having cut off the water supply of the castle, and the daily rations of the garrison having been reduced to half-a-pound of meat, Poyer's soldiers mutinied and obliged him to make terms.

On the 11th of July the castle was surrendered, Langhorne and Poyer[1] yielding at mercy, while the other officers were forced to leave the kingdom, and the soldiers, about 2,000 in number, were allowed to return to their homes. Thus Pembroke Castle, one of the strongest fortresses in England, was taken almost without the use of artillery, for the wind being unfavourable, the guns could not be brought up in time from Bristol; no ordnance save the Lion's guns was therefore available, beyond a few mortars, which were used to throw shells into the town.

On the 14th of July Cromwell prepared to move from Pembroke, and on that day dispatched 600 horse and dragoons by way of Chester, to serve as reinforcements to Lambert, who was as far as lay in his power retarding the advance of the Scots. With the remainder of his force Cromwell, being as yet uncertain as to whether his aid might not be even more needed about London than in the north, marched on Gloucester, where for the present we must leave him, in order to bring up to date the narrative of the Scottish invasion.

South Wales was now subdued, but some further fighting took place in North Wales, where in June, Mytton, the Parliamentary major-general, had been besieged in Carnarvon Castle by Sir John Owen; on the receipt of relief from Chester a skirmish ensued, which resulted in the capture of Owen and the raising of the siege. In August Lord Byron, having levied a force for the King, pushed with it on Anglesea, which he succeeded in occupying without difficulty, but which was in October retaken by Mytton, whereupon Byron fled to France.

### 3. The Campaign against the Scots

It was known in London on the 3rd of April that the Scots proposed to raise an army of 40,000 men, for the purpose of rescuing the King and of putting down the sectaries, but the first hostilities were commenced by the English Cavaliers who, on the 28th of April, under Sir Marmaduke Langdale, succeeded in

---

1. Powell, who was at first reported to have been killed in action, was taken prisoner at a later date.

surprising Berwick.

On the 3rd of May letters were received from Scotland, demanding the safety, honour, and freedom of the King, a personal treaty with him, the disbanding of the army, the suppression of the Independents, the enforcement of the Covenant, and the establishment of Presbyterian government, and more than hinting that the rejection of these demands would be followed by an invasion of England.

Most, if not all, of these points were such as the Presbyterians would have been but too happy to grant had it been in their power to do so, and they may indeed be considered to express the wishes of the majority in the Parliament, who took early advantage of the absence of the army to pass votes releasing those of the eleven members who were still in prison (June 3rd), to annul the vote not to treat further with the King (June 30th), and to reopen negotiations with the latter for agreement (August 2nd).

But at the time of the receipt of the letters from the Scots, the army was still in and around London, and the only answer returned to the demands was an order to send reinforcements to the north, where in the meantime further complications had arisen. Glenham about the 5th of May captured Carlisle, whereupon Langdale declared himself to hold a commission from Prince Charles as General of the five northern counties.

The Scots, when reminded that Berwick and Carlisle had both been taken by troops which had found a refuge and a base in their country, refused to give any explanation of their intentions, and matters rapidly moved towards war, which became certain when the latter town was delivered by Langdale into the hands of a Governor appointed by the Duke of Hamilton, the Scottish General.

Lambert, who commanded for the Parliament in the north, hurriedly threw garrisons into Appleby and Raby, while the majority of the opponents of the King found refuge behind the fortifications of Newcastle. On the 9th of May Fairfax was directed to march to the north, but this order was, as has been already noted, countermanded by reason of the insurrection in Kent.

During June various causes delayed the equipment of the Scottish army, while Langdale, who had by that time raised a force of about 5,000 men, received direct orders from Hamilton to refuse to engage the enemy until their arrival; orders to the same effect, based on his comparative weakness, were despatched by the Parliament to Lambert. He, however, being reinforced from Lancashire advanced towards Carlisle, into which city Langdale, obeying the orders which he had received, retired before the Roundhead troops.

Pontefract Castle, having been seized by stratagem by the Cavaliers, was at once closely besieged by 800 of the Parliamentary party; but the garrison, daily gathering strength, sallied out in all directions and continually beat up the quarters of the besiegers. Colonel Rossiter, while advancing with assistance to Lambert, engaged these raiders and completely defeated them at Willoughby Field. In such skirmishes, attended with varying success, passed the month of June and the first half of July, but about the middle of the latter month information of the approaching advance of Hamilton compelled the concentration of the Parliamentary detachments upon Lambert's command.

On the 14th of July news arrived in London that Hamilton with 10,000 men was at Carlisle, where he was joined by Langdale with a force of 3,000. As the Scots moved forward Lambert, by order of the council of war, retired before them, but lost no opportunity of delaying their advance by the skilful use of his cavalry; in one of the skirmishes thus brought on, Colonel Harrison was wounded, and a Captain Cromwell [2] killed.

---

2. It is an undoubted fact that Oliver Cromwell lost a son in the Civil War, but when and where he was killed is uncertain. Carlyle considers, on the ground of some words in a letter to Colonel Walton written after Marston Moor, that young Oliver had been killed before that date, but it is possible that the expression there used, "you know my own troubles this way" (Colonel Walton's son having been killed in action), may have referred to the death of Robert, the Protector's eldest son, who died in 1639; and this more especially since Cromwell himself referred on his death-bed to the misery which that loss occasioned to him: ("my eldest son died, which went as a dagger to my heart, indeed it did.") [Continued next page.]

On receipt of information of the invasion, orders were at once given by the Parliament to reinforce Lambert, and Cromwell, having despatched a small body of horse by way of Chester, moved himself to the north from Gloucester on the 26th of July; about the same date the former troops succeeded in reaching Lambert, who received further reinforcements from the counties of Nottingham, Leicester, and Derby.

The Scots advanced but slowly for the same reason as induced them to delay their original departure, namely, that they were anxious to restore the King by their own unaided efforts, and thus to obtain the right to shape the policy of the replaced Government to their own wishes on a purely Presbyterian basis, without any interference by the Royalists or Episcopalians. With this object they purposely held back until the conclusion of the contest in Wales, and were now desirous not to commence action until the surrender of Colchester should render them the only force in arms for the King.

This delay was deservedly as fatal to themselves as to those whom they failed to aid. The manner of march also of the Scottish troops invited disaster, for they straggled on in such loose order, that a distance of twenty miles frequently separated the headquarters from other parts of the force; the advanced guard was invariably formed by Langdale who, with 4,000 foot and 700 or 800 horse, preceded the main army by at least a day's march.

Cromwell, having determined to move to the north, pushed on from Gloucester to Warwick, whence, on the 31st July, he marched on Leicester; on August the 3rd he was at Nottingham, and thence advanced by Mansfield and Rotherham on Pontefract, to which place he came with the object of adding to his force the troops who were besieging that town, leaving the siege to be conducted by the county militia.

---

The probability that the Captain Cromwell mentioned as being killed at this time was Oliver, the eldest surviving son of his father, and a cornet of Cavalry at the commencement of the war, gathers strength from the fact that the event is recorded in *Whitelocke* (p. 322) who is not in the habit of mentioning the loss of officers of low rank unless they were remarkable for some special reason.

On his arrival at Pontefract Cromwell ordered the town to be stormed, which operation was conducted with such success, that most of the Royal infantry failed to secure their retreat into the castle, the gates being shut to prevent the entrance of the enemy, who were pressing in closely behind. Having organised the force of militia which was to contain the garrison, Cromwell continued his march on Leeds, where he met Lambert, who had fallen back from Ripon for the purpose of joining him.

Cromwell was now at the head of a body of about 8,600 men, and found himself on the flank of the long column of the Scots, who were straggling on towards London. On the 16th of August the position and numbers of Hamilton's army were as follows: The main body, consisting of about 10,500 foot, was at Preston, about to cross the Ribble on its southward march on Wigan, where lay, at a distance of sixteen miles, the Scottish horse, which were 3,500 strong; in rear, moving by Lancaster from the north, was Monro with the Irish contingent, 1,200 horse and 1,500 foot, while on the left flank of this chain of scattered troops stood Langdale, with the English Cavaliers, 2,500 foot and 1,500 horse, in a position in the upper valley of the Ribble about Longridge. It remains only to add that Hamilton, having no system of scouting, was entirely unaware of the advance or the position of Cromwell, who on the night of the 16th was on the Hodder, a small river which divides Yorkshire from Lancashire.

The lieutenant-general of the Parliament at once saw the advantage which his position gave him, acting as he did with a concentrated force on the flank of a column, of which the head was separated from the rear by a distance of about thirty miles, and determined to strike at that portion of the enemy which was nearest to him, to cut the straggling mass in half, and, having done so, to hold back if necessary so much of the hostile army as lay to the north of him, while with his main force he should drive the remainder farther and farther from their native country and from relief. It was not defeat but disaster which he proposed to inflict on Hamilton's army, and the vigour which he showed in the execution of his project was equal to the boldness of its conception.

On the morning of the 17th, having passed the previous night on the Lancashire bank of the Hodder, Cromwell moved on Preston, pushing forward an advanced party of 200 horse and 400 foot to clear the way, and to detain the enemy until the main body of the army could come up. This "forlorn hope" was soon engaged, and was at first held back by superior numbers, but the whole force being pushed into action an attack was made on Langdale's troops, who gallantly resisted, though Hamilton refused any assistance to them, being still obstinate in his belief that the Parliamentary army could not yet have arrived at a position so near to his line.

After four hours of hard fighting, in which almost all the loss suffered by his force during the three days of battle was incurred, Oliver pushed back Langdale into the town of Preston. Hamilton, finding that matters were going against him, then proposed to draw off his foot to a junction with the cavalry at Wigan, and with this object passed the bridges over the Ribble and the Darwent. By this retirement of the Scots the flank of Langdale's position was left exposed to attack, and the Parliamentary horse at once charged it, while their foot held him in front; under this stress the English contingent broke and fled, some over Ribble with the Scots, others towards Lancaster to join Monro.

The latter were pursued for about ten miles, many prisoners being made in the chase, while Monro, in place of advancing to the assistance of his leader, fell back into Cumberland without a blow, and thus relieved the Parliamentary army from the chief risk which attended Cromwell's plan, namely, the chance that they might, while attacking one half of the column, be themselves attacked in rear by the remainder.

By nightfall on the 17th Cromwell had taken Preston, had obtained possession of the bridges over the Ribble and the Darwent, and had beaten back the tail of the enemy's column beyond striking distance, with a loss to it of 1,000 killed and 4,000 prisoners. During the night Hamilton retired on Wigan with the remainder of his force, amounting to about 7,000 or 8,000 foot and 4,000 horse, and was on the morning of the 18th pursued by Cromwell with 3,000 foot and 2,500 horse and dragoons, the rest of the army having been left at Preston to guard against any attack from Monro, whose flight was not yet known.

Oliver's cavalry under Lambert were pushed to the front, and during the whole day harassed the rear of the retreating enemy, taking many prisoners; but the infantry being slow in movement did not arrive in time to prevent the Scots from occupying Wigan in front of which the Parliamentary army passed the night, being "very dirty and weary," but full of fight, as was shown on the following day.

On the 19th Hamilton, either in ignorance of the only end which could be to such a retreat, or in despair of any better fate, fell back towards Warrington, and, in order probably (though it is not expressly so stated) to gain time for the passage of his disordered army over the river Mersey, attempted to hold Winwick with a rear-guard. This force fighting well contrived, at the cost of 1,000 killed and 2,000 prisoners, to detain Cromwell's advanced guard until the arrival of his main body, but were then beaten in before the infantry of the Scottish column had succeeded in crossing the river. Finding further resistance useless, Lieutenant-General Baily, who commanded the Scottish foot, now about 4,000 strong, begged for terms, and surrendered with his whole force.

Hamilton with the remnant of his army, about 3,000 horse, fell back on Nantwich; but being hotly pursued by Lambert with the English cavalry, while the whole country was roused by letters from Cromwell, he turned, after losing about 1,000 men on his way, into Staffordshire, where before the end of the month he and all his companions, including Langdale, were captured by their pursuers. The Duke, having been tried as a traitor, under his English peerage the Earldom of Cambridge, was found guilty, and executed with Capel and Holland in March, 1649.

All resistance by the Scottish main army being thus at an

180

end, Lambert was recalled by Cromwell, who now turned to the north with the intention of driving Monro from England. With this object Lambert was despatched with orders to march by way of Carlisle, while Oliver himself moved by Durham and Newcastle on Berwick, detaching as he went some troops to press the siege of Scarborough Castle.

Having driven Monro and his force of 7,000 men over the border, Cromwell now proposed to follow him into Scotland, where, by the destruction of Hamilton's army, opportunity had been given to the party of Argyll of which they were not slow to take advantage, for the Marquis, having collected about 2,000 men and having been joined by Lesley with 1,500 more, marched from his own country upon Edinburgh, whence he drove the Committee of Estates, and thus regained the whole of his former power in Scotland. To him Cromwell now applied for the recall of Monro (who indeed, on hearing of Argyll's advance, had sent troops to Edinburgh to oppose him), and himself moved forward to assist the Marquis to recover his position in the kingdom.

On the 14th of September Oliver was at Alnwick, whither he had collected all troops within reach, leaving only four regiments of horse with Lambert, and whence he shortly after marched towards the border. On the 20th he was at Norham, from which place, on hearing of a defeat of Argyll by Monro which occurred near Stirling, he had on the 19th despatched Lambert with three regiments of horse to the aid of the Marquis; he himself set out with the remainder of his force on the following day. Before crossing the border Oliver issued a proclamation in which he declared that death should be the punishment for any attempt to rob the Scots of money, cattle or food, and further stated that he entered Scotland for the sole purpose of subduing those who had lately counselled the invasion of England.

As Cromwell advanced into Scotland, he detached from his force two regiments of foot and one of horse, for the purpose of carrying on the blockade of Berwick. This town was surrendered on the 30th of September, in obedience to the order of

Argyll who, coming from Edinburgh, met Cromwell at a short distance from the border on the 22nd. A firm alliance was concluded between the Scottish and the English leaders, and by the action of the latter peace was arranged between the Marquis and Lord Lanark, the brother of the Duke of Hamilton, who had previously joined his forces to those of Monro.

Every event in the north now tended to peace, for Carlisle soon followed the example of Berwick, while all forces in Scotland, with the exception of 1,500 horse under the command of Leven, were by treaty disbanded. In the early part of October, Cromwell went in person to Edinburgh, for the purpose of concluding an agreement with the principal representatives of Scotland, by which it was determined, that none of those who had favoured the late invasion of England should be allowed any share in the government of that country. Lambert being left with a small force to assist in this settlement, Cromwell with the remainder of the army returned into England by way of Newcastle, where he arrived on the 19th of October, marching thence on the 20th to Durham.

On the 29th forty horsemen, sallying from Pontefract Castle made a raid upon Doncaster, where they seized Rainsborough, who commanded the besieging force, in his quarters, and on his refusal to follow them as a prisoner, murdered him in the street. This outrage, together with the complaints of the neighbourhood as to the excesses of the garrison, brought Cromwell to the spot. He on the 9th of November demanded the surrender of the castle, and on their rejection of his demand, dismissing the Yorkshire militia (to whom the siege had been before entrusted), gave the conduct of it to Lambert, who, having completed his task in Scotland, had arrived at Pontefract on the 20th. Cromwell himself moved southward, and reached London on the 6th of December. His arrival was most welcome to the Independents, for during his absence the tide of events had, owing to the strength of the Presbyterians in the House, moved steadily and swiftly in opposition to their wishes.

As has been already mentioned, the Presbyterian members of

the Commons had taken advantage of the absence of the army, in which the Independents found their chief support, and had in June recalled the ten[3] members, whom the latter had formerly driven from the House, and had proposed a personal treaty with the King. In July, the Commons having annulled the vote by which all negotiation with Charles was forbidden, the Common Council of London undertook to protect the King and Parliament during such time as might be needed for the completion of a treaty, while petitions praying for such an agreement flowed in from all sides.

By the 2nd of August matters had advanced yet farther, for on that date the Commons voted that a message should be sent to the King, desiring a treaty with His Majesty; while evidence was received by the House against Cromwell and Ireton from Major Huntington, who had been a close adherent of the former, but who now stated that, finding that the aims and designs of the two leaders were directed against the Parliament, he desired to resign his commission.[4] Though this matter looked at one time as if it might be pressed to an impeachment of Cromwell and his son-in-law, yet the signal victory gained by the former over the Scots, and the consequent depression of the Presbyterian party, caused it to be allowed to fall out of sight, and we hear no more of the likelihood of any action upon it.

But the treaty was still possible, and proof of the sincerity of the intentions of the Parliament may be found in the fact that at the commencement of September the treatment of the King was entirely changed; for after that date, in place of being confined in Carisbrook Castle, he was permitted to live in Newport under parole not to attempt to escape, while large sums of money were voted for his use, and for the maintenance of a sufficient retinue.

It was at first determined that the time to be allowed for the

---

3. Stapleton had died in Calais of the plague.
4. The space at our disposal will not permit of a full analysis of Huntington's papers (*Masere's Tracts*, page 397), though the subject is of great interest and well worthy of study.

completion of the treaty should be forty days, but this limit was considerably extended at a later date, and negotiations did not finally cease until the 27th of November when, it having been found impossible to induce the King to consent to the sale of the Church lands, the commissioners of the Parliament returned to London. On the same day Hammond was ordered to headquarters, and Colonel Ewers was sent by the army in his place to serve as the custodian of the King, upon whom a strong guard was now kept.

The army, though unable to act while still engaged in the field, had not seen unmoved the tendency of the King and the Parliament towards reconciliation. The first sign of their feeling of irritation was shown on the 13th of November, when Fairfax, in a letter to the Commons, declared the dissatisfaction of the troops with the course which events were taking; this letter was followed on the 18th by a petition from Ireton's regiment, which in veiled terms demanded the trial of the King; on the 20th a remonstrance was presented to the House which distinctly desired that the King should "be brought to justice." Petitions to this effect began to flow in from the troops in all parts of the kingdom, while letters from headquarters at St. Albans related that the officers "spent yesterday wholly in prayer," always an ominous sign for their opponents.

On the 30th it was decided in the House, by a majority of ninety, that no notice should be taken of the remonstrance, while on the same day the army formulated a declaration which, after complaints of the neglect of the Parliament and threats of an appeal to the people, ended with the statement that for these ends they were "drawing up to London." But already before this declaration the soldiery had shown the tenor of their wishes, for on the 29th the King was carried off from Newport to Hurst Castle, where he remained a close prisoner.

On the 1st of December the Commons forbade the army to advance on London, an order which had but little result, for on the 2nd Fairfax and his troops occupied St. James's and Whitehall. On the 5th the Commons voted that the King's concessions formed a good ground for a treaty, a proceeding which was answered on the following day by the occupation of Westminster by Rich's horse and Pride's foot, and by the arrest of forty-one members of the majority. This high-handed act, generally known as Pride's Purge, at once changed the tone of the Parliament, which henceforth voted exactly according to the wishes of the army.

However, on the 5th the remainder of the House sat to receive a proposal from the army, in which complaints were made of the readmission of the suspended members, and justice was demanded upon some of them by name. On the 7th (on which day Cromwell received the thanks of the House for his late action against the Scots) the treasuries of the City were seized by the troops.

On the 11th first appears the *Agreement of the People*, a document which was supposed to have been drawn up by Ireton, and the contents of which included the dissolution of the Parliament, a new distribution of seats, and other changes, while opposition to it was to be punished with death. On the following day the Commons revoked the recall of the suspended members (who were all made prisoners), and annulled the vote of agreement with the King, while on the 13th they passed a resolution against any further addresses to him.

Petitions now came in from various parts of the country calling for justice upon the "chief delinquents," and on the 23rd a committee of thirty-eight was chosen to draw up a charge against such, which by the 28th had become a charge against the King. Charles had in the meantime been brought from Hurst Castle to Windsor, at which place he arrived on the 24th under the care of Colonel Harrison, while orders were now given that he should no longer be served upon the knee, and that all expenses respecting his attendance, etc., should be reduced.

Thus ended the year 1648, which saw the King courted by each party in turn, only to be finally surrendered by the one to the hatred of the other. As regards the military history of the year, it is remarkable principally for the advancement of Cromwell to independent command, and for the consequent adoption of that system of war which in after days became characteristic of that leader. Oliver was a general capable not only of appreciating the smaller details of war, but also of forming such plans as in their execution should imply, not merely the momentary confusion of a beaten enemy, but also the infliction of blows so heavy and so well directed, that none could avoid them, while they destroyed those on whom they fell.

To Cromwell war was no light evil, of which the misery might be remitted or inflicted at the will of the general; it was, on the contrary, the scourge of God entrusted by Him to righteous hands for the punishment of sinners, and thus in him we shall find none of that mistaken philanthropy, of which in war the result is the infliction of suffering on a multitude of innocent heads; for by the terror of his unsparing arm he spared himself the need to strike, with the result that his soldiers, whose name became a word of fear, both shed and lost less blood when once that fear had been established. To prove the truth of this we have but to compare the casualties and the results of, let us say, Edgehill and Preston. There is probably nothing in war which leads to unnecessary slaughter with such absolute certainty as mistaken mercy.

The early part of the year 1649 contained but few military events, yet it may be well, in order to maintain the sequence of the narrative, to mention a few of the leading features of that season. On the 16th of January the first Act (as distinguished from an Ordinance) of Parliament was passed; on the 18th Massey, the whilom gallant defender of Gloucester, and lately one of the "secluded" members, escaped from his prison in St. James's; of him we shall hear again.

The latter part of the month saw the trial and death of the King, an act which was so hated by the majority of Englishmen, that it had probably a very large share in causing the restoration of his son, when once the restraining hand of Cromwell was cold, and the sympathies of the nation could find open expression. It had, moreover, at once an effect on the constitution of the army, for Fairfax, on his refusal to approve of the sentence on the King, lost to a great extent the confidence of his soldiers, a fact of which the consequence was plainly foreshadowed by the dismissal of the Earl of Warwick, for a similar reason, from the office of Lord High Admiral, which he had held since the commencement of the war.

Another result of the execution of the King was to be seen in the ill-feeling aroused by it between the Scots and the English Parliament, a sentiment which found its vent in a paper presented by the former to the latter, in which the Scottish Commissioners condemned in strong language the treatment by the Commons of the King, the House of Lords, and the banished members.

As a reply to this rebuke the Parliament at once dispatched guards in quest of the Commissioners, who were apprehended at Gravesend, a high-handed proceeding which did not tend to smooth matters, and of which the result was seen at once in the acceptance by the Scots of Charles II. as their King, and in the consequent campaigns of 1650 and 1651. It perhaps may be permitted to us to doubt whether some part of this indignation of the Scots may not have been caused by the refusal of the English Parliament to make good the second sum of £200,000 which was due for the payment of their army for their services in the war against Charles I. For since the commencement of Hamilton's campaign in 1648, all money raised for this purpose had been diverted to the support of the navy.

In the month of March the Marquis of Ormond, the Royalist Lord Lieutenant of Ireland, sent an invitation to Charles II. to pass into that country, promising him there support and loyalty; but the Parliament, alarmed at this prospect and being further weary of the condition of anarchy in which that island was, appointed Cromwell General of the Forces in Ireland; Fairfax being, however, retained as commander-in-chief. In March also Pontefract Castle surrendered, after a siege of which the details (for which we have not sufficient space) have more the air of a romance than of reality.

In this month Capel, Hamilton, and Holland were tried and beheaded for their shares in various attempts against the Parliament; while in April the leaders of the revolt in Wales, Poyer, Langhorne, and Powell, were condemned to death by court-martial, but having been permitted to draw lots for their lives, the two latter were reprieved, Poyer who had lost the cast being alone put to death; he was shot in Covent Garden. Goring and Owen, the other two Royalist prisoners of importance, were released.

In May affairs again came to a crisis in Ireland, Dublin, of which Colonel Jones was Governor, being then in great danger on account of the advance of Ormond (who was now in league with the original rebels) with an overwhelming force against the capital, and it became obvious that aid must be sent, and that speedily, to the Parliamentary troops. But any such relief was for a time delayed by the mutinous action of the Levellers, who in May broke out into open revolt. The first signs of this movement were, as usual, so trifling as almost to escape notice.

A soldier having been shot for mutiny, his funeral was made the occasion for a demonstration which was attended by some thousands of his comrades as a protest against discipline and law. This proof of sedition was however allowed to go unpunished, and thus encouraged the mutineers soon ventured on stronger and more open revolt. Scroope's regiment having been ordered to Ireland refused to march until the Parliament should have performed its promises to them.

In this act of insubordination they were joined by many discontented men from other regiments, and the movement gaining ground, their discontent at length found voice in a declaration against the Parliament and its policy, which was published at Banbury by a Captain Tomson, who had collected about 200 horse. Troops were at once sent to put down the Levellers, and after a short fight at Banbury the majority of them surrendered, while Fairfax moving in person in pursuit of a yet larger party, defeated them and forced them to yield at Burford in Oxfordshire, where they were brought to trial, and being all found guilty, were decimated.

Tomson fled to Northampton with the remnant of his party, and having been driven thence, was discovered by his pursuers in a wood near Wellingborough where, despairing of quarter, he charged three times on the troops which were sent to apprehend him, and died fighting desperately.

Similar troubles arose in many parts of England, but the Levellers being everywhere in a minority, were invariably suppressed without difficulty, and were without exception punished with an iron hand.

In the meantime Ormond was pressing yet closer on Dublin, in consequence of which Ireton, as second in command under Cromwell, was ordered to Ireland in the early part of June. On the 30th of June arrived the news that Dublin was actually besieged, and there being thus no time to spare if it was to be saved from capture, Cromwell started for Ireland on the 2nd of July, travelling in great state, with a life-guard of eighty, "who had all been officers."

We must here for a time leave the narration of events in England, and pass to the record of the Irish campaign of Cromwell, surely one of the most remarkable in his history, since in nine months he reduced to almost entire peace a country in which war had scarcely ceased during eight years; it is true that in so doing he made his name such a curse as is not yet forgotten, but it was perhaps scarcely to be expected that the proceedings of the conqueror should be appreciated by the conquered, while from a soldier's point of view he is entitled to the highest praise, since that which lie had to do he did, and did efficiently.

CHAPTER 7

# The Campaign in Ireland
# 1649 and 1650

It will be necessary, before entering upon the narrative of the campaign of Cromwell in Ireland, to relate, in as few words as possible, the events which had led to the miserable condition in which that country was in 1649. In the latter part of the year 1641, only six months after the death of Strafford, an event closely followed by the disbandment of the army which he had collected in Ireland, the whole of that country burst into a blaze of rebellion. The first notice which the rulers of Ireland received of the approach of such a catastrophe was given by one O'Conolly, who betrayed to the Lord Justice Parsons the existence of a plot, of which the object was the seizure by surprise of Dublin Castle and the arsenal within it.

Acting on his information measures were taken to prevent the success of this enterprise, and Lord Maguire, one of the leaders of the plot, having been made prisoner was sent to London, where he was afterwards beheaded.

But although Dublin was thus saved, no time existed for any effort for the safety of the remainder of the country, since on the very day on which the plot was revealed (October 23rd, 1641), the Irish rose in every part and massacred all Protestants, English and Scottish, under circumstances of the most revolting barbarity. The total number of victims amounted to about 40,000; men, women and children being indiscriminately murdered in a manner of which the details recall those of the massacre of Cawnpore.

The principal leader of the Irish was Sir Phelim O'Neale (or O'Neill), a member of the family of the Earls of Tyrone, who, having caused all the Scots and English in Ulster to be put to death, maintained an absolute rule in that province.

Of the whole of Ireland but little remained in the hands of the English beyond Dublin and Drogheda (then called Tredagh), and even the Irish of the Pale, who had at first been believed to be loyal, and had in consequence been supplied with arms, joined with the rebels and rivalled them in their worst cruelties; of these half-English Irish Lord Gormanston took the chief command.

The first enterprise attempted by the rebels was the siege of Drogheda, and a defeat inflicted by them on a small party which had been sent to relieve that town added greatly to their repute and numbers. The first engagement of note occurred on the 15th of April, 1642, at Kilrush in County Wexford, where the Marquis of Ormond the King's lieutenant-general, defeated Lord Mountgarret the leader of the Irish; this action had no very decisive result at the time, but Drogheda having been shortly before relieved, the English now began to hold their own, aided by some scanty help from England, where indeed there were but few troops to spare.

Our space will not permit of an account of the many engagements which took place during this war, up to the time when, in April, 1643, the King proposed to the rebels a cessation of arms for one year, an act which, as before mentioned, greatly increased his unpopularity and diminished his chance of success. This proposal was renewed by further letters in May and July of the same year, and was finally concluded on the 15th of September, at which date an order was issued that all officers and soldiers who were not absolutely required for garrisons should be transported to England.

The truce appears to have been well observed by each party, and resulted in a treaty of peace which was signed in July, 1646, by which the Roman Catholics obtained every demand which they put forward. This peace was nevertheless at once broken, and Ormond (who had been appointed Lord Lieutenant in January, 1643) was closely besieged in Dublin by a force, headed by Cardinal Rinuccini, the Papal Nuncio, who had assumed the command of the Irish Catholics.

Finding himself in so dangerous a position, Ormond, by express direction from the King, offered his submission to the English Parliament, to whom he surrendered Dublin, Drogheda, Dundalk, and such other garrisons as remained in his hands. This transaction was completed on the 25th of July, 1647, when Colonel Jones took command of Dublin for the Parliament, and was made by them commander-in-chief in Ireland; his total force however amounted to but 5,000 men.

The war now continued with varying success, the commanders for the Parliament being, in addition to Jones, Monk in Ulster and Lord Inchiquin in Munster. The latter in 1648 joined Ormond, who in September, upon the invitation of the Catholics, returned to Ireland, the Papal Nuncio having been driven from the country by his own party, who were alienated from him by his folly and insolence.

At the end of 1648 there were therefore two parties in Ireland; the Parliamentary, which had been the English, holding Dublin and a few garrisons, and the Catholics, who formerly rebels, were now held as Royalists, and whose new leader Ormond, on the death of Charles I., proclaimed the Prince of Wales, on the 16th of February, 1649, at Carrick, as King of England, Scotland, France, and Ireland.

The English Parliament now at last resolved to put an end to disorder in Ireland, and with this object, in March, 1649, appointed Cromwell to the supreme command; to him this command gave great satisfaction, as in it he found not only an opportunity for further distinguishing himself, but also a means of uniting all soldiers, of whatever denomination, in such affection and regard to himself as always attends a general who leads an army to successful battle.

On the other hand Ormond's position was by no means an easy one, for not only did Owen O'Neale (the son of Sir Phelim) and the Irish army whom he led refuse to join in the peace or to serve under the Marquis, but the Scots also, to whom he had sent for aid, though sufficiently willing to assist the King, declined absolutely to make any terms with the Roman Catholics whom Ormond commanded. Jones in the meantime received some little succour from England, but there was as ever very great difficulty in inducing any of the English army to volunteer for Ireland, or even to proceed there when ordered.

At length in May, 1649, Ormond, having collected 8,000 foot and 2,000 horse, advanced on Dublin, near which he arrived on the 19th of June, while shortly after Inchiquin captured Drogheda. Information having been now received of an agreement between O'Neale and Monk, who held Dundalk, Inchiquin at once marched to the north, defeated part of the forces of the former, and forced the latter to surrender that town.

In a few weeks all the smaller garrisons which the Parliamentary party held had been reduced, and there remained in their hands in the early part of August, only Dublin and Londonderry, while the safety of the latter place was due entirely to the action of O'Neale, for seeking alliance with whom, the Governor, Sir Charles Coote, was censured by the Parliament, who refused to recognise as possible any alliance with Papists. The same blame for the same reason was also lavished on Monk who, on his return home after the surrender of Dundalk, though well received at Chester by Cromwell who was then on his way to Ireland, was so treated by the House of Commons, that men believed that he never either forgot or forgave his reception.

Milford Haven was appointed as the rendezvous for the forces ordered to Ireland, whence, ere the main body was prepared to start, reinforcements to the extent of 2,000 men were sent to Jones, thus bringing up his strength, after deducting all losses, to a total of about 5,000.

On the other hand Ormond was weakened by the departure of Inchiquin, who had been detached to Munster in consequence of a report that Cromwell intended to land in that province. Being acquainted with this fact Jones on the 2nd of August sallied from Dublin, completely defeated Ormond at Rathmines, and forced him to raise the siege of the capital, inflicting upon him a loss of 4,000 killed and 2,500 prisoners.

Ormond after adding to the garrisons of Drogheda and Trim, fell back himself to Kilkenny, whereupon Jones undertook the siege of the former place, but was, upon the return of Ormond to Trim, shortly afterwards obliged to abandon that enterprise. The Marquis, satisfied with this effort, and having heard of the landing of Cromwell, fell back about the 15th of August to his former position.

It had originally been intended that Ireton, with his troops, should land at Kinsale, but this project being abandoned on account of the weather, he sailed to Dublin, and there united his force to that of Cromwell. The new Lord Lieutenant was enthusiastically received at Dublin, which city, now that its garrison was reinforced with the 9,000 men whom Oliver had brought with him, at last felt itself safe from attack.

The total force at Cromwell's disposal amounted to seventeen regiments of foot and 5,000 horse, in all about 15,000 men; with 10,000 selected from these, after issuing a proclamation against swearing and lawlessness, he on the 30th of August marched directly upon Drogheda, intending either to take that town or to fight Ormond should he attempt to relieve it. Sir Arthur Aston, who it may be remembered was Governor of Heading in 1643, was in command of the garrison of Drogheda, which consisted of 2,000 foot and one regiment of horse; every effort had been made to put the place into a good condition for defence.

Cromwell, on his way to Drogheda, detached 1,000 foot and 500 horse under Colonel Venables to reinforce the garrison of Londonderry; this force marching to the north successfully effected a junction with Sir Charles Coote, the Governor, who with its assistance sallied from the town, and cleared the enemy from the adjacent country for a distance of fourteen miles.

On the arrival of the English army before Drogheda, which

took place on the 2nd of September, Ormond with 5,000 men again advanced to Trim, but confident in the strength of the former place, made no effort to come thence to its aid. On the 9th of September Cromwell summoned the town, and on the 10th, having made a breach on either side of St. Mary's Church, he ordered a storming-party of 1,000 men under Colonel Castle to commence the assault.

The storm began at 5 p.m., while a second party of forty or fifty men, under Captain Brandly (of the Navy), attacked a tenaille, which by its fire flanked one of the breaches. This latter work was carried at once, but the postern to the tenaille through the curtain was found to be blocked by the corpses of the slain of the garrison, to such an extent that no entrance could be forced by that way.

The main attack, after having carried the breaches was stopped by entrenchments, which the besieged had made on either side, and was finally driven out by a counter-attack with the loss of its leader. The day was now drawing to an end, while it was essential, above all for moral reasons, that the Parliamentary army should not appear to have received a check from the Irish; for these reasons Cromwell immediately ordered a fresh attack, which he led in person, and which stormed the breaches, the retrenchments, and the church.

The cavalry, which were at first unable to enter the town, owing to the fact that the breaches had not been cut down sufficiently low, now poured into the streets, from which they quickly drove the enemy, who fled across the Boyne, or into the Mill-mount, a defensive palisaded work on an eminence, which formed apparently a species of citadel. The victorious troops pressed on, the Mill-mount was stormed, and all whom it contained, including the Governor, were put to the sword.

Those of the garrison who had escaped across the river, however, still held three points, namely, the steeple of St. Peter's Church, the West Gate, and a tower near the latter called St. Sunday's. Since these men refused to surrender, the steeple with all in it was burnt, while a strong guard was set to watch the towers; these both surrendered on the following day, when the officers and every tenth man of the defenders of one tower, whence the troops had been fired on, were shot at once, while the remainder of that garrison, as well as the whole of those in the other tower, were made prisoners and sent eventually as slaves to Barbadoes.

Of the entire force of the Royalists, not fifty men escaped from death or captivity, direct orders having been given by Cromwell to spare none who might be found in arms; the loss of the English army was 100 killed, which, following the ordinary ratio of casualties, would imply an addition of about 200 wounded.

Much has been said with respect to the slaughter which Cromwell ordered on this occasion (a slaughter certainly not without a parallel in our own day), and while his detractors point to it as an instance of his cruelty and intolerance, his admirers lament it as unworthy of his greatness, and endeavour to find excuse for it in that, by his own statement, we know that it was ordered "in the heat of action."

But no blame or excuse is really needed, for war cannot be made on humanitarian principles, and Cromwell, being a soldier and having specific work to do, did that work in the way that seemed to him, and was, the most effectual and complete. He says himself, "Truly I believe this bitterness will save much effusion of blood;" and that this was its true tendency is shown by the immediate surrender of Dundalk and Trim, due almost certainly to the warning taken from the terrible fate of the defenders of Drogheda.

That war is an awful and horrible thing those who have seen it most often testify most distinctly, but it is unfortunately still as unavoidable as disease, and like disease must bring with it suffering and death; so long as these attendants upon war strike only the actual combatants, pity is wasted on the fate of those who endure only that which they strive to inflict. But the true sadness of the matter lies, not in those details of it which affect the paid and professional ministers of war, but in such as ruin, starve, and slay the innocent inhabitants of the theatre in which the deadly tragedy is played out.

After reading Cromwell's graphic account of the storm of Drogheda, the mind, though fully realising the horror of such slaughter, finds a yet more awful horror behind this, in the thought of the hideous sufferings of the inhabitants of the town, who, Protestants and Catholics, were harried in turn by the Catholics of Ormond and by the Puritans of Cromwell, and this in an age when less pity was shown by each to any form of heresy, than to the most heinous and devilish crime.

After the fall of Drogheda Ormond fell back to Kilkenny, while Cromwell returned to Dublin, whence, about a fortnight later, the English army marched to the south, with the object of reducing Wexford; it was compelled however to leave garrisons in Drogheda, Dundalk, and Trim, by which detachments the strength of the field army was much reduced.

The army moved, paying, by special order of Cromwell, for all provisions, along the sea-shore to Killincarrig, where a post which had been abandoned by the enemy was garrisoned with a company; thence they passed through a country desolated by the war to the river Darragh,[1] near Arklow, where a castle (query Clenart Castle?), which was the property of Ormond, received a similar garrison. There leaving the sea, to which they had probably clung on account of the convenience of supply from their ships, the army marched on Limerick, a small town where the enemy had a strong garrison, which however retired before the approach of Cromwell and burnt their post; the next point was Ferns, of which the castle surrendered on summons, and was garrisoned, as was also the castle of Enniscorthy.

Thus after a march of eight days Cromwell arrived in front of Wexford on the 1st of October. On the 3rd he summoned the town, but Colonel Simcott, the Governor, who had but lately occupied it with a garrison, endeavoured to temporise, until, having received a reinforcement of 500 foot from Lord Castle-

---

1. So says Carlyle, but it seems more probable that it was the Derrywater, a stream which runs into the Avoca.

haven, he should be in a position to refuse to conclude any treaty without the consent of that nobleman. In the meantime Jones, who was now Cromwell's major-general, had been sent with troops to the mouth of the harbour, where he captured a fort, and further, with the assistance of some of the sailors of the fleet, compelled a frigate of twelve guns which lay near it to surrender.

On the receipt of Simcott's answer Oliver abruptly broke off all negotiations, and the guns having arrived on the 6th, had by the 10th of October armed the whole of his batteries. He directed that the fire of his ordnance should be concentrated on the castle, which stood 300 or 400 paces outside of the walls at the south-east angle of the town, being convinced that should the castle fall the town would soon follow.

On the 11th Simcott asked for terms of surrender; in answer to him, Cromwell offered quarter for all, the officers to be prisoners, the non-commissioned officers and soldiers to be allowed to go to their homes, and the townspeople to be protected from violence and plunder. But before this answer could be accepted, the Governor of the castle, "being fairly treated," basely surrendered his charge. The defenders of the town walls, seeing their enemy on the battlements of the castle, were seized with a panic and deserted their posts; observing this a storming party at once escaladed the walls and pushed into the town.

A stand which was made by the garrison in the market-place served only to inflame the passion of the assailants, who "put all to the sword that came in their way," and finding that most of the townspeople had fled, plundered their houses of everything portable. The loss of the English did not exceed twenty men, while about 2,000 of the enemy perished.

Having placed a garrison in Wexford, Cromwell marched to Ross, which he summoned on the 17th of October, but the Governor, having received a reinforcement of 1,500 men from Ormond, hesitated to ask for terms. On the 19th, therefore, the English batteries opened fire, but when a breach had been made and all things had been prepared for a storm, the Governor evacuated the town and retired with his garrison to the west across the river Barrow.

During the whole of this time Ormond was lying quiet at Kilkenny where, having now come to an agreement with. O'Neale, he was awaiting the arrival of reinforcements from the north. But the Royal or Catholic party was fast losing heart, having found that their troops were no match for those of Cromwell, and from all sides flowed in offers of surrender and submission. Before the middle of November Cork and Youghal were in the hands of the Parliament and duly garrisoned.

All was thus going well in the south of Ireland, while in the north Coote, with the assistance of the reinforcements sent to him by Cromwell, had almost succeeded in driving the enemy from Ulster. On the 14th of November Cromwell was still at Boss, engaged in constructing a bridge across the Barrow, with the intention of marching up the Nore, and of endeavouring to force Ormond to give battle.

About this time Prince Rupert, who was in command of a remnant of that portion of the fleet which had, upon the appointment of Rainsborough to their command, deserted the cause of the Parliament, but who had been cooped up in the harbour of Kinsale by Admiral Blake (the defender of Lyme Regis and Taunton), succeeded with the loss of three ships in breaking through the blockading squadron, and sailed for Portugal, thus for ever passing from the history of the war; of Maurice also we shall hear no more, for he, towards the end of the year 1649, disappeared in the West Indies with his ship and his whole crew, no trace of their fate having been ever found.

At this period occurred one of the few actions in which the Irish ventured to meet the English troops in the open field, which for other reasons is not without some little interest. A column composed of soldiers who, having been left sick at Dublin, had been on convalescence ordered to rejoin the army, was on the 1st of November at Arklow. Its total strength amounted to only 800 foot and 350 horse, and the enemy, having heard from the country people of its approach, determined to cut it off from the main army.

With this object, Inchiquin was ordered to attack it with a force of 3,000 men, but, directions having been sent to the commander of the little column requiring him to march as quickly and in as close order as possible, the Irish leader succeeded only in overtaking him with the cavalry of his force, who came up with the English at about seven miles from Wexford.

On the receipt of a report from their scouts that the enemy was in pursuit, the Parliamentary troops were drawn up on the sands, between the sea and the cliffs, thus securing their flanks and preventing any possibility of an attack on their rear; in this position they awaited the onset of their opponents.

The Irish force consisted of about 1,500 cavalry, who overwhelmed the English horse with their numbers and at once drove them back in disorder; but the foot, though "miserably weary," stood fast, and with-holding their fire until the enemy were within pistol-shot, repulsed them with severe loss. The horse, which had in the mean time been rallied, gallantly charged again, and drove off the Irish in confusion.

This trifling skirmish has a certain value in military history from the fact that a similar affair at the present day might be reported in almost the same words; and further, because it proves that, even in those days when the foot were badly armed, cavalry not of the best were unable to break really good infantry; but on the other hand, Cromwell himself owns that, had the enemy's dismounted troops arrived before the conclusion of the action, the English column must have been destroyed.

At about the middle of November it was determined to advance upon Ormond, and to endeavour to force him to accept battle. With this object Lieutenant-General Jones and Major-General Ireton, leaving Cromwell sick at Koss, moved to Inistioge, which was abandoned on their approach; at this point they had hoped to be able to cross the river, but, finding it so swollen by rain as to be unfordable, they passed on to Thomastown, where there was a bridge. This, however, the enemy broke down before retiring from the town, after which check, since nearly all their supply of food was exhausted, the English troops returned to Ross.

This expedition was not, however, altogether a failure, for a force consisting of twelve troops of horse and three of dragoons, detached under Colonel Reynolds from the main column, succeeded in surprising Carrick-on-Suir. On coming near the town in the early morning of the 20th, Reynolds divided his command into two parties, of which he sent one openly against the enemy, while the other, their attention being thus diverted from it, made a dash at one of the gates; this they surprised and occupied and, upon the threat of a further advance into the town, all those of the garrison who could escape fled; 100 prisoners were taken, while the occupants of the castle, about 90 Welshmen, joined the Parliamentary army.

Thus with but little loss of life was captured a town of such strategical importance that Cromwell at once (on the 21st and 22nd) occupied it with his entire force; its value lay in the fact that it afforded a point of passage over the Suir, thereby giving free access to Waterford, and, which was perhaps for the moment even more important, offering a means of communication with the fleet, and thus ensuring a supply from them of ammunition and food. Of these the former was at the time much needed, for the reason that, Waterford Harbour being held by the enemy, no ships could come up the Barrow to Ross.

On the 23rd Cromwell moved on to Waterford; on the following day Reynolds, who had been left at Carrick-on-Suir with 150 foot, six troops of horse and one of dragoons, was attacked by the enemy, who fully appreciated the advantage which had accrued to the English by the capture of this town. The little garrison defended itself with great bravery against the attack of a far superior force, and the assailants, though they succeeded in burning the gates and sprang a small mine under the walls, failed to effect an entrance, and were, after four hours of hard fighting, repulsed with the loss of some hundreds of men.

The garrison of Waterford, having been lately reinforced, was too confident to yield without a struggle, while Cromwell, on account of the approach of winter, decided not to commence the siege. He however sent Jones, with a regiment of horse and three troops of dragoons, to gain possession, if possible, of the fort at Passage; this was surrendered by the Governor without difficulty, and the English thus obtained the power to use Waterford Harbour, which was commanded by the guns of the fort.

Immediately after this success (on December the 3rd) the army went into winter quarters; these included Bandon Bridge, Kinsale, Cork, and Wexford, the headquarters being at Youghal. At Dungarvan, on or about the 10th of the month, died Lieutenant-General Jones, to whom the present favourable position of the Parliament was largely due. One only episode varied the monotony of the winter quarters; this was an effort made by Colonel Wogan, the Governor of Duncannon, to join with Ferral (or Farrell), the Governor of Waterford, in an attempt to retake the fort at Passage.

On obtaining information that such an enterprise was intended, Cromwell ordered Colonel Zanchy, whose troops lay on the northern bank of the Black water, to advance with his regiment of horse and two guns to the relief of the garrison. With this small body (in all 320 men) Zanchy entirely defeated the Irish, of whom about 100 were killed, while the prisoners, among whom was Wogan himself, were 350 in number, and thus actually exceeded their captors in numerical strength.

One incident with regard to this skirmish is interesting, as showing how remarkable were the terms on which Ormond stood with the Irish who nominally served under his command; the townsmen of Waterford in their mistrust of their leader, who was present in the town during the action, absolutely refused to permit any of his troops to pass through their streets to the assistance of their discomfited friends, nor would they accept, even in their hour of need, of the addition of any fraction of the marquis's force to their garrison. Owing to their rejection of all such aid Wogan's regiments were entirely routed, while Ferral was driven hastily back into Waterford.

In the early part of the month of January, 1650, Ireton was

appointed by the Parliament President of Minister, while a few days later, on the 12th, a letter was written by the Speaker to Cromwell, by which he was recalled to England, in consequence of the proposed reception of Charles II. by the Scots, and of the threatening attitude of that nation, against whom, as was well known, Fairfax was unwilling to fight. Rumours of the above proposal had on the 8th of February already reached Ireland, but the actual letter did not come into Cromwell's hands until a considerably later date.

At the end of January, 1650, the weather being favourable, the English army again took the field. Oliver now determined to divide his force into two parts, of which one, consisting of 2,000 infantry and fifteen troops of horse and dragoons, was to march under Colonel Reynolds, followed by Ireton with a reserve, by Carrick into Kilkenny; the other under his own leadership, and containing twelve troops of cavalry, three of dragoons, and between 200 and 300 foot, was to attack Tipperary. It is interesting to note how, having now obtained a firm footing in the country, Cromwell does not hesitate to leave the sea-coast, to which, and to the shifting base afforded by the ships, he had formerly clung closely.

Following first the fortunes of Cromwell's column, we find that he marched from Youghal on the 29th of January, crossing the Blackwater, and inclining to the right at Clogheen, passed the Suir with much difficulty. Thence coming to Fethard, he after nightfall occupied a portion of the suburbs and summoned the town; the garrison in answer, fired angrily upon the English forces, saying, "that it was not a time of night to send a summons," but, after the negotiations had continued until the morning, the Governor surrendered upon such terms "as we usually call honourable."

Cromwell, hearing that Reynolds was now at Callan, marched to that place, which though guarded by three castles, had been taken before he arrived; leaving in the town a garrison of one company and one troop, he returned by the middle of February to Fethard and Cashel, having previously despatched Reynolds to take the Castle of Knocktopher, which lay about half-way between Callan and Ross, and interrupted the communication of one with the other; this service was efficiently performed. Ireton's column had taken for the object of its action the occupation of some passage over the Suir, which at present the English were unable to cross except by boat, or in weather sufficiently dry to make the fords passable; they therefore attacked Ardfinnan, where was a bridge defended by a strong work, and after a short struggle, in which they lost only two men killed, possessed themselves of that town. The conquest of this post was of the very greatest utility, since in all the course of the Suir, this was the nearest bridge to Cappoquin, where the English lines of communication with Youghal crossed the Blackwater.

One point only remains to be noted; it was considered that during the absence of the English army, the enemy might very probably make an inroad into County Cork. To prevent any such danger Lord Broghill was left with a force at Mallow, from which position he could guard the county against any attack from Limerick or Kerry. He, finding himself idle in consequence of the failure of Inchiquin to advance, employed his time in capturing Castletownroche, of which the surrender placed all the country between the Mallow and the Suir in the hands of the English.

In the course of March the whole County of Tipperary submitted to the Parliament, and agreed to pay a monthly contribution of 1,500; while a letter from Cromwell, March the 5th, relates how he has "taken in" all the castles on the upper waters of the Suir, and had also gained a strong hold on Limerick County, in which Broghill and Colonel Henry Cromwell had defeated Inchiquin near the town of Limerick.

The Irish forces, under Lord Castlehaven, had by this time been driven back on Carlow, Leighlin Bridge, and Kilkenny. Cromwell intending to besiege the latter place, which he knew to be of great strength, called Colonel Hewson from Dublin to his aid. The colonel, marching with a body of 3,000 men, succeeded without much difficulty in effecting this junction, since he met with no resistance of importance, except from the castle which guarded Leighlin Bridge.

This he carried, and thus rendered unnecessary the assistance which might have been afforded to him by a detachment of 800 horse and dragoons with 500 foot, which, under the command of Colonel Shilbourne, Cromwell had sent to meet him, in case the enemy should attempt to delay his march. It was fortunate that their aid was not needed, for by some accident they failed to find him, and therefore returned to Wexford, taking on their way Thomastown and two other castles on the Nore.

Ireton with his forces now passed to Waterford in order to continue the siege of that place, while Cromwell, having met Hewson near Gowran, secured that town, and on the 22nd of March, advanced on Kilkenny, upon which movement Castlehaven fell back up the river Nore by Ballyragget to Castletown.

Cromwell at once commenced the attack on Kilkenny, against which he threw up a battery, which on the 25th opened fire from three guns. These in about 100 rounds made a breach, which appeared practicable, but which was so swept by the fire from some retrenchments, that the storming party was repulsed from the assault with the loss of an officer and twenty or thirty men.

A simultaneous attack made on the Irish town, a suburb of the place, was, however, completely successful. Another suburb situated on the opposite side of the river was captured without difficulty by eight companies, which were sent for that purpose; but the officer in command having ordered an attack on the city, to which the only road lay across the bridge, the troops which attempted this dangerous operation were repulsed with the loss of fifty men, for the bridge up to the gate, which he desired to burn, was fully exposed to the fire of the defenders. After this failure Cromwell, wishing to have recourse to surer if slower means than that of open assault, commenced to prepare a second battery; but on the 28th the garrison surrendered upon terms.

The Speaker's letter, by which Cromwell was recalled to England, was received by him on the 22nd of March; but not finding its message confirmed by another letter of a later date, he wrote on the 2nd of April from Kilkenny to ask for further instructions.

Munster and Leinster being now practically subdued, Ireton was sent into Connaught with the object of preventing the junction of Lord Clanricarde, who commanded there, with Castlehaven, who was General in Leinster; Cromwell himself in the meantime prepared to reduce Clonmel, which was, with the exception of Waterford, the last important garrison of the Irish in the south.

On the 27th of April the English army, which had been employed in the interval between this and the last date mentioned in the reduction of many lesser posts, took up its position before Clonmel; on the 30th the guns arrived, and by their fire a practicable breach was made by the 9th of May. But the garrison, which numbered about 2,000 infantry, in nowise dismayed, retrenched the breach with parapets, which were flanked from the adjacent houses, with the result that, on the attempt of an assault, after four hours of hard fighting the storming party was driven back with heavy loss.

Thus ended the day of the 10th; during the night the garrison contrived, without being perceived, to escape from the farther side of the town; while in the morning, before their departure had been discovered, articles of surrender had been agreed upon with the few who remained. Finding themselves thus tricked, the English at once sent cavalry in pursuit of the fugitives, but they had obtained too long a start to allow of their being caught, and thus escaped with the loss of but 200 of such as straggled from the column.

With this success ended Cromwell's share in the reduction of Ireland; the *President* frigate having been specially sent to convey him to England, he left Ireland towards the end of May, and arrived in London, by way of Bristol, on the 31st of that month, having left behind him Ireton as his Lord Deputy. During his short stay in Ireland of barely nine months, Cromwell had succeeded in regaining possession of Leinster and the greater part of Munster, while Coote and Venables, acting under his orders, had almost driven the Irish from Ulster. Connaught alone remained in the possession of the Catholics and Royalists.

The cause of the King in Ireland was now lost, but it may be of interest to relate shortly the farther history of that country up to the date of the final extinction of the war.

We have first to take notice of some minor actions. A short time after Cromwell's departure, Ormond, Clanricarde, and Castlehaven met at Ballymore, in West Meath, for the purpose of consulting on the progress of events. Their meeting was, however, disturbed by the coming of Colonel Reynolds, who, having been informed of the intended gathering of the Irish leaders, attacked their guards with a force of 2,500 men, dispersed them, and forced the members of the Council to fly in all haste into Connaught.

After this exploit, Reynolds, having been reinforced by troops from Dublin, devoted his attention to the reduction of the isolated strongholds which still remained in the hands of the Irish. An effort made by the Bishop of Ross to relieve Clonmel, while that place was being besieged by Cromwell, was disastrously repulsed by Lord Broghill, who at Bandon utterly defeated the Irish forces, and, having captured the person of the Bishop, hanged him without ceremony as a rebel.

Ormond now began to find his position intolerable, though, in addition to the Province of Connaught, many large towns and forts still held out against the Parliament, for the jealousy of the Irish in the fortified towns against the English Royalists was so great, that they refused altogether to receive them into their garrisons. The marquis was thus totally unable to arrange any organised system of defence, from which it resulted that the several fractions of the Irish force were destroyed in detail.

In the north of the island the Parliamentary party obtained similar success to that which attended their arms in the south, for Sir Charles Coote, having been attacked near Londonderry by the Bishop of Clogher, who led a force of 5,000 men, entirely defeated him on the 20th of June. The Bishop, flying from the battle, was taken prisoner near Inniskillen, and at once hanged.

The fortified towns now fell fast from the hands of the Irish. Carlow surrendered on the 19th of August, Waterford a few days later, as also did Charlemont, Coleraine, and twenty others. In August also, Ireton, sweeping all the cattle from Wicklow County as provision for the siege, and calling Sir Hardress Waller to his aid, advanced to Limerick, while he sent Sir Charles Coote to besiege Athlone. With the view of interrupting the siege of Limerick, Lord Clanricarde, gathering together such forces as he could command, advanced from Connaught towards the borders of Leinster, but was on the 25th of October entirely defeated, upon which his troops dispersed. As the weather now began to change rapidly for the worse, while Limerick showed no signs of any intention to yield, the Lord Deputy withdrew his troops from the siege of that place and took up his winter quarters at Kilkenny.

By the end of the year 1650 Ormond's position became untenable; on the one hand the Irish refused to obey him, being at one time even threatened by their bishops with excommunication should they do so; on the other, Charles II., being under the influence and in the hands of the Scots, was compelled to publish a declaration against the peace of 1648, and to declare that void which formed the sole bond, even in name, between the different parties who professed to be allied under the Marquis against their common enemy the Parliament of England.

All action being thus rendered impossible, Ormond, in the middle of December, embarked at Galway and retired to France, leaving to Lord Clanricarde the task which had proved too hard for himself. Inchiquin also at about the same time, abandoning all hope of ultimate success, fled to Holland. Towards the end of February, 1651, the English troops again took the field; in May Ireton having sent Coote into Connaught by way of Sligo, himself crossed the Shannon, and on the 4th of June recommenced the siege of Limerick.

An effort was made by Lord Muskerry to relieve the town, and with this object he advanced with a considerable force from

County Kerry, but Broghill on the 22nd of June fell upon him at midnight near Dromagh, drove the Irish across the Blackwater, and, on their attempting to make a stand on the farther bank, utterly routed and dispersed them.

The line of the Shannon now formed the boundary between the possessions of the English and the Irish, and on this line, towards the end of May[2] was fought the last serious battle of the war. Clanricarde having heard that Coote was advancing from Athlone, called Castlehaven to him, with the intention of attacking the Parliamentary leader with their combined forces; but Coote, by a forced march of thirty miles, succeeded in reaching Castlehaven's troops before the latter had completed his junction with Clanricarde, having previously delayed this junction by blocking every passage of the river which ran between the two Irish armies.

Having fallen upon Castlehaven, who was thus isolated, Coote entirely routed and dispersed his force, and then, after receiving some reinforcements from Ireton, turned upon Clanricarde, whose troops fled in a panic without a blow. Thus the last field army of the Irish ceased to exist, for never again could any such force be reassembled.

In July, 1651, on the arrival of a messenger from the Duke of Lorraine, the Irish endeavoured to conclude a treaty with that Prince, who was offered the title of Protector Royal of Ireland; this proposal had, however, no effect, owing to the success of the Parliamentary party, which made any such office impossible.

The siege of Limerick dragged on slowly, its monotony being relieved only by a few sallies on the part of the garrison, until the 23rd of October, when at a meeting in the Town House it was decided to treat with Ireton. This decision was naturally much opposed by those who knew that their names were on the list of persons excepted from mercy, and the Bishops of Limerick and Emly, who were in this condition, solemnly excommunicated any who should negotiate a surrender; but nevertheless,

---

2. Not only is the date of this action very uncertain, but the scene of the battle is doubtful.

one Fennel, a colonel of the Irish, having seized by force one of the gates of the city, yielded it, with a fort which formed part of the defences, to the Parliamentary forces, who marched in on the 29th.

But Limerick, though captured, proved fatal to Ireton, who died there on the 26th of November, from a fever which had been brought on by the fatigue of the siege and the unhealthiness of the camp of the besiegers. He was succeeded for the time by Major-General Ludlow, under whose command Galway was attacked by Sir Charles Coote. This town however held out its defence until the 12th of May, 1652.

After this latter date there was but little further effort at resistance on the part of the Irish, though the Rebellion was not officially declared to be at an end until the 26th of September, 1653.

Thus did this war, begun with murder, and continued in strife more sanguinary than skilful, end in quarrels, disunion, and treachery among the Irish, who, being incapable of combination, were likewise incapable of success, since their distrust of each other enabled their enemy to crush each faction in turn.

After the funeral of Ireton, who was buried in Henry VII.'s Chapel, on the 6th of February, 1652, Lambert was declared Deputy in his place; but this appointment not meeting with the approval of Cromwell (who well knew that Lambert was a bold, capable, and ambitious man), advantage was taken of the termination of Oliver's commission as Lord Lieutenant, in April, 1652, to announce that that of the Lord Deputy must cease at the same time, and Lambert therefore retained only the office of Commander-in-Chief in Ireland.

Of this post also he was deprived in July, 1652, when the appointment was given to Fleetwood, a good soldier, but a weak man and no politician, who had married Ireton's widow, Bridget, the daughter of Cromwell.

In 1656 Fleetwood was succeeded by Henry, the son of the Protector, who laid down his office in 1659, at about the same time as his brother Richard resigned the Protectorate.

CHAPTER 8

# The Campaigns in Scotland, 1650, and of Worcester, 1651

The Scottish people, yet full of shame for the part which their army had taken in the surrender of Charles I., were fiercely agitated by the news of his death. Not all the power of Argyll, now as ever the firm friend of Cromwell and the Independents, could prevent the nation from declaring Charles II. the King of Scotland. But the sovereignty thus offered to him was not such as he desired, hampered as it was by the necessity of taking the Covenant, and by the consequent abandonment of his position as King by divine right.

For this reason Charles was rather inclined to trust those who heartily supported his cause because it was the cause of the King, and preferred the assistance of Montrose and Middleton to that of the rigid Presbyterians, who wearied even when they did not insult him. After some hesitation as to whether he should land in Scotland or Ireland, on finding that the latter was closed to him by the success of Cromwell, Charles reopened negotiations with the Scottish Government, but, desiring to have it in his power rather to demand than to entreat their assistance, he, while in communication with them, favoured the unfortunate efforts of Montrose.

The latter landed in Caithness in April, 1650, but, being met by Colonel Strahan with the vanguard of Lesley's army, he was defeated at Corbiesdale on the 28th of April, and, having been betrayed by one of his former adherents, was two or three days later taken prisoner. After the semblance of a trial, the Marquis was hanged at Edinburgh on the 21st of May.

On hearing of the defeat and disaster of Montrose, Charles had the meanness to deny to the Scots that he had in any way favoured his enterprise, and, their invitation to him being renewed, set sail from Holland, and arrived in Scotland on the 16th of June.

The Parliament of England had long foreseen the certainty of war with Scotland, since the latter country had not spared their protestations of horror at the death of the King, while it was an open secret that many of the Presbyterians in England were willing to join with the Scots, and even to accept Charles II., if only by such means the power of the Independents and of the army might be broken. It was therefore determined by the House of Commons not to await the advance of the Scots, but to strike the first blow, a mode of proceeding which would have the additional advantage of transferring the theatre of war into Scotland.

But Fairfax was known to be averse to any quarrel with the Scots, and, as a Presbyterian with a yet more bigoted wife, was believed to be rather favourable to them than the reverse; in this difficulty it was determined to recall Cromwell from Ireland, and a letter to this effect was written to him in January by the Speaker. As has been already mentioned this letter was long in arriving at its destination, and Cromwell himself did not return to London until the 31st of May.

On the 4th of June he received the thanks of the House for his success in Ireland; but this honour, though great, was not the most important gain which he had obtained in that war, for he had won the esteem and respect of the army, no less by his powers of administration than by his talent as a general in the field. Recognised now as the first soldier in the country, he required only the nominal rank to be the leader of the army; nor had he long to wait for this addition to his position.

At a meeting of the Council of State, held at the latter end of

June, it was decided, for the reasons given above, to invade Scotland, and thus to force on war. Fairfax, though at the moment he appeared inclined to agree with this decision, finally declared, under the influence of his wife and her Presbyterian ministers, against such an invasion, though he professed his willingness to engage the Scots, should they enter England.

When this feeling on the part of Fairfax became known, a committee, consisting of Cromwell, Harrison, Lambert, and two others, was directed to endeavour to induce the General to change his opinion; but after a long discussion, he still stated that such action against Scotland would be contrary to his conscience, and so impossible to him.

For this reason he at once resigned his commission, and Cromwell was, on the 26th of June, appointed captain-general and commander-in-chief of all the Parliamentary forces.

Oliver, having obtained his rank, did not long delay action, for he at once ordered all available troops to the north, and himself left London on the 29th of June; by his orders bodies of cavalry were pushed forward to watch the border, and preparations were made for the defence of Carlisle and Berwick against a sudden attack.

The Scottish forces were estimated at from 7,500 to 10,000 infantry, and from 2,700 to 3,000 horse, and rumour further said that already they were advancing towards the border. Cromwell moved to the north by way of York and Durham, and at the latter place was met by Sir Arthur Haselrigge, the Governor of Newcastle, who accompanied him to that town, whence a letter was addressed to the "Saints" in Scotland, explaining the reasons for the advance of the English.

On the 22nd of July the army crossed the border, on which occasion Cromwell issued a proclamation, declaring that no harm should be done to any who stayed quietly at home, while at the same time he promulgated a strict order against straggling and marauding.

But the country, as the army advanced, was found to be deserted, for the Scottish Government had warned the inhabitants that the coming of the English would be the signal for the murder of all between sixty and sixteen. The army marched by Mordington, Cockburnspath (26th July), and Dunbar (27th), to Haddington, and as they advanced the people in rear rose in arms and cut off all communication with England, except such as could be kept up by sea.

On the 28th of July Cromwell moved westward from Haddington, in expectation to find the enemy, who were reported to be 36,000 strong, in position on Gladsmuir; after a forced march, made with the object of seizing this line before the arrival of the Scots, he found that the latter were retiring before him towards Edinburgh. Pushing forward therefore a body of 1,400 horse, under Lambert and Whalley, he advanced his main army to Musselburgh.

At this point the English force found itself in front of the enemy, who were drawn up in a strong position between Edinburgh and Leith, the line being flanked by the fire of the latter place. On the 29th an effort was made to bring the enemy to action, but after some slight success on the part of the English, who captured a small post, it was found that the hostile position was proof against an assault.

After having waited during the remainder of the day and through the succeeding night in front of the Scots, with the hope of drawing them on to fight, Cromwell was forced by the severe weather, and by the want of provisions, to fall back on Musselburgh, whence he could communicate with the ships, and could thus supply his army.

Now, according to the proposed plan of the Scots, occurred their opportunity, for they had no intention of committing their troops to an engagement except at a decided advantage, but wished by the strength of their position to force the English to halt, to oblige them to retire by starvation, and then to fall upon their rear and harass the column on its retreat, while holding the passes in front on the road to England.

Accordingly, as Cromwell drew off on the 30th, the Scottish horse dashed upon the column, but were met by Lambert and Whalley, and so decisively repulsed that they gave no more trouble that day. The fight while it lasted was severe, and Lambert having had his horse killed and being himself wounded, was made prisoner, but was soon rescued by his own men.

During that night the English army lay at Musselburgh, where it is impossible to say that they "rested," for in addition to the discomfort caused by the constant rain, an attack was made by the enemy between 3 and 4 a.m. Their cavalry, about 1,500 strong, led by Montgomery and Strahan, drove in the outposts and defeated a regiment of English horse, but were soon repulsed, and were pursued to within a quarter of a mile of Edinburgh, with the loss to the Parliamentary troops of only one officer and four men.

Lesley, the Scottish leader, now fell back on his old position, giving out, although he had a force of 6,000 or 7,000 horse, and about 16,000 foot, that he would not attack until reinforcements had come up. It is more probable that, as Cromwell suggested in a letter, he hoped either that the English would run their heads against his impregnable position, or would be starved into retreat and surrender. Cromwell's troops lay quietly at Musselburgh until the 6th of August, at which date, the ships on account of the bad weather not being able to get to that port, they were compelled to fall back on Dunbar, whence, having received from the fleet a supply of tents and provisions, they returned on the 12th to Musselburgh.

The general, having thus refreshed and revictualled his army, now proposed another plan by which he hoped to force the enemy to attack him, and with this object, marching round the south side of Edinburgh, took up a position on the lower slopes of the Pentland Hills, within sight of the capital, and so placed that it commanded the road to Stirling, by which the Scottish army received its supplies. At this point the English arrived on the 14th, and the Scots at once drew off the greater part of their force from Leith towards the west, but still resolutely refused to fight.

On the 27th, in further hope of making them move against

him, Cromwell pushed yet more to the west and towards Stirling. The Scots followed his movement, and, after some skirmishing of the advanced guards, the English troops, desiring to bring matters to a final issue, attempted to attack, but soon found that this was impossible, on account of the boggy ground which divided the two armies, and thus the engagement died out in a cannonade which was kept up with vigour by either party.

The supply of bread again falling short, and reports arising of a movement of the Scots on Musselburgh, Cromwell, careful of the safety of his line of communications, returned to the latter town, where he arrived on the 29th, the enemy having at the same time made a parallel march on interior lines, but not having attempted an attack. The weather being very bad, and there being much sickness in his army, Cromwell, fearing lest his ships might not be able to come to Musselburgh, determined to retire to Dunbar, at which place there was a convenient harbour.

Charles had by this time signed the declaration, which the Scots had demanded as the price of their assistance, and in which he "confessed his mother's idolatry and professed his father's blood," and had thus, at the price of his honour, bound to his service many who were on the point of opening negotiations with Cromwell.

On the retirement of the English from Musselburgh on the 31st, the Scots at once fell upon their rear, and fighting continued during the whole night as the army fell back on Haddington. On the 1st, after a demonstration to the south of Haddington, Cromwell retired to Dunbar, while the Scots, leaving the coast road, took up a position on the Boon Hill, a spur of the Lammermoor Hills, which commanded the English line of retreat, while to make the intended action yet more fatal to his enemy, Lesley had occupied the Pass of Cockburnspath, by which alone any retreat was possible or any succour could arrive to the English. The nearest hope of the latter lay with Haselrigge at Newcastle at a distance of about 100 miles.

Cromwell's force, deducting 500 sick who had been embarked at Musselburgh, amounted to about 12,000 men, and

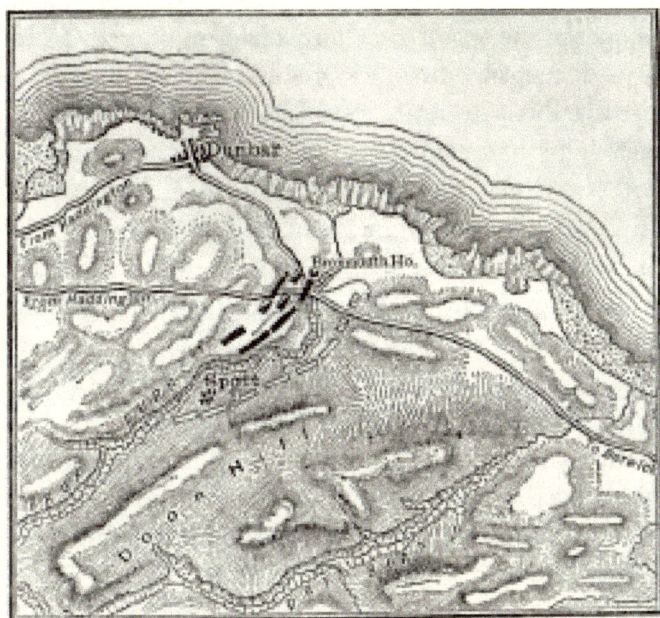

THE SCENE OF THE BATTLE OF DUNBAR,
SEPTEMBER 3RD, 1650

was posted in line facing south, on the undulating ground to the south of Dunbar, being divided from the Scottish army by the Broxburn, which, running in a channel cut by its own waters, formed at this time a ditch forty feet wide and as many deep.

The Scots, who numbered about 23,000, were posted on the lower slopes of the Doon Hill, in such a position that Cromwell, should he attempt to move towards England, must of necessity either attack them in front at every disadvantage of ground, or must march by their right flank between their army and the sea, a movement which was almost certain to entail disaster. The Scots, fully realising the advantage of their position, looked upon the English army as already lost, and spoke of them with contempt, arranging even the terms of surrender which should be demanded of them.

There were, it is true, some wiser heads about Lesley, who urged the advisability of offering a golden bridge to an enemy whom they knew to be more than their equals in war; but this advice was overborne by the exhortations of the ministers, who urged on their general in strains resembling, when they were not culled from, those of the old prophets of Israel.

On the 2nd of September, Lesley moved his whole army down the hill towards the Broxburn, hoping that by so doing he might induce Cromwell to risk the disadvantage which he must suffer from being obliged to pass the ravine, and might draw him on to attack; the Scots further threatened an advance of their troops to the north of the burn, for pushing forward a party in that direction, they seized the garrison of a small cottage which lay in front of the English army.

But Cromwell stood fast, for indeed it would have been madness to have sent his small force, which must have been disordered by the passage of the obstacle, against the strong front of the Scots.

At about 4 p.m. Lesley threatened an attack on the English left, for reinforcing his right wing with two-thirds of the cavalry of his left, he edged down towards the sea, with the intention of occupying the only easy passage of the ravine, which lay where the road now crosses the Broxburn. The Scottish foot and train also took ground to their right, and it became obvious that, unless forestalled, they would in the morning assault the English flank, and would thus, if successful, cut the army completely from its base, and drive them back upon the sea.

But Cromwell, from the grounds of Broxburn House, saw this movement, and at once realised the use which he might make of Lesley's mistake. For the Scottish leader had committed the capital error of abandoning a position on the flank of the defile, in order to take up one in rear of it, and had thus exposed his right, which had originally threatened the march of the English from ground on which it was itself absolutely secure.

The Scots were, in consequence, now so placed that no advantage of position remained to their right wing, to which again it was extremely difficult to bring up reinforcements since, the army being in occupation of the comparatively level ground at the edge of the ravine, any movement of troops to their flank must be conducted over the rocky and broken side of the hill. There thus existed to the Scots on their right flank only such hope of victory as might be found in a fight, in which they were, as far as regarded their position, on equal terms with their enemy, and that hope Cromwell, knowing the worth of his own men and despising the Scots, felt with certainty to be but forlorn.

It was true that, should the Scots succeed in passing the burn without opposition, they would be at once in a position to roll up his line by an attack on his left flank, but this, substituting only the word "right" for "left," was exactly the advantage which he proposed to gain for himself by attacking at the break of day.

Lambert and Monk, on being consulted, at once agreed to the plan of their leader, and it was decided that the former with Fleetwood and Whalley, should lead six regiments of horse across the ravine, while Monk should command the three regiments and a half of foot, who were to make good the advantage gained by the charge of the cavalry. The force named above was directed to advance at daybreak across the burn, and was to clear a passage for the remainder of the army; this done, the whole were to push in upon the right flank of the Scots, and were to roll it back upon the main army. Lambert further added to Cromwell's plan a suggestion that, before the commencement of the advance, the English artillery should open fire on the Scottish left, in order to attract attention to that flank, and thus to delay the despatch of support to the right.

On the morning of the 3rd of September the troops accordingly paraded before it grew light; but Lambert being detained on the English right while giving the necessary orders to the artillery, the attack did not commence until six o'clock, greatly to the annoyance of Cromwell, who knew well how much depended upon the assumption of the initiative. At 6 a.m. the foremost of the troops named above crossed the stream, and the cavalry, who led the way, were at once engaged with the enemy's horse, from whom they met with a stout resistance; the first attack of the infantry was also checked for a time, though the issue of the struggle between the half-trained Scots and the veteran English was never for a moment doubtful.

In rear of the leading regiments passed two brigades of infantry and two regiments of cavalry; these, after crossing the ravine, bore away a little to their left, in order that their advance might not be disordered by the fight which was raging in their front; when clear they wheeled up to their right and fell directly upon the enemy's flank.

For awhile the fight was hot; but after the leading Scottish troops had been repulsed, each successive body as it advanced against the English was broken by the weight of the fugitives, who were flying in disorder towards the hills; thus each force in turn was thrown into confusion before the critical moment of the contest, with the result that each in turn added to the number of the flying.

The action had not lasted for more than an hour before the Scottish army was entirely routed, and the scattered troops were in full flight in every direction, some seeking refuge in Edinburgh, while others, finding their retreat on that city cut off, fell back upon the detachment at Cockburnspath, which was to have destroyed the last remnant of the English army.

The pursuit extended over a distance of eight miles, and the total loss of the Scots amounted to 3,000 killed and 10,000 prisoners, while 30 guns and 15,000 stand of arms were taken; the casualties of the English army did not exceed 20 men. Of the prisoners, 5,000, being wounded, old men or boys, were allowed to return home; the remaining 5,000 were sent into England, whence, after enduring terrible hardships, they were, as had been the prisoners taken at Preston, sold either as slaves to the planters or as soldiers to the Venetians.

On the day following that of the battle, Lambert pushed on to Edinburgh with six regiments of horse and one of foot; Cromwell himself, after a rest of a few days, advanced on the capital, which at once surrendered to the victors. The example thus set was followed by Leith, but Edinburgh Castle still held out against the English.

The remnant of the Scottish army (but 1,300 horse remained of the 6; 000 who took part in the battle) retired on Stirling, while Charles himself took up his residence at Perth. To the King the effect of this defeat was, strange to say, not unwelcome, as by it he obtained some relief from the weariness of his position; for since the blow inflicted by Cromwell had fallen most heavily on the Ultra-Presbyterians, of whom Argyll was the chief, the result of the battle tended to increase the influence of the more moderate party, of whom the representative was Lord Lanark, who had now, by the death of his brother, become Duke of Hamilton. About this date the more bigoted of the extreme Presbyterians seceded from that portion of the Scottish army which attended the King, and under the leadership of Strahan and Ker commenced independent action in the south-western counties.

Having made Colonel Overton the Governor of Edinburgh, and having arranged for the blockade of the castle, Cromwell on the 14th of September marched towards Stirling with his main army, which had been recently reinforced with 1,500 foot and

1,000 horse. On the 15th, though much delayed by bad weather and worse roads, he reached Linlithgow; thence on the 16th he passed to Falkirk, of which the garrison, when summoned to surrender, returned for answer that they would follow the fate of Stirling.

At the latter place the army arrived on the 17th, but it, upon being summoned, refused to accept any terms; whereupon Cromwell, doubtful of his ability to storm so strong a fortress, fell back on the 19th to Linlithgow, which he now fortified and held as an advanced position in front of the capital. On the 20th the English returned to Edinburgh and sat down to a formal siege of the castle, which ran its course without much incident.

Ker and Strahan were in the early part of October about Dumfries, and Cromwell, possibly with a view to some arrangement with them, for they were known to be but ill-satisfied with the King, marched from Linlithgow at the head of seven regiments of foot and nine of horse, and moved in the direction of Glasgow; at that city he arrived on the 18th, and there remained until the 21st, when, hearing that the Scottish leaders, far from wishing to conclude an agreement with him, proposed to move upon Edinburgh in his absence, he hastily returned to the capital, and had arrived there by the 25th.

During the remainder of October and the greater part of November little of note occurred; the siege of Edinburgh Castle dragged on, while the army, which was cantoned in the capital, in Leith, and in the villages within a radius of eight miles, was principally occupied in throwing up fortifications for the purpose of rendering its position impregnable.

Towards the end of November it was decided to undertake an expedition against the moss-troopers, who, hanging on the outskirts of the army, plundered and murdered all who fell into their power. The task of suppressing these robbers was entrusted to Lambert and Monk, who quickly reduced them to submission. On their return from this expedition the former was sent in company with Whalley, and in command of 3,000 horse, under orders to move on Glasgow by way of Peebles, along the south bank of the Clyde; Cromwell himself marched on the north bank of that river, and had arranged to meet Lambert at Hamilton on the 29th of November, with the intention that the combined forces should search for and defeat the Scottish western army.

The general arrived punctually at the appointed spot, and not finding Lambert, waited for him at Hamilton until 7 a.m. on the 30th; thinking that some unforeseen floods must have delayed the march of his subordinate, Cromwell on the latter day retired on Edinburgh, while on the same date Lambert arrived at Hamilton. The Scottish army under Ker (for Strahan had already submitted to the Parliament) hastened to seize the opportunity thus given of falling upon Lambert's force while it was still at a distance from any succour, and with this object, marching all the night of the 30th, attacked the quarters of the English troops at 4 a.m. on the morning of the 1st of December.

The Scots at first succeeded in entering Hamilton, but the soldiers of the Parliament, in no way dismayed, formed up their ranks in the dark, in their turn attacked their enemy, and drove them in confusion from the town. The Scottish troops lost 100 killed, 100 prisoners (among the latter was Ker himself), and were soon scattered in headlong flight before their pursuers.

Thus was destroyed the western army, which, but for their ill-advised attack upon Lambert, might without difficulty have baffled for months the pursuit of Cromwell. It never again rallied as a whole, but the soldiers which had composed it spread abroad over the country in small bodies, robbing and murdering the inoffensive and unprotected peasantry.

The batteries of guns and mortars in front of Edinburgh Castle being now ready to open fire, Cromwell on the 12th of December summoned the garrison to surrender; after negotiations, which continued until the 18th, the Governor agreed to yield, and the defenders accordingly marched out on the 24th, leaving as trophies to the victors a total of 52 guns, among which was the "great iron murderer called Muckle Meg."

The year being now too advanced to allow of movements in

the field, the English army took up its winter quarters around Edinburgh and Leith. Here they remained quiet throughout January, 1651, the 1st of which month saw Charles crowned, "but not with much state," at Scone. About the middle of January rumours reached the general of the intention of the Scots to "slip into" England, while reports were rife of an expected increase of their army, which, being now composed of 8,000 horse and an equal number of foot, was to be raised to 50,000 before giving battle to the English. Of this force the King was, it is said, to be the Captain-General, Hamilton the lieutenant-general, and Lesley the major-general, while Middleton was to command the cavalry, and Massey to lead the contingent of English Royalists.

Cromwell broke up his winter quarters on the 4th of February, on which date eight regiments of foot and nine of horse set out towards Stirling, and were on the 5th at Falkirk; but the season was not yet sufficiently advanced to allow of the opening of the campaign, and the army, after much suffering from cold and wet, returned on the 8th to their cantonments.

This excursion cost the English something more than discomfort, for Cromwell, having caught cold from over-exposure, fell sick with fever and ague, and became at one time so ill that he was even reported to be dead; about the middle of March his health improved, and by the end of that month he was, though still weak, at length able to take the field.

During his illness the army as a whole remained idle; but a detachment captured Tantallon Castle, which, lying at the mouth of the Forth, had much disturbed the communication with England; a little later Blackness Castle, which lay a short distance to the north of Linlithgow, also surrendered to a force which was sent against it.

Great activity now began to reign in the Scottish quarters; the King went north, as far as Aberdeen, for the purpose of seeking for recruits, while Middleton was reported to be also stirring with the same object. On the receipt of information in London of an intended rising in Lancashire, which was supposed to have been caused by the rumour of an approaching invasion by the

Scots, Harrison was sent to the North of England by the House of Commons, in command of a strong force of horse and foot.

So general indeed was the belief in the probability of a Scottish inroad on England, that on the 11th of April an Act was passed to press 10,000 men during the current year; while Fleetwood, who held the command at home during the absence of Cromwell, published an order that all officers and soldiers should at once join their respective regiments.

On the 16th of April a parade of the whole of the English army in Scotland was held at Musselburgh, on which occasion their strength was found to be 8,000 to 9,000 horse, and an equal number of foot; this number did not, however, include a force which had been sent to attack Burntisland, an expedition which had been undertaken with a view of gaining a footing in Fife, in order thence to act against the Scottish army from the east.

After this parade the troops moved on Glasgow, either with the object of drawing Lesley out to fight by threatening him also from the west, or with a view of preventing any intended advance of the Scots into England; this march was altogether uneventful, and the army, having reached Glasgow on the 19th, was again in Edinburgh by the first week in May.

About the middle of the latter month Cromwell suffered a serious relapse, brought on in all probability by the fatigues of the above march; and news of this illness having been received in London, a letter was written on the 27th, desiring him if necessary to resign the command, while two physicians were sent by the House to take charge of his health; but by the 3rd of June he was sufficiently recovered to write a letter of thanks for the offer, and by the 24th was able to again take the field.

During the pause in hostilities, caused by the illness of the English leader, the Scots had pushed to the south from Stirling, and in June occupied a position at Torwood, from which Cromwell now proposed to drive them. With this object the English field army, consisting of twelve regiments of foot and thirteen of horse, moved on the 25th of June from Edinburgh, and encamped that night on the Pentland Hills; thence they pressed on to the west, and leaving Linlithgow on the 2nd of July, marched on that day, skirmishing all along the line with the enemy, beyond Falkirk towards Torwood; but the position of the Scots being found on a nearer approach to be too strong to permit of a successful attack, the army fell back again on Linlithgow.

On the 13th of July a similar movement was made with a similar ending, except that, some annoyance having been received on the march from Callender House, in which was a Royal garrison, this post, after having been summoned, was on the 15th bombarded, breached, and stormed in full sight of the enemy, who made no effort to relieve it.

Finding that the Scots were not to be drawn from their position, which was itself too strong to admit of the certainty of success should he attack it, Cromwell now determined to offer his enemy such advantage as might induce even them to assume the offensive, and thus to bring matters to a crisis. With this object he voluntarily weakened his numerical force by detaching troops into Fife, whence they might attack the Scottish left flank, which was not so well defended as was the right, and might thus, should the enemy decline to be tempted from his position, carry their lines of defence from the weaker side.

Accordingly on the 17th of July, Colonel Overton with 1,600 infantry and four troops of cavalry, a force which was intended as an advanced guard to a larger body, crossed the Forth at Queensferry, and with the loss of six men secured a footing on the north bank; in order to cover this movement Cromwell threatened an attack on Tor wood, but the enemy held fast in their position. The Scots, however, sent five regiments of horse and the same number of infantry against Overton, who was in some danger of being swept into the sea; but Lambert, crossing on the 19th, with two regiments of horse and two of foot, brought the total of the Parliamentary forces up to 4,600 men, while the Scots had but 4,000.

Under these circumstances the English, who had at first stood on the defensive, advanced against the enemy, who posted their troops on a hill a little to the north of Inverkeithing. Finding the Scots unwilling to attack, Lambert ordered his troops to storm the hill, and after a short but sharp fight entirely routed his opponents, killing 2,000 of them and taking 1,400 prisoners, among the latter being Browne, the Royal general, the same who in the earlier war had served the Parliament in conjunction with Waller. Lambert, after the action, received further reinforcements from Cromwell, which brought the total of his force up to at least 7,000 men.

On the 21st of July, on the receipt of the news of this victory, Cromwell pressed on to the west, while the Scots, abandoning two of their defensive lines, fell back on their main position about Stirling. This advance was made in the hope of forcing the enemy to assume the offensive either to the east or to the west. In the former case Cromwell intended to push at once across a ford and attack, while in the latter Lambert was to pursue the same tactics; but the Scots, realising this plan, had, though at one time on the point of marching towards Fife, on seeing the movement of Cromwell's army, returned to their original impregnable position. From this it became evident to the English general that, unless the war was to be permitted to drag on unsatisfactorily into another winter, some more active measures must be adopted.

For this reason he determined to pass his main army over the Forth into Fife, leaving only four regiments of horse and as many of foot on the southern side, and interposing his forces between Stirling and Perth to vigorously attack the Scottish position from the east. By the 26th of July 13,000 to 14,000 men had crossed the Frith, and the campaign had entered upon a new phase.

Cromwell evidently realised the possibility of a movement of the Scots in the direction of England (though the contrary might be imagined when we consider how small was the force which he had left in front of Edinburgh), for before commencing the transport of his army across the Forth he had sent a message to Colonel Rich, who lay in the north of England under Harrison's command, directing him to close up his troops towards the border.

By the 28th Cromwell himself was in Burntisland, which had been abandoned by the enemy; thence he determined to advance on Perth in order thereby to cut off all supplies from the Scottish army about Stirling. But the latter, having completed their levies, and having brought their strength up to 15,000 foot and 6,000 horse, suddenly abandoning their position, marched on the 31st of July to Hamilton, and so burst, by way of Biggar, upon Carlisle, which they reached on the 6th of August. Cromwell had in the meanwhile taken Perth, which, after a short bombardment and the delay of one day wasted in negotiations, surrendered on the 2nd of August, on which day news arrived of the sudden outburst of the Scots on England.

There is much that is difficult to unravel in the state of affairs at this time, and it is a hard question to answer whether Cromwell was surprised at this movement or had intended it to take place. On the one hand it was a daring, not to say a rash step, to thus permit his enemy to interpose in force between himself and his base, more especially since that base was London, where all were not friendly to him, and where the near approach of the King might probably excite a counter-revolution; on the other it may be urged that Cromwell had the delight which all strong men take in thorough measures, and had so great confidence in his army that he felt that any battle must result in a victory to them, while he further knew well that such a victory in Scotland implied the slow hunting down of fugitives in the then pathless wilderness of the Highlands, whereas in England it must be followed by the absolute destruction of the entire Scottish army.

On the whole we are inclined to believe that this apparently desperate piece of strategy was intentional, for a general who would dare to deliberately weaken his army for the purpose of inducing his enemy to fight, as Cromwell had already done when he detached Lambert into Fife, would certainly not hesitate to lure his foe into destruction by, as it were, making him a present of a distinct strategical advantage. It is further not unlikely that, in addition to his military plan, Cromwell had also political reasons for permitting, and even inviting, the Scots to thus plunge into the heart of England, for the Parliament and city might be assumed to be in all probability inclined in the future to show gratitude as great as their present fear, while decisive success in such a campaign as this could leave no possible competitor with him for the position of the leader of England.

Cromwell spared no pains to ensure that the success should be decisive; he had already provided a force of 3,000 men, with which Harrison and Rich might delay the march of the enemy. Lambert was at once despatched, with all the cavalry that could be got together, under orders to harass the Scottish column; while the general himself, crossing the Frith on the 6th of August, with the remainder of the horse and nine regiments of foot, hurried by the shortest road to the border, leaving Monk and Overton, with five regiments of horse and four of foot, to continue the subjugation of Scotland, which now, in the absence of her army, must become an easy prey. As a matter of fact the town of Stirling surrendered at once, and Monk sat down undisturbed to the siege of the castle.

By the 10th of August the Scots, reported to be about 12,000 in number, were in Lancashire (probably near Preston, a name of evil augury), and were much disappointed at finding no disposition among the English people to join them. On the other hand Lambert was but a few hours behind them; Harrison, whose force had been swelled by troops from Cheshire and Lancashire, was in front, and Fairfax, willing to act now that England was actually invaded, was raising troops in Yorkshire, while 3,000 infantry stood ready to defend the passage of the Mersey at Warrington; Oliver in the meantime was hastening from Scotland with a force estimated at 10,000 men.

By the 16th of August Lambert had completed his junction with Harrison, and stood with 6,000 horse in front of the enemy's column, proposing to defend Warrington Bridge, of the possibility of which defence he had, however, much doubt. Indeed, on the approach of the Scots, the position was abandoned after a short struggle, and as there had not been time to entirely destroy the bridge, the invading army passed on it and endeavoured to pursue Lambert's retiring cavalry. Their attack was, however, met by the rear-guard, who charged three times upon them and compelled them to desist from their enterprise.

The object of Lambert's action was to delay and "amuse" the enemy until Cromwell should come up, and though his force, amounting as it did to 9,000 horse and 3,500 foot, might have been sufficient to defeat the Scottish army, he had distinct instructions to avoid battle until the main army had come up into line. For these orders there were probably two reasons; Cromwell had no wish that England should be saved by another hand than his, while the greater the distance from the border at which the foreseen victory should b gained, the more certain would be the absolute destruction of the doomed Scottish army.

During this time Cromwell was advancing at the highest possible speed, his men marching twenty miles a day "in their shirt sleeves," while their arms and clothes were carried for them by the country people. By the 19th he was at Ferrybridge near Pontefract, where he was met by Fairfax, who "went with him three miles in his coach." At this point Cromwell decided to leave such of his foot as were tired or sick after the long hot march, and to move yet more quickly with the remainder.

Information having been received that the Earl of Derby had landed in Lancashire from the Isle of Man, Colonel Lilburne was detached with ten troops of horse to prevent him from recruiting his forces, which were at present too small to be of much effect, for he had only 250 foot and sixty horsemen with him, having trusted in his influence in the county to raise more.

By the 21st the Scots were at Nantwich, or on the road thence by Newport on Lichfield, but were so worn out with the length and the heat of their forced marches that the King, it is said, "came to them cap in hand desiring them to march a little farther;" for he had yet the mad hope that he might reach London and find help there, though at this very time 14,000 of the city trained bands had been called out, and now stood paraded against him.

Lambert and Harrison looked on quietly from Uttoxeter. Pressing on still through the heat of the August weather, Charles about the 23rd arrived at Worcester, and his troops having without difficulty driven out the few defenders, occupied that city. Beyond this point his men could not be persuaded to march, and it was perforce determined to repair the fortifications, which had been broken down after the surrender in 1646, and to endeavour to hold them against Cromwell. Efforts were further made to secure the passages of the Severn above and below the city, with the object probably of fighting on the line of that river, and of thus preserving communication with Wales, whence Charles might hope for reinforcements.

Cromwell pushing on in haste was near Mansfield in Nottinghamshire about the 21st, at Nottingham on the night of the 22nd, and at Coventry by the 25th. At this latter place he was joined by Lambert and Harrison.

Moving thus in a direction parallel to that of the Scots, and out-marching them, he was able, as was his object, to interpose between them and London. The line of the King's march, on the other hand, was probably influenced, now that he realised that England as a whole was not well disposed towards him, by a wish to keep near to loyal Wales, and if possible to draw troops from yet more loyal Cornwall, on the way to which Massey proposed to raise a party in Gloucester, where his popularity, as he hoped, might not yet be exhausted.

Since Charles had halted at Worcester the problem became easy for Cromwell, for he had only to place his far superior forces between the Scots and London, in order to ensure safety to the capital, and proportionate gratitude from its citizens to himself, and could then at his own time crush the prey which he held in his toils. With this object he marched by Warwick (where he met Fleetwood and Desborough) through Stratford-on-Avon to Evesham, where he was on the 27th, and where he was joined by Fleetwood's London forces, who had moved by way of Banbury.

On the 28th the greater part of the army was in front of Worcester on the eastern bank of the Severn; that portion of it which had followed Cromwell from Scotland had therefore marched about 350 miles in twenty-four days, for, as the crow flies, it is 260 miles from Edinburgh to Worcester.

On this same date Cromwell received news that Whalley, to whom at his request he had despatched reinforcements, had before their arrival completely defeated the Earl of Derby at Wigan, after a smart fight, which lasted about an hour, and had there taken about 400 prisoners; orders were at once sent to the colonel to hold Bewdley Bridge on the Upper Severn, with the object of cutting off the retreat of the fugitives from the intended battle.

Cromwell now found himself at the head of the largest force which had been assembled during the whole of the Civil War, for he had at least 30,000 (some say 40,000) men under his command; being in such strength, he was in no mood to allow any formed body of the enemy to escape; and the road to the north being sufficiently provided for by Whalley's position, it remained only to close Wales to the remnants of the defeated army.

In order to effect this, it was first necessary to obtain possession of a passage across the Severn, over which the only available bridge lay at Upton, about eight miles below Worcester; thither Lambert marched on the 28th of August, and on arriving about 10 a.m., found the bridge broken down, a plank serving as the only means of passing the river.

Attacking at once he surprised the enemy, and his horse and dragoons, partly swimming and partly fording the Severn, crossed it, and posted a small detachment in the church at the foot of the bridge. The enemy, who were under the command of Massey, at once swarmed down upon them, but were repulsed by musketry fire, their leader having his horse shot under him, and being himself wounded in the hand and arm.

The remainder of the Parliamentary cavalry having crossed, the enemy drew off towards Worcester, and Lambert, sending

THE COUNTRY NEAR WORCESTER,
WHERE THE BATTLE OF WORCESTER WAS FOUGHT,
SEPTEMBER 3RD, 1651

word of his success to Fleetwood, who was four miles in rear, set his men to work to repair the bridge. Fleetwood mounted 300 infantry behind as many troopers, and pushed on to Lambert's help; all working well, and the enemy not interrupting, the bridge was soon in a fit state for use, and the whole force marched over it before nightfall.

On the following day Fleetwood's cavalry were pushed three miles towards Worcester, their scouts being a mile-and-a-half yet further in advance; on the march Maxfield (Madresfield) House was taken and occupied. On the 29th Cromwell reviewed his troops, and assembled a council of war for the purpose of deciding upon a plan of attack.

Before entering into a description of this plan, we must for a time return to the Scots. Their army stood astride the river, the horse being for the most part in the suburb of St. John's on the right bank, while the foot held the defences of the town. These consisted of an old wall with towers, which had been partially demolished, and of a line of earthworks, having somewhat of a bastioned trace, which lay to the south of the town; to the south-east, on rising ground, stood the Fort Royal, a quadrilateral bastioned work with very acute salients, which connected the line before mentioned with a second line which trended back to the walls of the city.

With the exception of the Fort Royal, which appears to have been for the times a formidable work, the fortifications could not have been of any great strength, since there had not been sufficient time in the ten days of the occupation of the city by the Scottish army to make them storm-proof, especially when we consider that the cavalry, being for the most part gentlemen, were little likely to put their hands to the work, while the infantry were mostly Highlanders, who may be presumed to have been of small use as sappers.

Forced labour of the country-people was indeed resorted to, but even that must have been in a military sense unskilled. In addition to the works above mentioned, the bridge between St. John's and the city was covered by a redoubt on the western side, while each of the gates in the city walls was protected in a similar manner.

Many sallies took place during the first days after Cromwell's arrival, but they were all repulsed with loss, and the spirits of the defenders were further damped by the coming (on the 31st) of the Earl of Derby, who was himself wounded, with the news of his own defeat by Whalley. He was accompanied by only about 30 horse, the sole representatives of the reinforcements which he had been expected to bring. Charles, it is reported, despairing of success, would have marched away with his cavalry, but a hint of this intention roused the infantry to mutiny, and they stoutly declared that all should fare alike.

According to the plan arranged by the Parliamentary leaders Fleetwood was to open the battle by an attack on the western side of the city, which if successful would drive in the enemy on that flank, and would thus confine the remainder of the struggle to the other bank of the river; there the action was to be taken up by Cromwell, with whom it lay to storm the enemy's works, to assault the town, and to drive the defenders through and out of it.

On the 1st or 2nd of September, a party of the Scottish horse, sallying from St. John's, destroyed two bridges on the Teme, hoping thus to render an attack on the western side of the city an impossibility, but Cromwell had already given orders for the collection of boats and of the material for the immediate construction of any temporary bridges which might be needed. On the 3rd of September, between 5 and 6 a.m., Fleetwood, who had on the 2nd passed 10,000 men over the Severn at Upton, advanced from that village towards Worcester; but before he could reach the city he was of necessity obliged to force the passage of the Teme, over which there was now but one bridge, that at Powick.

Owing to some unexplained delay, Fleetwood did not arrive at the Teme until between 2 and 3 p.m., and his left wing, which he had intended to pass at Powick, found the enemy at that point in strength, and was by them at first repulsed with some loss. But at about the same hour, boats having been brought up the Severn, Cromwell threw a bridge across the latter river just above the junction of the Teme. Over this he in person led three regiments of foot and one of horse, which were followed after a time by four or five other regiments.

The enemy, being thus taken in flank, began on their left to give way, and Fleetwood's right wing at once passed the Teme on a second bridge of boats; but the bridge at Powick having been broken down, and the ground being suitable for defence, the Scots at that point still held their own even after their left had been routed. From this it followed that, when they were at length driven in after severe fighting from hedge to hedge, they at first retired towards Hereford, but eventually, not being closely pursued, wheeled off into Worcester and took refuge behind the fortifications of that city.

No sooner had this portion of the action come to an end than the Scots, imagining that most of the English force was by this time on the western bank of the Severn, poured out from the Sudbury gate and from the Fort Royal. At the first onslaught the Parliamentary troops gave ground, but Cromwell rapidly brought back his regiments from across the river, and after three hours of "as stiff a contest as ever I have seen" drove back the enemy into Worcester. By 7 p.m. the Fort Royal had been stormed, and the guns within it were at once turned on the fugitives who, blocking Sudbury Gate with a wagon of hay, managed thus to gain sufficient time for the escape of such of them as were mounted.

Fleetwood, having in the meanwhile fought his way up to the city on the opposite side of the Severn, had by this time carried the suburb of St. John's, and his men, pouring over the bridge, pushed on through the streets until they had effected a junction with their comrades.

The whole of the baggage and of the artillery of the Royal army was captured, as were also a large number[1] of prisoners,

1. The number of prisoners taken is variously estimated; some authorities say 6,000, while others give a total of 10,000.

while strange to say, in so severe a battle, "much of it at push of pike," the Parliamentary loss was reported as amounting only to 200 men, while that of the Scots was stated to be nearly 3,000.

On the morning of the 4th the pursuit was taken up by Harrison with about 4,000 cavalry, with such success that no formed body of troops crossed the border, while of the chiefs of the Scottish army Charles was almost the only one who escaped. The force at Bewdley secured 1,200 prisoners, while a detachment from it which was at Shifnall in Shropshire captured the Earls of Derby and Lauderdale, with others of the leaders, who surrendered without a blow to a captain of horse.

The Duke of Hamilton, whose leg had been broken in the action, died of his wounds; Massey took refuge with the Countess of Strafford, who delivered him to the Parliament, while Middleton, who escaped from the battle with a considerable body of troops, was routed and captured before he had made his way into Scotland. The story of the escape of the King is too well known to need repetition. Of the captives the Earl of Derby alone suffered death on the scaffold, being beheaded at Bolton about the 16th of October, but 1,500 of the rank and file who were taken, were given to the Guinea merchants as slaves to work in their mines; better by far for these had they been killed at Worcester or by the axe.

After this "crowning mercy" the hopes of the Royalists were at an end, and before the year was out, the islands of Jersey, Guernsey, and Man, which had up to this time held out for the King, passed into the hands of the Parliament. Ireland, as has been already mentioned, was shortly after completely subdued, while Scotland practically lost its independence before the end of 1651.

Of the doings of Monk it is necessary to say a few words. Having been left in command after Cromwell's departure, he succeeded by the middle of September in securing the surrender of Stirling Castle, of which the garrison, scared by the to them novel fire of mortars, mutinied against the Governor, and commenced to sack the castle, upon which the former yielded it to Monk, who found in it the records and regalia of Scotland.

After dispersing some forces which the Scots were endeavouring to organise about Perth, Monk stormed Dumfries and Dundee, in which latter place, following the example of Cromwell at Drogheda, he put almost the whole of the garrison to the sword, and in addition gave up the town to be plundered. St. Andrews and Montrose shortly afterwards sent to ask for terms, while Aberdeen was abandoned by the enemy, and the spirit of resistance died quickly away throughout the country.

The party of the Remonstrants, of which Argyll was the head, having anew gained the upper hand, owing to the result of the battle of Worcester, the marquis in November assembled a Parliament for the purpose of offering terms of submission to that of England. Lambert and Deane were accordingly sent to Edinburgh to act with Monk and others as Commissioners to arrange a treaty of peace, and on the 1st of May, 1652, the union of England and Scotland was proclaimed at Edinburgh Cross. This union was extremely unpopular in Scotland, coupled as it was with a declaration of submission to the authority of the Parliament of England.

Thus at length, after nine years of almost continuous war, which had spared but few spots in either Great Britain or Ireland, the three nations agreed (if that can be called an agreement which was forced upon the two weaker) upon such union as may be possible between the lord and the serf, jarred and riven by such hatred as divided the Independent, the Presbyterian, and the Roman Catholic.

War indeed ceased, resistance being crushed down by the strong hand of Cromwell, but the materials for confusion were ever present; and unhappy England, though outwardly powerful, knew no true peace under his rule who, if he relieved his country from a tyranny, substituted for it a yoke no less harsh than that of the Stuarts, while it altogether lacked so much right as law and custom can give to an abuse.

# After Years

It is proposed to detail briefly the fate of the several leaders of the Parliamentary party, whose names have been prominently mentioned in the foregoing pages.

Of these, three had passed away before the termination of the Civil Wars.

Essex died on the 14th of September, 1646, at the age of fifty-four, having lived sufficiently long to feel that the storm, which he had proposed to rule and guide, was too fierce for such as he, and that the men whom oppression had forced to arm against their King, were no tools to serve the purpose of one who intended to lay them aside as soon as they had done their work for him.

The Earl of Essex died in outward honour, but from the date of the Self-denying Ordinance had lost all influence and power.

Ferdinand, Lord Fairfax, whose repute has been over-shadowed by the fame of his son, was a man of another type; well as he served his party in the north, his name was but little known beyond his own county, and on his death in March, 1648, the event was noticed solely on the ground that he was the father of His Excellency the Lord General.

The death of Ireton, as has been already mentioned, was an event of great political importance, on account of the influence which he possessed over his father-in-law, the future Protector.

He died at Limerick on the 26th of November, 1651, and was buried in Westminster Abbey, whence at the Restoration his bones, together with those of Cromwell and Blake, were removed and burnt at Tyburn.

Oliver Cromwell, the Lord Protector of England, has made far too deep a mark on the history of his country to render it necessary for us to enter into the details of his accession to that rank.

The first of the rulers of England, as he was one of the foremost of her generals, his name will never be forgotten, for though to a superficial examiner it may appear that at his death the work of his life was levelled with the dust, yet the principles which he invoked still rule, and will ever rule, the people of England.

He died on the 3rd of September, 1658, on the anniversary of his victories of Dunbar and Worcester.

After the resignation by Sir Thomas Fairfax of the command of the army, we hear of him on only two occasions; one when, as already mentioned, he raised troops in Yorkshire for the purpose of repelling that invasion of the Scots which led to the battle of Worcester; and the second when in 1659, after the death of the Protector, he called out levies to assist Monk against Lambert, at which time he found that sufficient of his old reputation had survived his retirement to induce 1,200 cavalry to desert from the latter to his leadership.

He died in the 60th year of his age, on the 12th of November, 1671, having passed all his later years in retirement.

Sir William Waller survived his repute, and outlived the animosity or the recollection of the Royal party, for, after sitting for Middlesex in the Parliament of the Restoration, he died in obscurity in 1668.

Fleetwood, who, after the death of Ireton, was appointed Lord Deputy of Ireland, held that post until November, 1655, when he was displaced in favour of Henry Cromwell, on the occasion of the renewal of the office of Lord Lieutenant. He was then made Lord General of the Forces, and was in 1657 created a peer in the Protector's new House of Lords. After the death of Oliver and the resignation of Richard Cromwell, Fleetwood was by station the foremost man in England; but he was of a disposition too vacillating and feeble to hold the reins of power with a firm hand.

In December, 1659, it was suggested to him that he should restore the King, but he had no heart for work of such difficulty, and refused to move in the matter without the consent and the aid of Lambert. With the commencement of 1660 all his authority departed, and at the Restoration, he sunk into obscurity so complete, that it is uncertain whether he died in America or in Stoke Newington.

Lambert, whose energy, determination, and lack of scruples were well known to Cromwell, was early marked by the latter as a capable but dangerous man. For this reason he was deprived of the position of Lord Deputy in Ireland, which had been at first granted to him on the death of Ireton, and for this reason did the Protector, while denying him all power, keep him always near him and under his own eye. In 1657, being suspected of the knowledge of one of the many plots which embittered the later years of Cromwell's Protectorate, Lambert was deprived of his commission, and forced to retire into private life; but after the death of Oliver, he was, on the resignation of Richard, held to be a possible claimant for the succession.

In 1659 Lambert crushed with ease a premature Royalist rising, which, under Sir George Booth, took place in Cheshire, but having a little later quarrelled with the Parliament, was by them cashiered; in answer to this act of the Commons, he marched to Westminster and dissolved the House.

On hearing of Monk's advance from Scotland, he moved against that leader with a force of 10,000 men, but owing to the opposition of Fairfax, was deserted by his troops and fled into hiding.

On the 9th of January Lambert was made a prisoner, and was on the 25th carried to Holmby House, which had at a former period served as a place of confinement for Charles I.; escaping thence, he was proclaimed as an outlaw, and having been recaptured, was committed to the Tower. On the 9th of April he again escaped and raised a few horse, of whom half deserted on the approach of Colonel Ingoldsby, who had been sent to apprehend him; upon this his wonted courage abandoned him, and he surrendered himself without a blow.

He was after the Restoration tried and condemned to death; but, being reprieved, was confined during the remainder of his life as a prisoner in Guernsey, where he devoted himself principally to gardening. He died about 1690.

Blake, the defender of Taunton and Lyme Regis, is the next to present himself to our notice. He became a soldier at the age of forty-eight, and a sailor eight years later, yet he succeeded in obtaining an assured position as the one, while as an Admiral his name will be remembered for ever.

After a succession of engagements with the Dutch, he raised the flag of England to supremacy at sea; he terrified Algiers, then a formidable power; he bombarded Tunis, and in 1657 cut out a Spanish fleet from the harbour of Vera Cruz. But this was his last action, for, while on his return home from this victory, he died, August 17th, 1657, as his ship, the *St. George*, entered Plymouth harbour.

The history of Monk deserves narration at greater length than our space will permit, for his career was one of the most remarkable of the times.

In 1644 we find him a Royalist colonel; taken prisoner at Nantwich, he remained in confinement until 1646; at that date he was appointed a colonel in the Parliamentary army; in 1649 he fell into disgrace on account of his treaty with the Irish rebels; yet, he was in 1650 selected by Cromwell to command a regiment in the army which invaded Scotland in that year; there, as appears from the fact that he was consulted by Cromwell with regard to the plan for the battle of Dunbar, he attained considerable importance, as is farther proved by his selection as commander in Scotland on the advance of the general into England.

In Scotland Monk remained until 1653, when he was, after the manner of the time, which assumed that a man who could perform one duty well was equally capable of all, recalled from his military command to serve under Blake in the English fleet. As a naval officer he was present at the actions of February the 18th and July the 31st, 1653, in the latter of which he acted as Admiral, Blake being at the time sick on shore.

On the death of Oliver, Monk, being then again in Scotland, proclaimed Richard Protector; on the resignation of the latter he joined the party of the Parliament against Lambert, and marched his troops into England to their support. But his own inclination, urged on by the advice and arguments of his wife, who was an ardent Royalist, was towards the Restoration of the Monarchy; this in due time, as is a matter of history, he effected.

For this high service he was created Duke of Albemarle, under which title he distinguished himself in 1666 in a series of successful actions at sea against the Dutch. He died in 1669, aged 61 years.

The fate of most of the minor leaders of the Parliamentary forces is lost in the obscurity from which their deeds for a time raised them.

# ALSO FROM LEONAUR

## AVAILABLE IN SOFTCOVER OR HARDCOVER WITH DUST JACKET

**THE JENA CAMPAIGN: 1806** *by F. N. Maude*—The Twin Battles of Jena & Auerstadt Between Napoleon's French and the Prussian Army.

**PRIVATE O'NEIL** *by Charles O'Neil*—The recollections of an Irish Rogue of H. M. 28th Regt.—The Slashers— during the Peninsula & Waterloo campaigns of the Napoleonic wars.

**ROYAL HIGHLANDER** by *James Anton*—A soldier of H.M 42nd (Royal) Highlanders during the Peninsular, South of France & Waterloo Campaigns of the Napoleonic Wars.

**CAPTAIN BLAZE** *by Elzéar Blaze*—Elzéar Blaze recounts his life and experiences in Napoleon's army in a well written, articulate and companionable style.

**LEJEUNE VOLUME 1** by *Louis-François Lejeune*—The Napoleonic Wars through the Experiences of an Officer on Berthier's Staff.

**LEJEUNE VOLUME 2** by *Louis-François Lejeune*—The Napoleonic Wars through the Experiences of an Officer on Berthier's Staff.

**FUSILIER COOPER** *by John S. Cooper*—Experiences in the 7th (Royal) Fusiliers During the Peninsular Campaign of the Napoleonic Wars and the American Campaign to New Orleans.

**CAPTAIN COIGNET** *by Jean-Roch Coignet*—A Soldier of Napoleon's Imperial Guard from the Italian Campaign to Russia and Waterloo.

**FIGHTING NAPOLEON'S EMPIRE** by *Joseph Anderson*—The Campaigns of a British Infantryman in Italy, Egypt, the Peninsular & the West Indies During the Napoleonic Wars.

**CHASSEUR BARRES** by *Jean-Baptiste Barres*—The experiences of a French Infantryman of the Imperial Guard at Austerlitz, Jena, Eylau, Friedland, in the Peninsular, Lutzen, Bautzen, Zinnwald and Hanau during the Napoleonic Wars.

**MARINES TO 95TH (RIFLES)** by *Thomas Fernyhough*—The military experiences of Robert Fernyhough during the Napoleonic Wars.

**HUSSAR ROCCA** by *Albert Jean Michel de Rocca*—A French cavalry officer's experiences of the Napoleonic Wars and his views on the Peninsular Campaigns against the Spanish, British And Guerilla Armies.

**SERGEANT BOURGOGNE** by *Adrien Bourgogne*—With Napoleon's Imperial Guard in the Russian Campaign and on the Retreat from Moscow 1812 - 13.

www.ingramcontent.com/pod-product-compliance
Lightning Source LLC
Chambersburg PA
CBHW032043080426
42733CB00006B/174